PDF Printing and Workflow

PDF Printing and Workflow

Frank J. Romano

Prentice Hall PTR
Upper Saddle River, New Jersey 07458
http://www.phptr.com

Library of Congress Cataloging-in-Publication Date
Romano, Frank J.
PDF printing and workflow / Frank J. Romano
p. cm.
Includes index.
ISBN 0-13-020837-X (alk. paper)
1. Printing - - Data processing. 2. Adobe Acrobat. I. Title.
Z249.3 .R655 1998
005.7'2--ddc21 98-43390
CIP

Editorial/Production Supervision: Craig Little
Acquisitions Editor: John Anderson
Buyer: Alexis R. Heydt
Cover Design: Talar Agasyan
Cover Design Direction: Jerry Votta

Prentice-Hall, Inc.
A Simon & Schuster Company
Upper Saddle River, NJ 07458

Prentice Hall books are widely used by corporations and government agencies for training, marketing, and resale.

The publisher offers discounts on this book when ordered in bulk quantities. For more information, contact the Corporate Sales Department, phone: 800-382-3419; fax: 201-236-7141; email: corpsales@prenhall.com or write:

Corporate Sales Department,
Prentice Hall PTR
One Lake Street
Upper Saddle River, NJ 07458

Printed in the United States of America

10 9 8 7 6 5 4 3 2 1

ISBN 0-13-020837-X

Prentice-Hall International (UK) Limited, *London*
Prentice-Hall of Australia Pty. Limited, *Sydney*
Prentice-Hall Canada Inc., *Toronto*
Prentice-Hall Hispanoamericana, S.A., *Mexico*
Prentice-Hall of India Private Limited, *New Delhi*
Prentice-Hall of Japan, Inc., *Tokyo*
Simon & Schuster Asia Pte. Ltd., *Singapore*
Editora Prentice-Hall do Brasil, Ltda., *Rio de Janeiro*

INTELLECTUAL PROPERTY

Adobe, the Adobe logo, Acrobat, the Acrobat logo, Acrobat Catalog, Acrobat Capture, Acrobat Exchange, Acrobat Distiller, Acrobat Reader, Acrobat Search, Adobe Accurate Screens, Adobe Extreme, Adobe Type Manager, Adobe Type Set, Adobe Illustrator, Aldus, ATM, the ATM logo, Display PostScript, PageMill, the PageMill logo, Photoshop, the Photoshop logo, PrintMill, Pixelburst, PageMaker, PostScript, and the PostScript logo are registered trademarks of Adobe Systems Incorporated.

Agfa, the Agfa rhombus, Agfa Balanced Screening, Mainstream, AgfaType, AccuSet, Alliance, Alto, Apogee, Arcus, Avantra, ChromaPost, Chromapress, ChromaWatch, ChromaWrite, Cobra, CristalRaster, DuoProof, FotoLook, FotoTune, Galileo, Horizon, IntelliTrack, LUTGen, MultiStar, OptiSpot, PhotoWise, ProSlide, Python, QuickLink, SelectScan, SelectSet, Setprint, Star, Taipan, and Viper are trademarks of Bayer Corporation or its affiliates.

AppleTalk, EtherTalk, ColorSync, ImageWriter, LaserWriter, Mac, Macintosh, Macintosh Quadra and QuickTime are trademarks of Apple Computer, Inc. registered in the U.S. and other countries and AppleScript, Power Macintosh, PowerBook, QuickDraw, System 7, System 8, and TrueType are trademarks of Apple Computer, Inc.

Ethernet is a registered trademark of Xerox Corp.

Freehand is a trademark of Macromedia Corp.

HP, LaserJet and PCL are registered trademarks of Hewlett-Packard Company.

IBM and OS/2 are registered trademarks of International Business Machines Corporation.

Kodak is a registered trademark of Eastman Kodak.

Linotype, Hell, Optima, Helvetica, Palatino, Times, and Univers are registered trademarks and HQS Screening, LinoPress, LinoServer, Linotype Library, and RT Screening, are trademarks of Linotype-Hell AG and Heidelberg Druckmachinen and/or subsidiaries.

Microsoft and MS-DOS are registered trademarks and Windows, Windows 95, and Windows NT are trademarks of Microsoft Corporation.

Novell and NetWare are registered trademarks of Novell, Inc.

OpenWindows, Sun, and SunOS are trademarks of Sun Microsystems, Inc. Solaris is a registered trademark of Sun Microsystems, Inc. SPARCstation is a registered trademark of SPARC International, Inc., licensed exclusively to Sun Microsystems, Inc. and is based upon an architecture developed by Sun Microsystems.

Post-It is a registered trademark of 3M.

Scitex and Scitex Brisque are registered trademarks of Scitex Corp.

UNIX is a registered trademark licensed exclusively through X/Open Company, Ltd.

QuarkXPress and QuarkXTension are registered trademarks of Quark, Inc.

All other company and brand and product names are trademarks, registered trademarks, or service marks of their respective holders. If we inadvertently missed anyone, any word with a capital letter is probably a trademark of somebody's so please respect their intellectual property.

ACKNOWLEDGMENTS

Thanks to Mattias Andersson, William Eisley, Amie Howard, and Mark Witkowski. They helped to develop the first version of this book which has evolved from a PDF primer to a digital workflow primer.

Thanks to Mike Jahn, PDF Evalgelist, and Gary Cosimini of Adobe Systems.

Thanks to Thad McIlroy and the Seybold organization for great sessions on PDF.

Thanks to Craig Little, Fiona Candlish and John Anderson at Simon & Schuster.

Frank Romano
Salem, NH

CONTENTS

DIGITAL WORKFLOW

Unlike other manufacturing assembly lines, graphic arts workflows do not follow a general model of the production process. Every printing plant is different. Every workflow is different. And every job is a surprise.

With conventional workflow, the production process used to start with the printer or the prepress house. They received different kinds of artwork or raw text, and their job was to set type, scan images, build pages, make film and plates, and finally print the job. They knew how to scan the images, whether transparencies or reflections, positives or negatives. They knew what colors were "reproducible," what the variability of the process was, and what file formats to use. The printer and/or the prepress service had almost everything under control.

Today we see the integration of the image creator with the production process itself. Most jobs today arrive in digital format. Designers and graphic artists are integrating computers into their work. Content creators are now doing some tasks that used to be done by printers or prepress houses, so printers and prepress services are losing control over file preparation for printing. And that file preparation controls the entire process.

BITMAP files contain both screening and dot gain compensation information, and reside as a 1-bit, pixel-by-pixel discription of "laser on, laser off" commands. They reside with the dot gain compensation and screening "threshold array" already mapped out for final imaging. These files are typically referred to as being "locked" because you cannot alter the screening or dot gain compensation information without reprocessing the pre-bitmap data.

RASTER files have resolution (same as bitmap), but now the individual picture elements (pixels) have color depth, that is, levels of gray. These levels of gray will eventually be mapped into some type of "threshold array" as part of the screening process prior to (or during) exposure. Raster formats as they stand do not contain screening and/or dot gain compensation information. These parameters are defined as part of the exposure dialog. When you take a raster file, superimpose screening and dot gain compensation, and then store the mapping of the individual laser on, laser off commands, you create a bitmap file format. Raster files are not "locked" in that you may adjust (manipulate, edit, etc.) individual gray level components for each and every pixel. You may also apply screening and/or dot gain compensation at will, based on whatever circumstances are required.

CT = Continuous Tone (Contone)
LW = Linework

But even while everything seems to be a lot easier to artists as they apply computers, and every image looks very good on the computer monitor, there may be a problem. Chances are that those beautiful images will not print correctly. Let's get basic.

Digital workflow for printing often comes down to two basic approaches: raster and vector. There are almost 20 different raster-based file formats available in the Macintosh version of Photoshop 5.0 alone, many with configurable subsets—plus vector formats.

All of these formats come together in a *container* of sorts, which holds all page elements and combines them. The container application may vary throughout the workflow, which results in two distinct types of job control—*component* files, which are created by the designer or creative professional in the initial preparation, and *consolidated* files, which are used for various steps in the final production process.

Component Files

Component files for high-end printing are assembled using QuarkXPress or PageMaker or Illustrator or FreeHand (the latter two for packaging) and FrameMaker or Corel Ventura Publisher for object-oriented, text-intensive documents. The components are raster and vector files.

Consolidated Files

Consolidated files are used to bring all of the component files, both raster and vector, into a single format—a container—that is accepted by an output processing system, a RIP or CEPS system. The consolidated format has been PostScript, but PDF (Portable Document Format) is now an alternative. PDF and PostScript come from the same roots. Font handling, color handling, resolution, target output device, and compression must be set up in advance in order to achieve an acceptable consolidated file.

In PostScript, altering the consolidated file after creation requires re-creation from the original component files. PDF started the same way, but now there are many tools for editing PDFs. When PDF lacked these tools, CT and LW formats, either in CEPS native formats, or as TIFF/IT files, found a reason to remain in production. These formats stayed in use because of the requirements of specific output devices. However, raster files are uneditable and voluminous and this can affect network performance. CEPS raster-based CT and LW files have a limited set of editing tools, usually based on proprietary systems. TIFF/IT has no editing tools. PostScript never really lent itself to interactive editing, although there were some attempts on the part of third-party developers. PDF is moving rapidly via plug-ins to provide high levels of editability.

TIFF/IT = Tag(ged) Image File Format/Image Transfer

CEPS = Color Electronic Prepress System (high-end, proprietary color image manipulation systems linked to high-end scanners)

Embedded Elements

Vector files are usually saved in EPS; raster files have loads of options, with production efficiencies such as image replacement, data compression, and color management. It is almost impossible to control the file formats from clients; it is useful to try to control those used in internal operations.

Editability

The need to make changes to a job (sometimes after it has been shipped) is not really funny. Author's alterations, printer's errors, or Murphy's law make editability an issue at every stage in the process. With automated production processes it is vital that we get the job right as far up front as possible and then have the ability to make changes at each step if necessary.

Embedded Elements

While vector files are usually saved in EPS, raster files have many options, changing not only the specific format, but enhancing production with items like image replacement, data compression, and color-managed files. Now that we are moving to digital photography and scanning very early in the process, we must rethink the way in which we capture and apply our files. It is almost impossible to control the file formats from clients; it would be useful, at least, to try to control them in our internal operations.

If technology helps us work faster, better, and more efficiently, why is it that it does not always work, particularly in graphic arts? Because we have too many variables.

In the printing industry there are many variables that affect the production process. Although is important to notice the amazing technological developments that are helping printers and service bureaus to serve their clients better and faster, it is also very important to point out that this is a developing industry, which lacks a great deal of standardization. Every user is king.

Technological Pitfalls

Because there is a lack of standardization, especially on digital file preparation, the window for mistakes is enormous. Many of these mistakes come from the ignorance of the file creator about workflow issues and file preparation. In other words, the content creators should have enough knowledge about prepress basics and production workflow to avoid mistakes downstream in the process. Some do; many don't.

On the printer side, new technologies become outdated as fast as they emerge. Keeping up with these changes is one of the biggest challenges that services in this industry face. For example, digital workflow is becoming more common. However, production in a digital environment is dependent not only on the equipment, but also on the intellectual ability of the people running that equipment.

This means that the productivity of a printing company is directly proportional to the level of employees' knowledge of digital technologies and to their commitment to productivity. It is crucial that both printers and content creators receive enough training in these issues to achieve high performance and improve throughput. There is no advantage in having progressed in technology if it is not accompanied by progress with people.

Islands of Automation

The ultimate and ideal workflow is totally digital. Unfortunately in this industry, this is the case in only a few instances. Traditional print publishing is plagued by incompatible equipment and disconnected islands of automation that electronic publishing has created, unintentionally, as entirely new forms of digital bottlenecks.

This last sentence contains two key terms, "islands of automation" and "bottleneck." *Islands of automation* refers to those highly automated processes inside the workflow that do not have continuity with the other steps or processes that follow in the workflow. It is like having computer-to-plate technologies and not having reliable digital proofing. The benefits of having a filmless and time-effective platemaking process are diminished by the fact that some customers require a film-based proof.

A *bottleneck* is any process or workstation with capacity less than or equal to the demands placed on it. Capacity is the measure of the system output. For example, on a printing press, it is the number of impressions that it can produce in a time frame, usually an hour.

Every system is composed of many steps. Every step or production operation has a certain capacity. The capacity of each of these operations is not the same. Some stations work faster than others, meaning that at some point some workstations will be idle while others will be overloaded.

In the case of islands of automation, we may have very fast, highly automated processes linked with slower processes that will constitute system bottlenecks. The problem with bottlenecks is that they determine the capacity of the entire system. If in my system I have very fast workstations linked to others that are not so fast, the capacity of my system equals the capacity of the slowest workstation, not the fastest. To be effective, workflows should be entirely automated. In the printing industry, we talk about automation, digital files transfers, etc, but the full benefits of the technology will not be seen if fully digital workflow is not in place.

Why Workflow Automation?

Automation permits the combination of complex and simple tasks that do not need manual intervention. The reason we should automate is it results in lower costs and faster deliveries. However, in graphic arts, there are probably as many exceptions as rules. Exceptions are those jobs that do not run easily through the workflow. Managing exceptions is more difficult. They are more expensive than managing regular standardized processes because they require operator expertise and intervention. This concept applies not only for the production process alone, but also for customers, since they now have to archive, retrieve, manipulate, and reuse digital information. They must also deal with exceptions and non-standardization.

Workflow Design

We can have as many workflow models as we wish. The bottom line is that when designing a workflow, it is necessary to analyze the different steps that are encountered most commonly. Then, identify the processes to produce the desired results, and finally design a workflow, or a group of workflows, which can handle those steps in an efficient way. The idea of workflow design is not to streamline each task in order to save time in each step of the process, but rather to automate the entire process. The whole is the sum of its parts.

Typical Tasks in a Print Production Environment

Preflighting

Preflighting a job is nothing more than checking if the digital file has all the elements necessary to perform well in the production workflow. Many software programs are designed for this task. Among other elements, these programs check if the fonts are embedded, if all images are present, with the right format (RGB or CMYK), etc. The idea of preflighting is to avoid mistakes before the job reaches the first output production steps. Preflighting attempts to avoid problems by fixing them up front.

Color Management

Color management has been an issue of controversy. It has became more popular recently due to the fact that digital printing and digital proofing are becoming more popular. As it is described in this book, color management is an effort to match color as it is output from different output devices in a given system. It is important to maintain the consistency of the same image across different media and output devices. Today, color management is based on profiles for encoding color.

PostScript File Creation
Most jobs are created in some sort of page layout application like QuarkXpress or PageMaker. Most RIPs (Raster Image Processors) do not understand applications—they "speak" another language, PostScript. Therefore, at some point, it will be necessary to transform those application files into PostScript code. When you click *Print* the application program builds a PostScript file from your screen image, the underlying data, and some information from the operating system. In the graphic arts, when you print, you are sending PostScript code.

PDF File Creation
PDF is an excellent file format for file exchange. As we will discuss later in this chapter it is one of the most versatile file formats due to its portability and cross-platform characteristics.

Trapping: When you have adjoining elements of different colors, registration is critical. The problem is that press registration is not 100 percent perfect, therefore it is necessary to overlap these colors to compensate for misregistration, and we call this image trapping. Today trapping is accomplished using different software packages. Some are more sophisticated than others, but the question is when in the workflow trapping is done. Some do trapping before RIPing, some do it while RIPing, and others after. Approaches depend on the configuration of the workflow but, for the most part, it will depend on the kind of applications and products service providers provide.

Imposition
Imposition is the arrangement of individual pages on a press sheet, so that when it is folded and trimmed, the pages are in correct orientation and order. To impose is a responsibility that should not be taken lightly. As in the case of trapping there are advanced imposition software packages that do this automatically. However, this task can be done manually in the application software, depending on the type of operation.

RIP
The RIP takes in high-level page description files and outputs low-level data streams that can be fed directly to a digital

printer, imagesetter, or platesetter for image rendering, or to a video display to be viewed. The RIP has three main functions: Interpretation, Creation of the Display List, and Rasterization.

Interpretation: in this stage the RIP interprets the PostScript code that has been sent. It decodes PostScript and prepares the information to the following step, the display list.

Creation of the Display List: creation of an intermediate list of objects and instructions before rasterizing. It is a list of objects in a page description file that have a determined order. The order the page elements have in this display list is the same order in which they will be displayed or imaged.

Rasterization: the conversion of graphic elements into bitmaps for rendering on a monitor, digital printer, or imagesetter. In other words, the RIP takes the display list and converts it into pixels. This stage is a necessity because every output device needs to generate pixels.

Proofing

A proof is an output of the job before it gets printed. There are different kinds of proofs available, ranging from conventional, which is film-based; soft proof, which uses a calibrated monitor; and digital proof, from a digital proofing printer.

Remote Proofing

Sometimes the person who OKs the proof is in a remote location. To avoid mail delays some graphic arts service firms use remote proofers in their customers' sites. Files need to be transmitted over a digital telecommunications network. Once the client receives the file they can output it on paper, using a digital printing device, or simply display it on a monitor (soft proof). The file that is sent can be an application file, a PostScript file, or a PDF file. This file can either have just the resolution necessary to output on the proofing device, or the full resolution of the final reproduction device. File size is an important issue for file transmission over digital networks, therefore it makes more sense to have just the resolution needed to output on the proofing device.

In any case, the most important consideration is to have the proofing devices accurately calibrated to the printing conditions of the press or digital printing device on which the job will ultimately be produced.

Corrections
The aim of a proof is to detect any error or mistake in the file prior to printing the job. When corrections need to be done, decisions have to be made quickly. It is necessary to have excellent communication between customer and producer. Remote proofing, and digital proofing in general, is helping to speed up the process of correction and re-proofing. Therefore it is important to have corrections as a task in the workflow with a clearly defined methodology.

Film Output
If film is still used, it is outputted by an imagesetter, after the RIP stage. Film can be output either on single spreads or on full size imposed page. The film is then used for plate exposure, or for making analog proofs.

Plate Output
Today there are two methods for producing a plate: the conventional way, using film, and the digital way, using a computer-to-plate device, also known as platesetter. With a totally digital workflow the second way is more suitable, however many printers still use film due to the capital investment required. With computer to plate technology, film is eliminated from the production workflow, which represents many advantages for printers, and eliminates one level of variability in the system.

Another issue with computer-to-plate is proofing, which has to be done digitally. Digital proofing has improved in the past couple of years, but is still not completely accepted as a contract proof by some critical customers who continue to demand a halftone dot-based proof.

Blueline Proof
Its purpose is to check final imposition and verify if there is any element missing or misplaced.

The blueline can be printed in many paper formats: it can be a print of single page or a big print of the entire press sheet imposition. These proofs are not intended to judge color or print quality in any aspect, they are just to verify the position of the different elements in the page or the imposition.

Printing

Printing is the last task in a print production environment. Today we not only output using conventional printing methods, like offset lithography, flexography, or gravure, but we also have a variety of optional digital printing devices available. Digital printers and presses use different technologies, and instead of ink, they use toner or inkjet ink.

Storage

Storage refers to the warehousing of electronic files from already outputted jobs. Files can be stored on central computerized systems, CD-ROMs, tapes, or magnetic diskettes. Many storage technologies have been developed in the last years, however graphic arts files are known for their huge size, and therefore storage can still be a problem more in the finding and retrieval than in the actual storage.

These are the most typical tasks in a print production workflow. Some others are omitted here but probably they are a subcategory of the ones we just mentioned. As you see, each one of the tasks has its own requirements. Workflows can be very different from one print shop to another, each one may combine tasks that are highly automated with conventional or manual methods or they can have a fully digital workflow. Therefore the content creator must be aware of these issues before creating the file for printing.

One of the promises of PDF does lie with the originator. If he or she converts the layout program pages into PDF properly—and properly is the operative word—then workflow can be truly automatic. We must assume that some originators will not make good PDFs (and they probably did not make good application files either), so PDF may begin when a job is accepted by the prepress or printing service.

Variable Data Printing

Print will no longer have to be simply a long-run, broadcast-oriented information distribution medium. Print will have to deliver a specific, targeted message to a specific, targeted audience.

At the front end, master pages must be formatted, with provisions for entering information that will vary from printed unit to printed unit. Information must be imported from a database to fill the variable areas of the layout. Most of the programs for variable data printing provide some way to define portions of QuarkXPress or PageMaker layouts as subject to variation.

Personalization is an outgrowth of the mail merge features dating back to word processors of the 1970s (and to "player-piano" typewriters of the 40s and 50s), which made it possible to merge a standard letter with a list of names, addresses, and personalized salutations. Personalization on today's digital color presses mostly takes the form of supplementing name and address data with other text in specific areas of a static page layout. The source of the variable information is a database or delimited, sequential list of fields. A more advanced approach to personalization is adding not just text, but other content objects to the page, such as photos, graphics, scanned signatures, etc. They are retrieved from a database for placement in the layout. This makes the page "dynamic" in that it can change both content and layout for each recipient.

A different aspect of variable printing is sometimes described as custom document assembly, or versioning. This has been done in the office for years. Word processors in the 70s assembled individual paragraphs into reports, customized insurance policies, and other materials.

Short runs of specific layouts can incorporate variable data with some of the data varying from page to page, while other content is common to a series of pages. Many programs define the variable objects on the master page as a variable content box. Data areas on the page must be predefined (usually must be rectangles of a predefined size). The database data is then linked by a variable data program and the master layout and the variable data are combined, either in the page (which then needs to be rasterized for each impression) or in the RIP.

Soon pages and layouts will be generated on the fly according to the defined content. The static master page must be rasterized and each of the variable page components must also be rasterized fast enough to keep up with the print engine.

The RIP task becomes more complex as graphics and color-separated photos are included as components that vary from unit to unit. Print server configurations such as Barco's and new multiprocessor RIP configurations such as Adobe's Extreme are working in this area. For now, most pages to be printed are pre-rasterized, assembled on the fly, and input to the print engine.

The ability to pass these huge amounts of raster data through the pipeline to the print engine in such a way as to ensure that the device can run at its rated speed is the other major challenge. This task is complicated by the size of the pipeline to the print engine, i.e., the maximum speed of data transfer to the engine, which at this stage of technological evolution of engines is generally much slower than is required for true productivity.

The suppliers of digital color printers and presses have chosen a slightly different method for handling variable data and outputting custom documents. They all face other technical considerations that contribute to the complexity of the overall variable printing workflow, including the ability to handle input from a variety of database formats and mechanisms for ensuring and verifying job integrity.

Digital workflow is evolving rapidly to meet the demands of automated presses, printers, and systems. The printing industry must be competitive with mass media. It must be able to handle long and short runs, static and variable data, now not later.

2

It all started with PostScript

It was not apparent that fateful day in 1985 that PostScript would be what it has become. It was Spring and Apple Computer introduced us to Desktop Publishing, a combination of the Macintosh, PageMaker, and PostScript. PostScript gave us a laser printer that thought it was a typesetting machine and links to film imagesetting.

It was not apparent that PostScript would do what it has done because there were many competitors in the page description language arena in 1985. But PostScript had one thing going for it: the high end. From that vantage point it could control the emerging film imagesetters and then work down to laser printers on the desktop.

After a decade of competing typesetting machines, each with a different encoding system, and an equal number of front end systems, each with a different user coding system, the industry was ripe for some standards. That got us to PostScript and once there we started to pick at it and push it and extend it. And that's what the PDF does. With Acrobat 3.0/3.01 it extends its franchise into high-end printing while maintaining its lead in document transmission and viewing. It is now a tool for both print and nonprint communication.

Stone tablets, Gutenberg bibles, glossy magazines, newspapers, and even memos are all information containers. Although the form of each container is radically different, the end purpose is the same—to carry, share, and distribute information and ideas to some audience.

It is ironic that PDF started out as a tool to eliminate paper. Now it is seen as a tool for the salvation of paper.

Today, we call these information containers *documents*. To have value, these documents and the information contained within them must be easily shared and distributed. The printing industry converts that information into paper.

The printing industry looks inward in that it looks for a method for getting information from those who create the documents in order to replicate that information on paper for distribution. There is another—and competing—world that wants to distribute the document in electronic form. The ability to share documents with a large number of people is the goal.

From movable type, to phototypesetting and imagesetting, to 16-page computer-to-plate signatures, to digital printing, the publishing/printing industry strives for faster and more effective ways of mass producing documents across all media and all platforms.

In the Beginning (No, Not *that* Beginning)

As document creation evolved into computerized forms, document composition was primarily limited to proprietary Color Electronic Prepress Systems (CEPS). These systems, produced by companies such as Crosfield, Linotype-Hell, and Scitex, were not only expensive but difficult to use. Another drawback to these proprietary systems was the difficulty or impossibility of cross-platform file transfer. Each had a unique file system that precluded any compatibility.

The Revolution (No, Not *that* Revolution)

March 21, 1985 marked the date when easy, economical digital publishing became a reality. On this day Apple, Aldus, Adobe, and Linotype unveiled a working typesetting system with an open architecture. It was based on the Macintosh Plus computer, which was one of the first personal computers with a Graphical User Interface (GUI). The output was made with either a laser printer, the Apple LaserWriter, or a high-resolution laser imagesetter, the Linotronic 300, from Linotype. Both output devices operated with a new Page Description Language (PDL), called PostScript, from Adobe. The typesetting front end utilized software from Aldus PageMaker, which was a graphic-oriented page layout program operating on the Macintosh.

We were asked once when the digital age began for the printing industry. Our reply: March 21, 1985, when PostScript was introduced.

The strength and importance of this prepress system was that several graphic arts industry vendors worked together on an open-architecture system that would be available to everyone at a fraction of the price of a CEPS system. During the years after the introduction of the new system based on the PostScript page imaging model, more and more printer and imagesetter manufacturers implemented PostScript into their output systems.

Further developments in the prepress industry have produced devices and systems for scanning, page assembly, and output which are compatible with the prepress system based on PostScript. As a result of these combined efforts, digital workflows have been able to significantly speed up prepress production and related turnaround times.

Today, anyone with a computer can be a publisher. The publisher can choose from a wide range of applications, typefaces, and output devices, all speaking the same tongue, PostScript.

A Little About PostScript

The idea for PostScript began in 1976 at Xerox's Palo Alto Research Center (PARC) as a Computer Aided Design (CAD) language, and a language later called Interpress, for driving laser printers. When Xerox abandoned the project, John Warnock and Chuck Geschke left PARC and formed Adobe in 1981.

Their first product was PostScript. PostScript's power lies in the fact that it is a device-independent programming language. This means that the same PostScript file can be output on virtually any printing device regardless of its resolution, on film or plate or paper. As a programming language, PostScript can support almost any level of graphic complexity. Looping routines can be set to define extremely complex patterns and objects for pages and documents.

Actually, their first product was to be a document production system, but they saw a need for a common means of communicating from originating systems to output systems with an emphasis on type.

Phototypesetters
Character-based typesetters on film or photo paper.

CRT phototypesetters
Character, line art, and some photo using cathode ray tubes for higher speeds.

Laser phototypesetters
Character, line art, and photo output via lasers.

Laser imagesetters
Character, line art, and photo in color primarily to film—capstan or drum based.

Laser imposetters
Character, line art, and photo in color for imposed flats of 4-up, 8-up, and more pages.

Laser platesetters
Character, line art, and photo in color for imposed polyester and aluminum plates.

Laser imaged on-press plates
Character, line art, and photo in color for imposed plates in registration on press.

PostScript Interpreter
Parses and interprets PostScript codes and operators.

Display List
A list of all of the objects on a page.

Rasterizer
Builds the page from the list of objects in the Display List and creates a page bitmap for the output device.

While looping capabilities are a boon, they can also be a bane. PostScript files could contain loops that take two hours to process without ever placing a single mark on a page. Another boon/bane is PostScript's flexibility. Aside from syntax rules, the format of PostScript is very unstructured. There are an infinite number of ways to write code to perform the same task. Some of these ways are extremely efficient and others are not.

This relationship is best seen in the way some software applications generate "good, RIPable" PostScript data and other software generates "poor, problematic" PostScript data.

Due its unstructured nature, PostScript is an extremely page-dependent page description language. Page-dependence means that the entire file must be interpreted prior to imaging a single page. As a result, the individual pages described within a PostScript file cannot easily be extracted from that file. In other words, an object, like a circle, placed on the first page of a document may not be described by the PostScript code until the end of the file. The unstructured nature of PostScript and its page dependence leads to a very unpredictable file format.

The RIP

In a sense, the RIP, or raster image processor, is really the PostScript programming language compiler. It interprets the file and "executes" its commands, which are to draw objects on a page. A RIP is the essential element in any form of raster-based imaging which includes computer-to: paper, film, plate, cloth, plastic, metal, and perhaps epidermis. The end result of RIPping is a bitmap for the entire image that tells the output engine where to place spots.

The RIP performs three functions:

1. Interpretation of the page description language from the application program
2. Display list generation
3. Rasterizing (screening, color transforms, and making the page bitmap)

Almost every imaging device available today is a raster imager—using spots to build text, lines, pictures, etc. Thus, every imager must, out of necessity, have a RIP, whether it is a lowly desktop printer or a giant computer-to-plate (CTP) system. And every RIP is just a little bit different. Many are based on Adobe's design, with some additional features, and some are legally derived from public information on the PostScript language. These have been called PostScript clones. Most of the small or home office market is dominated by Hewlett-Packard's PCL printer language, a PostScript wanna be.

When you send a document to a printer the RIP does its job and out come the page or pages. But today's digital workflow is much more complex and multiple RIPpings are often the norm. In a CTP workflow, the document might be RIPped to a color printer for color proofing, RIPped to an imposition proofer, RIPped to a remote proofer, and finally RIPped to the platesetter. In most cases this involves four different RIPs and four different imaging engines. And four chances for variation.

Over time, two paths to RIP development took place by:

- Adobe licensees
- Adobe clones

In both cases, the RIP includes a core set of functions based on the PostScript interpreter. From there developers have added increasing functionality. Here are some of them:

- More efficient graphics handling
- More efficient picture handling
- Halftone screening with different dot structures, angles, and algorithms
- Stochastic screening
- Trapping
- Imposition
- Statistics and other reports

RIP Evolution

The PostScript page description language was developed to communicate the appearance of text, graphical shapes, and images to raster-based output devices equipped with a PostScript interpreter. PostScript has become predominant in the computer printing world because of its device-independence. Device-independence means that the image

Spots, dots, and pixels

For a vast oversimplification we give you this one minute lecture.

Most imaging recorders today use a laser. The laser creates a SPOT whose size is based on the resolution of the recorder. This is the basic laser SPOT and its width is measured in microns—thousandths of an inch. A SPOT is an addressable element and is either there or not there, zero or one, if you will. We say dots when we mean SPOTS, and resolution—the number of SPOTS in an inch—is expressed as dpi (dots per inch) instead of the more accurate spi (spots per inch).

DOTS should refer to halftone dots. There is no gray ink in a printing press or laser printer. About eight to ten of the spots are clustered to form a shape that gives the eye the illusion of gray. Halftones are measured in lines per inch, e.g. 133 line screen.

PIXELS are spots with gray levels. On a monitor the intensity of the beam controls the amount of light energy to create a level of gray. Thus Red, Green, and Blue PIXELS are combined at varying levels to display a picture. On color laser printers the intensity of the laser does the same thing for yellow, magenta, cyan, and black. A PIXEL is 100% dark or some percentage of gray. Some laser printers have both spi, spots per inch, and bit depth for gray levels. These are composite printers, as are all toner-based color printers. Film and plate printers output bilevel—zero or one—spots, which form type and lines and, through halftone dots, pictures.

To repeat:
The RIP, or raster image processor, is really the PostScript programming language compiler. It interprets the file and "executes" its commands which are to draw objects on a page. A RIP is the essential step in any form of raster-based imaging which includes computer-to: paper, film, plate, cloth, plastic, metal, or whatever. The end result of RIPping is a rasterized bitmap for the entire page image that tells the output engine where to place spots. The RIP performs three functions:

1. *Interpretation of the page description language code from the application program*
2. *Display list generation*
3. *Rasterizing (screening, color transforms, and making the bitmap)*

Almost every imaging device available today is a raster imager—using spots to build text, lines, photos, etc. Thus, every imager must, out of necessity, have a RIP, whether it is a lowly desktop printer or a giant computer-to-plate (CTP) system. And every RIP is just a little bit different. Many are based on Adobe's design, with some additional features, and some are legally derived from public information on the PostScript language.

(the page to print or display) is defined without any reference to specific device features (printer resolution, page size, etc.). A single page description can be used on any PostScript-compatible printer from a 300 dpi laser printer to a 3,000-plus dpi imagesetter or platesetter. In our opinion, another reason for its success is that it supports high-end printing. Computer-to-plate and digital printing as we know them could not have developed without a standardized page description language.

Most applications that can print to a PostScript printer also let you "print" to a file. Printing to a file means that the application (or the computer running the application, with the help of a PostScript driver) converts the job data into PostScript commands and saves the data as a file instead of transmitting the code over a cable to a printer. You can then download the file to any PostScript printer to print it out. Downloading is different from printing in that no data conversion (from job data to PostScript) takes place, the file is merely sent to the printer. This allows you to directly send PostScript streams to printers, without opening any application program. The PostScript file contains all font and image data and can be stored on a disk and sent to a graphic arts service. Most computer platforms have a variety of PostScript downloaders available.

PostScript Printer Description Files

Each application usually creates and stores files in its own internal format, not PostScript. When you print a job, the application uses a PostScript driver to translate its data into PostScript. Depending on what computer or application you use, the printer driver could be installed as part of the application, or, more commonly, the printer driver is installed in the System folder for any application to use.

PostScript is device independent ... to a point. When you print, you print to a specific printer that has very specific features such as certain resolutions, page sizes, minimum margins, choice of paper trays, etc. Although the PostScript driver can send the PostScript job to any printer, it can't specify a tabloid page for a printer that does not have a tabloid tray, for example. To access features specific to the printer, PostScript uses PPDs (PostScript Printer Description files) which are stored in the System folder.

Some printer-specific information that a PPD might include:

- Input paper trays
- Page size definitions
- Print areas for each page size
- Output paper trays
- Duplexing (double-sided printing)
- Default resolution
- Resolutions available
- Black and white or color output
- Halftone screening functions
- Default screen angles
- Screen frequency combinations
- Custom screening definition
- Default transfer functions
- Default font

QuarkXPress also uses another file to relate printer-specific information: a Printer Description File (PDF), which is not to be confused with the subject of this book, the Portable Document Format, also a PDF. (Confusing, isn't it?) QuarkXPress uses data from both the PPD and PDF to generate PostScript for output.

At print time, you select the PostScript output device and select a PPD (or a PDF in QuarkXPress). If you later want to print the same job to a different printer, all you need to do is select a different printer with a different PPD.

PostScript Interpreters and RIPs

When the RIP receives the PostScript file for processing, it needs to convert that file to bitmap data. PostScript printers, whether 300 dpi laser printers or 3,000-plus dpi platesetters, need a PostScript interpreter to translate the PostScript code into the bitmap data needed to print or image the page. Raster data prints a page as a pattern of tiny printer spots. To place these spots, the RIP maps out the page as a grid of spot locations—this is called a bitmap. Any specific spot can be defined or located by its address based on x,y coordinates. To image a page, the output engine either images a spot or does not—zero or one, on or off. Data of this type is called binary, because only two values are used. The term *bilevel bitmap* means spots. *Composite data* means pixels—spots with levels of gray.

The small or home office market is dominated by Hewlett-Packard's PCL printer language, which has almost never been used for high-end printing.

A RIP includes a core set of functions based on a PostScript interpreter. From there developers have added increasing functionality.

Today, many workflows use the Display List as the format of choice. In every case, it provides a flatter, more efficient file that can be handled automatically.

And the Acrobat PDF is based upon the Display List, which is why new workflows are evolving to apply it.

PDF, PPD, and PDF: What is What?

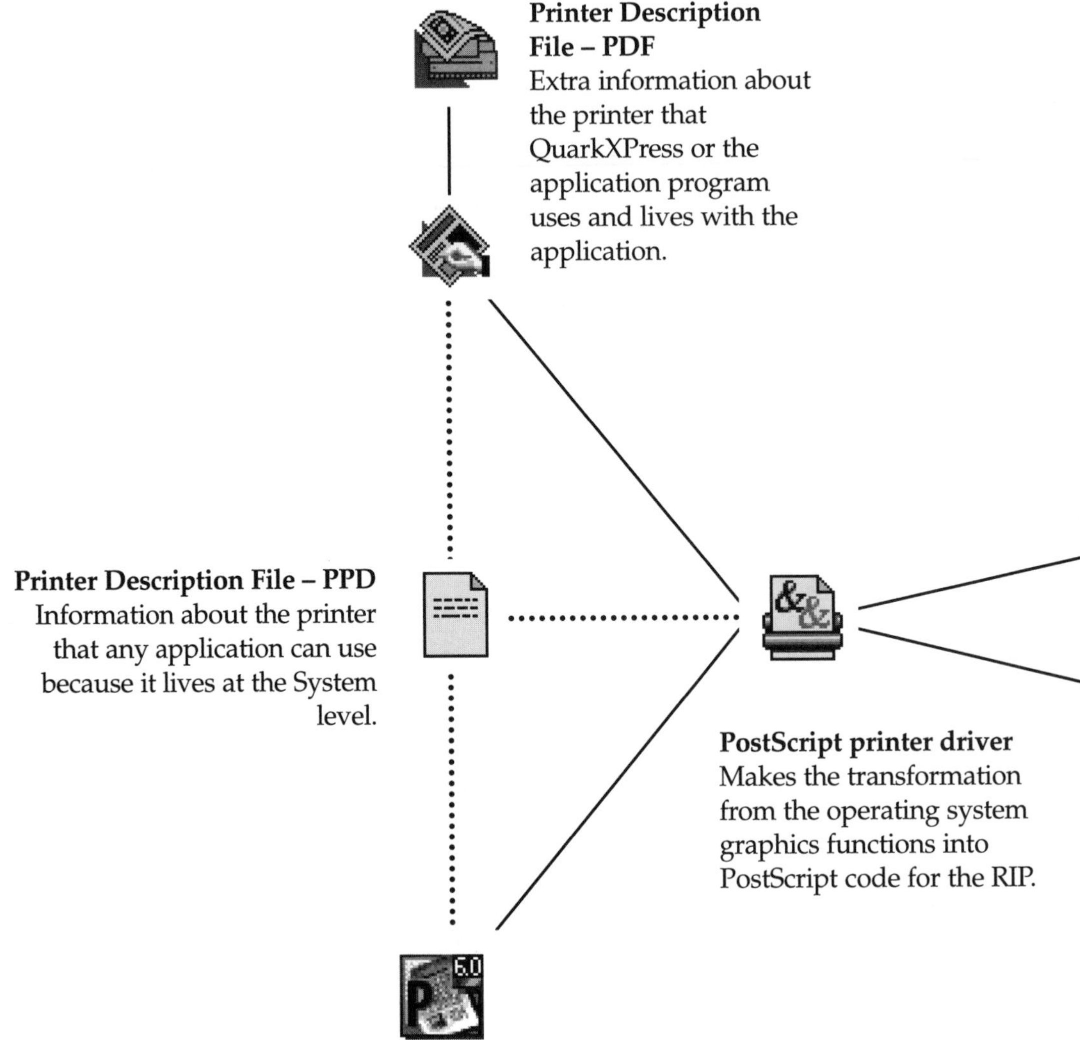

Printer Description File – PDF
Extra information about the printer that QuarkXPress or the application program uses and lives with the application.
Printer Description File – PPD
Information about the printer that any application can use because it lives at the System level.
PostScript printer driver
Makes the transformation from the operating system graphics functions into PostScript code for the RIP.
6.0

PostScript File
Includes the same information that would be sent to a PostScript printer but saved to disk.

Acrobat Distiller
Application that interprets PostScript data and builds a Portable Document Format file. Like a RIP but not a RIP.

Portable Document Format – PDF
A device-independent document format.

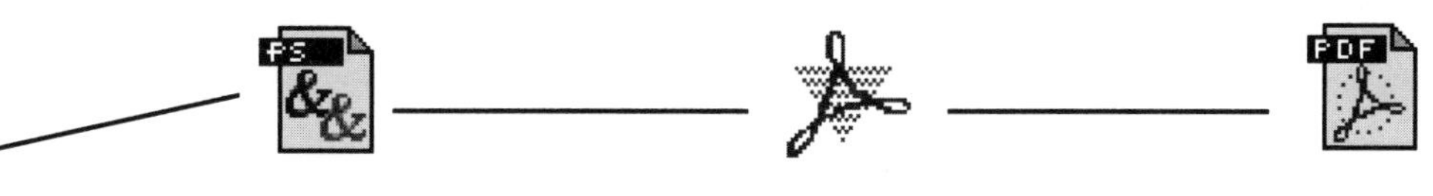

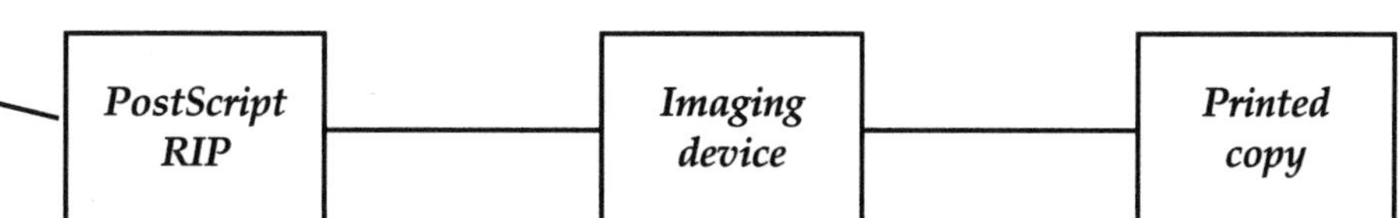

Bitmaps
A bitmap image is an image which is defined digitally by a number of pixels in a rectangular array. Because computers are binary entities they must break up images into a map of small pieces, called picture elements, or pixels. All images that are scanned into a computer are bitmap images whether black and white line drawings, or black and white or color photos.

Monochrome bitmap images are the simplest and the smallest in file size. Scanned black and white line drawings are monochrome bitmaps. Each pixel of the bitmap can either be black or white (on or off), so only two bits of computer information are required to define these bitmaps. For this reason, they are also called bilevel bitmaps.

LZW *stands for Lempel-Ziv-Welch (its developers)*
JPEG *stands for Joint Photographic Engineers Group*
RLE *stands for Run Length Enclcoding*

All are methods for compression.

LCD = Liquid Crystal Display

Bitmap data is what the output engine or recorder needs. But PostScript really describes pages not as a table of spots, but as a series of mathematically described shapes or objects. It takes a lot less data to describe a page by its shape, size, and location than by listing the state (on or off) of each individual pixel in the image. The PostScript interpreter converts the PostScript code to a list of objects. Then it rasterizes the objects to create the bitmap for actual outputting. The resolution of the output device determines how many spots are needed to image a page.

PostScript Level 2

Since the introduction of PostScript in 1985, Adobe and other developers have created extensions to the PostScript language. Color extensions were added in 1988 to better support printing color images. PostScript Level 2 was announced in 1990, and it integrated the original PostScript with all previous language extensions, and added new features. Included in PostScript Level 2:

- **Color Separation:** Lets a user send a full-color job, not already separated, to the PostScript Level 2 interpreter which converts the one-page color job into four files: one for each process color (cyan, magenta, yellow, and black).
- **Composite Fonts:** Type 1 PostScript fonts can encode 256 distinct characters but a typical Japanese font has over 7,000 characters. The composite font technology included in PostScript Level 2 supports these larger fonts.
- **Data Compression:** Network transmission is a large percentage of the actual processing time for a job. PostScript Level 2 supports several data compression schemes, such as LZW, JPEG, and RLE. Jobs sent over the network are sent in a compressed format, then decompressed by the PostScript interpreter. The amount of data transmitted is reduced, speeding up the network transmission portion of the job.

Hardware and Software RIPs

There are so-called hardware RIPs and software RIPs. The distinction is not always clear. Initially all RIPs were proprietary, with a CPU, disk, RIP software, and related hardware enclosed in a cabinet and attached to an imaging recorder. There was no monitor and no keyboard, although a keypad and LCD panel on the recorder did allow some level of interface. You connected your network to the RIP and away you went. Then someone decided that they could sell you the RIP software and you could install it in your own computer. Usually they supplied a special computer board and cable to connect to the imager. The latter approach was called a software RIP.

What is Adobe's CPSI? Adobe CPSI (Configurable PostScript Software Interpreter) is the core software RIP Adobe sells to OEMs, and which OEMs can include in a deliverable product.

OEM means Original Equipment Manufacturer, which means that one company (Adobe in this case) make a product, which is then incorporated in a product that is sold to an end user. Adobe is said to "OEM" CPSI.

How do Harlequin ScriptWorks 5.0 and Adobe CPSI differ? Both are aimed at OEMs and both include a PostScript language interpreter and a renderer. But the similarity ends there. CPSI does not include a user interface or a throughput controller or any form of media management. It has no drivers for specific devices, no color management options, no TIFF/IT-P1 support, etc. Adobe CPSI is a software kernel that requires development as a complete product by an OEM.

Configurable PostScript Interpreter (CPSI)

CPSI (Configurable PostScript Interpreter) from Adobe is the basis for many RIPs from many vendors. It is guaranteed to be fully PostScript Level 2-compatible since it comes from Adobe. Developers can set it up to generate output for specific output devices, such as imagesetters, color proofers, laser printers, high-speed printers, large-format imagesetters, plotters, and computer-to-plate devices. CPSI can be modified to drive a complete range of PostScript devices. CPSI uses the host workstation's operating system and can be used in RIPs for Macintosh, Power Macintosh, SPARCstations, and Windows NT as well as others. Although the core of the RIP is CPSI, each RIP vendor has its own user interface and device drivers. The user interface lets you tell the RIP how you want jobs output: you want to use 2,400 dpi, produce a negative image, have pages automatically color-separated, and have the imagesetter punch each page (if it can). The user interface provides you with status information: Job 1 took 4 minutes 10 seconds to RIP and contained no PostScript errors, as an example.

In 1991, Adobe introduced PixelBurst, a NuBus-based card coprocessor with an application-specific integrated circuit (ASIC) that speeds PostScript processing by freeing up the main CPU more quickly, accelerating halftone screening and generation of text and line art—particularly at high resolutions or when outputting large images. It is the basis for many RIPs.

Since its introduction in 1985 when Adobe PostScript software helped spawn the desktop publishing revolution, Adobe has continued to drive the industry forward with powerful printing solutions. The current version of the PostScript page description language developed by Adobe is publicly available to software and RIP developers. This has led to its adoption and recognition as a virtual industry standard. Although Adobe created the

RIPs today

On early imagesetters and on most color copiers with RIPs you will find a box with a set of plugs in the back and a small liquid crystal display on the front. Inside is a CPU; a disk, on which the RIP software was loaded, with special hardware in some cases for faster processing; and a special interface board to move data to the imaging engine very quickly.

However, most of these "boxes" have been replaced by an entire computer system, with monitor, mouse, and keyboard. Most of the other "stuff" is pretty much the same as the "box." Software upgrades are easier and the software itself is protected with a "lock" or "dongle" that has an encoded serial number.

Thus, the difference between a hardware RIP (the "box") and a software RIP (the whole computer) is pretty academic today.

original specification for PostScript and then Level 2, other RIP vendors were the first to ship PostScript Level 2 language compatible RIPs capable of both high and low resolutions running on all major platforms and operating systems. Some non-Adobe RIPs already have features which have not been announced as part of PostScript 3, such as support for symmetrical multiprocessing (SMP), TIFF/IT-P1 input format processing, integrated color management, and PostScript display list access and editing. Adobe's typical upgrade cycle is about eighteen months.

PostScript 3

In September 1996, Adobe Systems Incorporated announced its newest printing systems solution, which includes the next generation of Adobe PostScript called PostScript 3 (the word "level" has been dropped). Adobe's integrated printing system solution focuses on changing the printing experience by allowing OEM customers to build best-in-class printing solutions and providing users the ability to print complex graphics and Web content, when and where they need it. Adobe has gone beyond offering a page description language to providing a total systems solution for delivering and printing digital documents.

Adobe has developed an advanced level of functionality in Adobe PostScript 3 to accommodate the new digital document creation process which includes varying sources, complex composition and virtually unlimited destinations. Users are now accessing content for use in digital documents from varying sources including electronic mail, Web pages, Intranets, online services, content providers, and digital cameras. Document composition now includes not only text, but also complex graphics, clip art, corporate logos, Internet content, multiple fonts, scanned images, and color. Finally, the digital document's destination can be printing systems anywhere in the world, such as personal printers, network printers, service bureaus, pay for print providers, or data warehouses for electronic archival.

Enhanced Image Technology insures that documents print faster, easier, and with optimal quality. A key benefit to the user is that Enhanced Image Technology recognizes image objects and automatically optimizes processing to deliver the highest possible quality, and at the same time speed return to application. Adobe PostScript 3 will include new imaging features that support the increasingly complex documents available via the Internet, support for three-dimensional images, photo quality grayscaling, smooth gradients in graphic objects, image compositing, and full-color spectrums.

Adobe PostScript 3 with *Advanced Page Processing* increases the performance of an imaging system. As components in a document become more complex, the printing system will process each component as a separate object in order to optimize imaging throughput. PostScript 3 will support direct processing of Web content, including HTML and PDF. Advanced Page Processing will also extend the resident font set to provide compatibility with the resident fonts of all leading operating systems, enhancing performance by reducing font downloading. PostScript 3 provides users with a more robust ability to manage individual pages within a document, thereby improving control over the printing process.

Adobe's *NetWorks System* improves ease of use, ease of connection, and ease of printer management all in one environment through Adobe PostScript 3. A printer with NetWorks functionality will include a printer-based Web page, Web-based printer management, printing directly from the printer's Web page, support for all industry standard remote management technologies, and a single step CD-ROM installer for all drivers, fonts, and value-added software. Adobe's NetWorks System ultimately allows users to leverage the power and benefits of the Internet. Printer vendors and others are rushing to make any printer on the Internet accessible from anywhere, anytime.

Adobe PostScript 3 also offers what Adobe calls "Planet Ready Printing" to allow local language needs of users anywhere in the world. Users will easily display and print any language with any PostScript 3 printer. OEMs will develop complete imaging systems that are savvy to localized demands of language and usage. Specific features include drivers that are tightly integrated into the operating system, be it Microsoft Windows 3.1, Microsoft Windows 95 or 98, Microsoft Windows NT, or Apple Macintosh, and full support of international font requirements.

What is new about PostScript 3 and high-end printing?

- *Smooth Shading renders gradient fills at the resolution of the printing system.*
- *Selectable Separations enables color separations to be printed, even from low-end monochrome printing systems.*
- *More Gray Levels provide monochrome desktop printing systems with the ability to print photoquality grayscales (up to 256 levels of gray).*
- *For high resolution printing systems, delivers photoquality grayscales and 4,096 levels of each colorant.*
- *In-RIP Trapping.*
- *HiFi Color for more vibrant hues and richer colors.*
- *Improved Color Control provides greater control with respect to overprint between color components.*
- *Idiom Recognition converts less efficient legacy constructs into higher quality, faster Language 3 constructs.*
- *Fast Image Printing enables fast draft mode and near-final quality raster-image printing.*
- *Improved Font Technology and Extended Font Set.*

Adobe has completed Adobe PostScript 3 language feature development and is now beginning its system integration process. The product schedule included two internal quality assurance cycles before system delivery to OEM printing system manufacturers and third-party development partners in December 1996. In the second half of 1997 Adobe disclosed the Adobe PostScript 3 operators and language specific features. They were published in a rather large document that appeared on the Adobe Web site (in PDF form of course).

Extreme architecture

A PostScript Extreme printing system can take in PostScript or PDF files. When it takes in a file, the "Coordinator" evaluates the file to see what format it's in. If it's a PDF file, the Coordinator sends it to a "PDF Page Store" device (a disk or file system). If it's a PostScript file, the Coordinator sends it to a "Normalizer" component that converts it to PDF, and then sends it to the "PDF Page Store" device. Thus all files are in PDF form.

From there, Adobe PostScript Extreme feeds individual pages to as many as ten PostScript RIPs (which contain converters that quickly convert the PDF pages back to PostScript to rasterize them), staggering them in special ways if necessary to accommodate duplexing and other needs. Once they're rasterized into bitmaps, Adobe PostScript Extreme sends the pages to an Assembler and then to the print engine. Because PDF files create pages as individual elements, they can be handled very efficiently.

Extreme neé Supra and the Future of RIPs

The high-speed data requirements of digital presses, large-format film imposetters, and computer-to-plate systems demand radical changes in RIP and workflow architectures. Developers are also trying to eliminate PostScript processing bottlenecks and accelerate deadline production times. RIP suppliers have been converting PostScript into continuous tone (CT) and line work (LW) files via proprietary methods or converting PostScript into some editable internal format in an attempt to make the RIPing process more efficient.

There are lots of alternatives out there. Covalent Systems' Job Monitor Protocol is a standard framework for collecting data from jobs as they pass through a series of steps and for transferring the data to business systems. Prepress production environments could collect critical information, such as how much time was spent on image editing at one workstation and color correction at another, and transfer it to a business system for analysis and billing. All of this is available now if you stick with the selection of proprietary systems and custom interfaces between them. Another proposed standard, CIP3, covers the interaction among processes at the front-end prepress operation, the press itself, and the back-end finishing operation. CIP3 is being promoted by Heidelberg, with the support of other press and finishing-equipment suppliers, in addition to front-end system vendors such as Agfa.

Adobe's contribution to an ideal digital workflow is a printing architecture known as Extreme, formerly named Supra, which will use PDF as its backbone. Demands for last-minute changes in pages foster a concept known as "late binding." RIP developers are working toward a format that allows data to be changed after it has been interpreted by the RIP but before it becomes the bitmap. These changes take account of different printing or proofing requirements, or nonprint delivery.

Adobe's Extreme RIP architecture is a major step in RIP evolution. It is built around the 3.0/3.x version of Adobe's Portable Document Format. PostScript is an interpretive programming language; PDF is a compact, noninterpretive format designed for fast imaging to a screen. PDF has lacked the ability to handle high-resolution images easily and to handle screening for print—both of these are included within Extreme. Extreme also connects Web and print publishing, as both will use the new version of PDF used as the plug-in to Web browsers.

The PostScript of the Red Book is fading away. Extreme ensures that PostScript document files can be processed as separate but complete pages. Multipage jobs can be processed by several RIPs simultaneously. Extreme is aimed primarily at high volume applications and many firms are supporting Extreme.

Agfa, Autologic, and Monotype have already delivered the capability for allocating whole jobs among multiple RIPs and RIPed work among multiple imagesetters. The industry is getting excited because of Extreme's front-end processing.

Working with PostScript

Not all PostScript is equal; code generated by Photoshop conforms to Document Structuring Conventions (DSC), some from QuarkXPress does not. Page structure can't easily be determined. Extreme converts such files automatically into PDF format, allowing separate processing. Extreme incorporates both Adobe PostScript language and Adobe Portable Document Format for production printers, and Adobe PrintMill, an intranet-based printing and printer management solution.

When you create a page in QuarkXPress or PageMaker you are interfacing with the program as displayed on the screen. The GUI describes the page on screen for the user. However, when you click *Print,* it is PostScript code which defines that page as it is sent to the printer or imagesetter. You can even save the

PostScript file to disk and read it (if you can decipher it). But a page described in PostScript is nearly uneditable without an understanding of the programming language itself. Admittedly there are unique people out there who can edit PostScript.

PostScript is a voluminous file format. Placing a single "a" on a Quark XPress page and "printing" the page to an ASCII file produces at least 16 pages of 10/10 type. Not very digestible for humans, unless you speak geek.

Outputting PostScript

There are four choices for outputting a file from an application:

1. Click Print and send the file to a printer on your in-house network. This is a great option if you're publishing a single copy for yourself. Or even a couple of dozen copies for the staff.

2. Send the application file to an outside service, but make sure you send the image files and all of the screen and printer fonts. This file can be changed by the service bureau, making its integrity questionable.

The Four Choices for Outputting PostScript:

1. Click Print and send the file to a printer.

2. Send the application file to an outside service.

3. Save the file to disk as PostScript code.

4. Create a PDF of your file.

This second approach not only opens the door for further unpredictability, but it also raises some tricky legal issues. Due to font licensing, the service bureau must install the fonts you use and/or supply, print your job, and immediately remove those fonts from their system. This must be done for each job and each time the file is printed.

What if the service bureau has purchased a license to the same font? For instance, you supply a document which uses Garamond. Whose version of Garamond is it—Adobe's, ITC's, Monotype's, or some overnight type house's? If you don't specify and/or the service bureau doesn't have the correct version of your typeface, a font substitution will occur. Possible repercussions of an improper font substitution could be the reflowing of text, sometimes destroying the original design. Or maybe you like Courier, the ultimate font substitution.

But service bureaus deal with application files because they can open them, preflight them, and make changes.

3. Save the file to disk as PostScript code, which incorporates the images and fonts, and send it to an output service. This is a viable option if you have a very large external storage device to save all of that PostScript information. (Remember, a single "a" generates 16-plus pages of PostScript text. Well, that's not really fair, because the 16 pages of code could support many text pages. But, PostScript code is voluminous, nevertheless.)

A drawback to this method is the lack of "correctability." If the correct page setup options were not chosen at the time of PostScript generation, the page may not reproduce as desired. Often, designers don't know the specifications of the imagesetter or output device of the service bureau. Without this information, specifications regarding page size, crop marks, line screen ruling, and many other variables can't be set. And once the PostScript file for that document is generated, it's too late.

What if only a part of a page or a graphic created in a drawing program needs to be placed into a page layout application like QuarkXPress or PageMaker? Thus was born the Encapsulated PostScript (EPS) file—a file representing one page with—or in the early days, without—a preview image. This allows you to save a graphic in a standardized form and place it into a composite document where it can be scaled and manipulated to fit. However, the EPS file does not save font data and many artists have seen their beautiful graphics output with Courier because the original font was not available at the RIP. So, the EPS was portable only to a point. Adobe Illustrator now saves EPS with the font data as does Acrobat Exchange 3.x. And the new Placed PDF could replace EPS.

It has been said that EPS stands for Evil PostScript.

PostScript Conclusions

As a platform-independent page description language, PostScript has emerged as a de facto standard. Today, PostScript accounts for 95% or more of the final output of all commercial publications. On the downside, PostScript is extremely variable and page-dependent.

There's no doubt that PostScript has brought on revolutionary advances. But with every revolution comes the need for further refinement. Even Adobe admits that PostScript has many deficiencies for the role it is currently playing. The use of PostScript has far surpassed Adobe's original intention, and thus they are in the midst of solving problems and advancing their core technology in order to fulfill the expectations of today's digital workflow demands. The wide variety of applications, platforms, and typefaces has caused many headaches for the publishing industry. There are just too many places for things to go wrong.

While you can easily move documents around by e-mail, network, or disk, you can't assume that everybody has the right fonts on their system, or that they have the right program to open your document, or even (in a cross-platform environment) the right setup to receive the document. You could spend a lot of time and money installing the same software and fonts, plus the requisite extra hard disk space and RAM, on every system to allow document portability—and then train people on each program used to create the documents in the first place. But of course, this setup is inefficient and you don't have the capital to implement it, and neither does anyone else.

PostScript serves its purpose as a way to describe document pages in a design-rich fashion. But in today's world of ever increasing efficiency, the need for speed, and the customer's insistence on jobs being printed "yesterday," research and development into document handling is a never-ending process. Files need to be transferred from place to place, quickly, predictably, and efficiently. With the increasing use of digital presses, CTP technology, and completely digital workflows, the need for a platform-independent digital file transfer standards is becoming more and more necessary.

That brings us to the fourth alternative for communicating with graphic service providers and the outside world, the Portable Document Format.

4. Create a PDF of your file.

To understand its application and its value in digital workflows, we move on.

More information about PostScript and PDF than you many wish to know:

When you create a page in QuarkXPress or PageMaker you are interfacing with the program as displayed on the screen. Underlying what you see is what you get, and that is PostScript code. When you click *Print*, it is the PostScript code that is sent to the printer or imagesetter. You can even save the PostScript file to disk and read it. Here is some PostScript code. First, header information is output:

```
%!PS-Adobe-2.0
%%Title: PDF intro
%%Creator: QuarkXPress 3.32r5
%%CreationDate: Tuesday, November 26, 1999
%%Pages: (atend)
%%BoundingBox: ? ? ? ?
%%PageBoundingBox: 30 31 582 761
%%For: Onamor Knarf
%%DocumentProcSets: "(AppleDict md)" 71 0
%% © Copyright Apple Computer, Inc. 1989-92 All Rights Reserved.
%%EndComments
%%BeginProcSet: "(AppleDict md)" 71 0
```

In this case the system sets up some shortcuts to reduce the verbose PostScript program commands to shorter versions, e.g. the command "moveto" becomes "/m".

```
/m/moveto load def          /z/setmatrix load def
/rm/rmoveto load def        /t/translate load def
/l/lineto load def          /S/scale load def
/rl/rlineto load def        /g/gsave load def
/np/newpath load def        /G/grestore load def
/cp/closepath load def      /H/setgray load def
```

Then font data is loaded (this is just a snippet):

373A767D4B7FD94FE5903B7014B1B8D3BED02632C85
5D56F458B118ACF3AF73FC4EF5E81F5749042B5F9CF
1016D093B75F250B7D8280B2EACE05A37037F7BDF6E
12226D7D4E2DF2C52FAFD5FD40FE72A0D3AC4BD485
D8369D4C87636E920D1DAF222D92155A9CB1667E715
F0B82799B37CC8F5B32B74B39CF494536DC39C7EF04
A7BCB29E2CEC79073CADCCFB23B4AA1363F8

Each character in the fonts is defined:

```
/Adieresis/Aring/Ccedilla/Eacute/Ntilde/Odieresis/Udieresis/
aacute/agrave/acircumflex/adieresis/atilde/aring/ccedilla/ea
cute/egrave/ecircumflex/edieresis/iacute/igrave/icircumflex/i
dieresis/ntilde/oacute/ograve/ocircumflex/odieresis/otilde/ua
cute/ugrave/ucircumflex/udieresis/dagger/degree/cent/ster-
ling/section/bullet/paragraph/germandbls/registered/copy-
right
```

And then the position and copy are set::

```
43 533.53 m 3.02 -.18 2 19.3 (RIP)d
67.39 h 3.02 -.18 23 101.5 (is just a little bit dif)d
179.48 h 3.02 -.18 2 14.48 (fer)d
193.2 h 3.02 -.18 11 67.38 (ent. Many ar)d
264.25 h (e)M
43 548.16 m 1.55 -.18 8 50.33 (based on )d
266.01 h (-)M
43 562.79 m 0 -.18 12 65.04 (tional featur)d
105.49 h 0 -.18 14 81.86 (es, and some ar)d
184.43 h 0 -.18 16 88.46 (e legally derived)d
43 577.42 m 2.59 -.18 1 8.73 (fr)d
```

Both PostScript and PDF use a notation known as "postfix." That is where the name PostScript came from. Postfix is an old mathematical notation sometimes called reverse "Polish" notation. The "action" indicator, usually called the "operator," comes at the right-hand end of the expression (that is, after the variables) and complex expressions can be written without the use of parentheses. There is also a notation known as "prefix" notation where the operator comes first. Normal notation (e.g., a + b) is called "infix" notation because the operator is between or within the expression.

The default measurement system in both PostScript and PDF is in units of 1/72 of an inch and the starting point is in the lower left corner of the page or drawing area. An 8.5 by 11 inch page is 612 units horizontally and 792 units vertically—just like graph paper.

PDF objects are a construct that the PostScript Language does not have. The ability to randomly access portions of PDF a document and the page independence of PDF pages are based on the object structuring of PDF.

Color space resources are often called color profiles. This terminology has been promoted by the International Color Consortium or ICC. The color space resources in PDF and PostScript serve the same function and are roughly equivalent to ICC profiles. They aren't literally the same but contain the same or equivalent information. It is easy to convert from a PDF color space resource to an ICC profile and vice versa. Most color management systems consider color spaces as being derived from and belonging to color devices. The material in this PDF file is associated with two devices one L*a*b* and on a RGB device. Most color management discussion and color management software consider a whole job to be in one color space. This is a mistake that Adobe PostScript and PDF do not make. Any material in either language can be specified with respect to any color space.

The objects can refer or point to one another to form complex relationships and data structures. Streams of arbitrary unstructured data can be defined. The cross reference table that occurs at the end of the PDF file allows program to read selected objects out of the file at arbitrary positions. The objects don't have be in any particular order or place within the file. The cross reference table determines where each object has ended up in the file. This notation is powerful enough to represent many other kinds of structured data besides a PDF document. In fact Adobe has begun to use the notation for at least two other purposes: one for FDF files to hold the field name, field value pairs that result from filling in an Acrobat Form, and the second which is the *PJTF*, or Portable Job Ticket Format, used to control the workflow and post-processing steps.

PDF files require that they have a /Root which points to a /Catalog which points to a /Pages object which points to the documents pages. Not all uses of this notation should have to follow those document rules. In fact, both the FDF and the PJTF do not. So to be perfectly logical, each of PDF, FDF, and PJTF are using a notation and specializing it for their particular needs. Jim King of Adobe Systems has coined the term SDF or Structured Data Format for the general use of this notation and reserved PDF for the specialization having to do with representing documents in this particular way. Thus this diagram.

Structured Data Format (SDF)

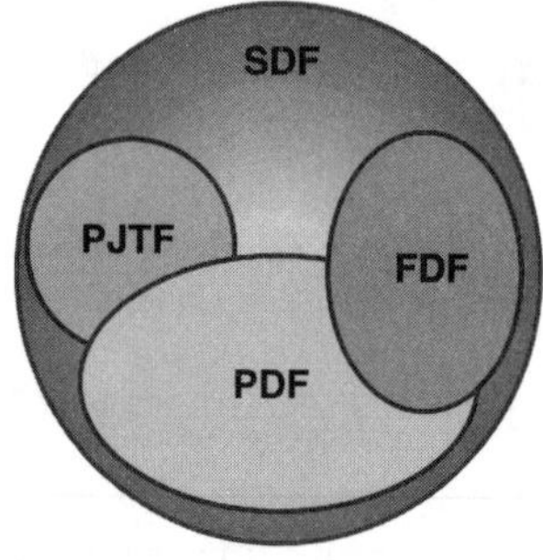

More information: http://www.adobe.com/ supportservice/devrelations/PDFS/TN/PDFSPEC.PDF

3

AN INTRODUCTION TO PDF

Paper is the culprit, we are told. The publishing industry's search for an ideal digital document had several software companies claiming they had the answer to paper documents needlessly killing trees, piling up unused in warehouses or filing cabinets, and causing frustration among business people lost in the sea of paper. With the increasing attention being given to the Internet, the idea of a paperless world seemed tangible. However, now that we know the truth of the statement there'll be a paperless office when there's a paperless bathroom. The ideal document must handle paper *and* pixels.

Yes, it's true: PDF prints three to four times faster than PostScript direct.

What is a Portable Document?

The underlying concept of document portability is that of printing to a file and distributing that file. As an analogy, take a sheet of paper with text and graphics on it and fax it. The sending fax converts the page images to dots and the receiving fax prints them out. If you have fax capability from your computer, a program takes the page image, converts it to dots, and sends it to the printer. Now, save the last file we created on the computer—a representation of the page as dots—and instead of printing it to paper, put it on the screen. This document can be sent, viewed, and digested on screen by a large audience without any hint or mention of paper.

Portable documents are self-reliant files that remain intact regardless of the platform they were created on. In other words they can be moved electronically from computer to computer, for viewing or printing, and retain their content and format integrity.

But there is something missing. Like any fax image, there is no underlying *intelligence* for the text. You could not search through it because it does not know an *'a'* from a hole in the paper. Searchability is something you want. You could use the application file but then the receiver must have the same fonts you had, and the images must be provided and the applications must be at the same revision level.

Some portable document approaches saved a bitmap of the page as it appeared on the screen, the underlying ASCII text, and the font data. By having the text in ASCII format you can search for words and phrases. This is a major advantage over print. After all, the material in a book or catalog is not really information until you find what you want.

Acrobat Distiller
Acrobat Distiller is used to convert any PostScript file into the Portable Document Format (PDF). Distilling a file is the best option when dealing with complex information such as high resolution images, gradients, and other artwork. The result is a page-independent, highly structured, small file size format ready for delivery. Acrobat Reader allows for viewing, navigating, and printing a distilled document.

Acrobat Reader
Reader's role is primarily for viewing as well as third-party proofing and approving. The client can retrieve a PDF via the Internet, view it and approve it without having the original application program. Adobe has made the Reader free and downloadable at www.adobe.com

Acrobat Exchange
Acrobat Exchange is also for viewing, however editing features are included. Hyperlinking, bookmarking, deletion and insertion of pages, and password protection are all possible. Version 3.0 also has added word editing.

A drawback to portable documents is analogous to some of the portable TVs of the 1950s when you had a unit that weighed hundreds of pounds with a handle on the top. Even with compression, some portable documents are six to ten times bigger than the original application file. True, the final file size is larger than the original application file counterpart, but the advantage is quite significant.

By creating an electronic document that carries all the needed components—fonts, graphics, and even a program to view and print the document—portable document software could eliminate the cost and time of printing, distributing, and storing paper copies, while adding the ability to find text and link multiple documents so information would be more accessible and more dynamic.

Whether for use within a company for document exchange and distribution, or for use on bulletin board systems, CD-ROMs, or fax-back services for user-requested documents, the possibilities for portable document software were beguiling.

The Portable Document Enters the Market
In 1990, developers introduced portable document software. First came No Hands Software's Common Ground. Adobe later shipped Acrobat and Farallon Computing followed with Replica. Other companies also had portable document formats.

Adobe's Portable Document

Adobe Systems dove into the competition in 1993 defining their Portable Document Format as a file format used to represent a document independent of the application software, fonts, hardware, and operating system used to create it. The software used to create this PDF was called Acrobat (actually, its original name was "Carousel").

Adobe's PDF was a third version of a PostScript file format. It took the PostScript file of the document and RIPed it (called distilling) to a new format that saved every page as an individual item, compressed the type and images, and cut out almost all the variability of the programming language. What remained was a portable document file that could be viewed on almost any platform, Mac or PC, running DOS, Windows, MacOS, or UNIX. But the first version of Adobe Acrobat did not fully support high-end printing for color separations.

The PostScript code needed for production printing was not included. This did not hinder the use of PDFs to view on monitors or to print to monochrome and color printers, but it was not able to output a composite CMYK file as four monochrome PostScript streams to be sent to an imagesetter or a platesetter.

The Ultimate Portability

The printing and publishing industry saw more potential in the PDF than just looking at pages on a screen. Like the success of PostScript itself, the success of the PDF was based on capturing the high end of the printing world. Competitors to Acrobat only saw viewing as the problem to be solved. They forgot that paper was and always will be the only form of communicating to everyone in the world regardless of their lifestyle or location. Paper is the only democratic form of communication, since it does not restrict access because of technology.

Toward the Ideal Digital Document

Adobe acknowledged the need to meet the demands of the high-end printing market. As a result of their working relationships with organizations such as the PDF Group and DDAP, Acrobat is emerging as the software capable of creating the near ideal digital document.

PDF Components
PDF files contain: a view file that displays the page as you created it, embedded type (Type 1 and TrueType), graphic objects (bitmaps and vector images), links for variable forms data, and links to sound and QuickTime or AVI movies—plus Job Ticket information.

PDF Group
A professional group of representatives from leading production and printing companies who have joined in support of the PDF in the areas of electronic delivery and pre-press workflow. The group members are working directly with Adobe to solve problems as well as provide input for necessary additions.

DDAP
Stands for The Digital Distribution of Advertising for Publications. Started in 1991 as an ad-hoc industry committee to implement various industry standards. Today DDAP is active in the role of including PDF as an industry standard.

Acrobat 3.0 and Acrobat 3.01
Adobe Acrobat 3.01 adds a PDF Writer driver, an Acrobat Capture plug-in, and macros to support Microsoft Office 95 and 97. For Windows 95 and Windows NT users, Exchange 3.01 and Reader 3.01 enable improved integration with Internet Explorer, including support for submitting PDF forms to Web servers and displaying search highlighting. For Windows 3.1 users, Exchange 3.01 and Reader 3.01 provide improved printing to non-PostScript printers.

For all Windows users, Exchange 3.01 and Reader 3.01 include enhanced security on links to external applications. When Acrobat 3.01 users view PDF files within Web browsers, they can find, select, and copy text, and use keyboard navigation. Acrobat 3.01 automatically installs the Netscape plug-in when used with Communicator.

For Power Macintosh users, Acrobat version 3.01 includes Acrobat Capture, Import Image, and Scan plug-ins. For all Macintosh users, Acrobat version 3.01 includes an improved ExportPS plug-in. Acrobat Exchange 3.01 and Acrobat Reader 3.01 include enhanced security on links to external applications. When Acrobat 3.01 users view PDF files within Web browsers, they can find, select, and copy text and use keyboard navigation. Acrobat version 3.01 runs on Macintosh System 7.0 and later (Acrobat 3.0 required System 7.1 or later).

The printing and publishing market expressed their needs, and Adobe listened. Acrobat 3.0 was released in November 1996 with added functions necessary for the high-end market. Acrobat 3.0 incorporates extended graphics state functions so that color separation can occur more effectively and OPI (Open Prepress Interface) image comments can now be preserved. The PDF pages can be exported as an EPS for insertion in a page makeup program, like QuarkXPress or Pagemaker—only this time the font data is saved. In late 1997, Acrobat 3.01 fixed a few glitches and added a few new features. 3.02 is coming.

The Ideal Digital Document

As presented in the previous chapter, the choices for moving documents from place to place are few and not very attractive. Thanks to Acrobat, we have an alternative to sharing large, bulky, and arbitrary information containers.

Imagine an ideal digital document. How many headaches would be avoided if there was a portable, page-independent, platform-independent file format which could not only preserve design richness, but also allow for repurposability, searchability, predictability, and even some editability? This ideal digital document describes the Portable Document Format. PDF not only may be the aspirin for your headaches, but also the refinement of the PostScript revolution. PDF documents:

- Preserve design richness
- Create predictability
- Maintain some editability
- Create searchability
- Allow repurposability
- Allow high-end printing

Design Richness

Preserving design richness entails maintaining the look and feel from creation to final output by properly reproducing all content information within the document such as bitmap, vectored line art, and text.

Bitmap or raster images

A bitmap image is an image which is defined digitally by a number of pixels in a rectangular array. Because computers are binary entities they must break up images into a map of small pieces, spots, or picture elements, or pixels. All images that are scanned into a computer are bitmap images whether black and white line drawings, or black and white or color photos.

Bitmap (Scanned) Line Art

Monochrome bitmap images are the simplest and the smallest in file size. Scanned black and white line drawings are monochrome bitmaps. Each pixel of the bitmap can either be black or white (on or off), so only two bits of computer information are required to define these bitmaps. For this reason, they are also called bilevel bitmaps.

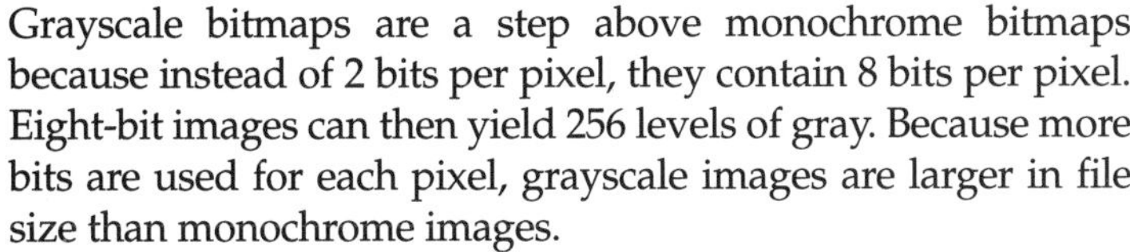

Grayscale bitmaps are a step above monochrome bitmaps because instead of 2 bits per pixel, they contain 8 bits per pixel. Eight-bit images can then yield 256 levels of gray. Because more bits are used for each pixel, grayscale images are larger in file size than monochrome images.

Grayscale Contone

Color bitmap images can be either 24 bit (RGB) or 32 bit (CMYK) yielding millions of possible color combinations for each pixel. Thus, color bitmap file sizes tend to be very large, humongous even.

Because the human eye cannot discern the individual pixels, we perceive the images to be smooth lines (monochrome bitmaps) or continuous tone (grayscale and color bitmaps). These digital images can accurately describe an original image, but tend to be very large in file size.

Line art

Line art is described as a combination of lines, curves, tints, and fills in vector or line form to allow it to be scaled, rotated, etc. and converted to a very compact version of the data that is independent of the final size of the image.

Unlike bitmap images which are defined in terms of pixels, vector images are defined by the curves used to create the shape. (Remember all that ugly geometry: $y=x^2 + 2$?) Think of it as lots of little electronic rubber bands which are anchored at some points and pulled apart at others. As the size changes the stretching compensates but the quality is not affected.

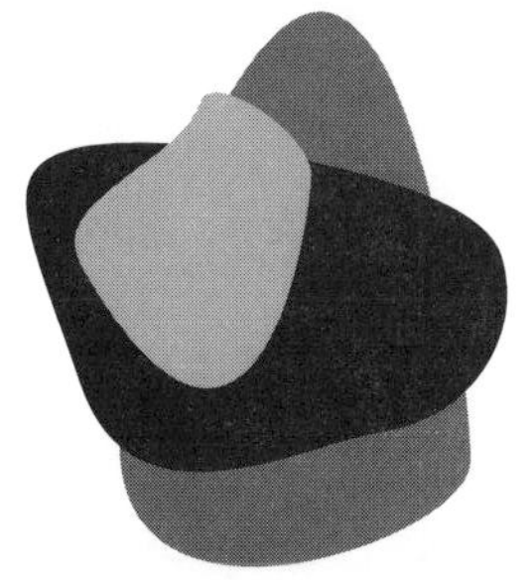

Vector-based line art

Text
Text is carried as character symbols with placement information, which can be converted to the final image through use of font drawing information. This allows the size of the text, and the font used, to be varied during the creative process.

PostScript allows users to design and create pages containing bitmaps, line art, and text without concern for a particular platform or output device. Acrobat Distiller transforms PostScript files from PC, Macintosh, and UNIX systems into all-inclusive bundles retaining all formatting, graphics, and photographic images that the original documents contain.

ASCII
The American Standard Code for Information Interchange is the most basic coding system for text and serves as the foundation for virtually every system that encodes information. Almost every document can be saved as ASCII which can then be imported to any other document.

Rich Text Format (RTF)
Microsoft format used to go across platform with fonts, style sheets, and graphics to some extent. Once thought to be a portable document format but it was not robust (rich?) enough.

Portability
Document portability is our concern. Computer users have suffered from a lack of formatted text, loss of graphics, and lack of proper fonts installed on particular computers that are used to view and print documents. Documents have been somewhat portable through the use of ASCII and Rich Text Format (RTF) files, but content alone does not always convey the true message without formatting or design richness.

PDF*ing* a file makes it "portable" across computer platforms. A PDF file is a 7-bit ASCII file, and may use only the printable subset of the ASCII character set to describe documents—even those with images and special characters. As a result, PDF files are extremely portable and compact even across diverse hardware and operating system environments.

Furthermore, PDF provides a new solution that makes a document independent of the fonts used to create it. Fonts can either be embedded or descriptors can be used. Embedding the fonts in the PostScript stage includes the actual font outlines in the file. Distilling this file will ensure that pages are displayed with type characters in exact position. The font descriptor includes the font name, character metrics, and style information. This is the information needed to simulate missing fonts and is typically only 1–2K per font. If a font used in a document is available on the computer where the document is viewed, it is used. If it is not available, two Adobe Multiple Master fonts are used to simulate on a character-by-character basis the weight and width of the original font, to maintain the overall color and formatting of the original document.

Font embedding does add some size to the document; however, it provides an important aspect of document portability—cross-platform font fidelity and the ability to print out at any resolution. This means that the receiver of the digital page could have a high-resolution color printer and print out pages as needed at a remote location. Pages could be created in one part of the world and then sent to a printer in the opposite hemisphere which uses the data to make high resolution films for printing. Plus, embedding all fonts assures text editability.

About Adobe Acrobat

- *View documents with guaranteed page fidelity. It is not necessary for the user to buy the application. The Reader is free.*
- *Time is saved by sending information and files over e-mail.*
- *Collateral and technical documentation can be stored electronically and accessed instantly, this is helpful with sales and customer service groups.*

Editability

Last minute changes to a PDF can be made via a new plug-in for Acrobat Exchange called Text Touchup. Since the PDF is vector-based and includes the font name, character metrics, and style information, small type changes are possible. Full paragraphs cannot be edited due to the lack of reflow capabilities, but those small yet sometimes crucial changes such as misspelled words or incorrect phone numbers or prices can be made on a last-minute basis within Acrobat Exchange or with other plug-ins, such as Pitstop.

Predictability

Acrobat PDF eliminates the variability of PostScript and provides a foundation for effective digital print production workflow. A RIP interprets PostScript, converts it into a display list of page objects, and then rasterizes the page into a map of on/off spots that drive the marking engine. When you distill a document into a PDF you are essentially doing the interpretation and display list functions as in the RIP process.

The resulting PDF is a database of objects that appear on a page and how they relate to each other—a print-specific file with extensions for OPI, image screening information, and more. The variability of PostScript is squeezed out and only the essence remains—which can be output back into the PostScript stream again for printout—just open the PDF and print it. If your document can be distilled to a PDF, the odds are that it will output reliably on most PostScript RIPs.

The PDF provides a solution to three information needs:

- *The need for an interchange format for viewing richly formatted documents.*
- *The need for a data format for archiving documents.*
- *A format for transmitting documents for remote printing.*

PDF is not your father's PostScript.
PDF defines basic types of objects, such as numbers, names, arrays, dictionaries and streams. Page descriptions, outlines, annotations and thumbnails are built from these objects, as in PostScript. Objects have an object number and a generation number, allowing multiple versions of an object to exist within a document. The object can be referenced indirectly by its object number.

PDF operators are mostly one letter, unlike the verbose PostScript operators. Several operators combine more than one PostScript operation. The 'b' operator in PDF does the work of PostScript's closepath, fill, and stroke verbs, as an example.

PDF does not have programming constructions for branching (if . . . else) or looping. The PDF interpreter runs straight through the code when it displays or prints.

The pages of a file may not follow each other in sequence and are accessed through a catalog/balanced-tree data structure, analogous to a disk directory system. When versions of a file are saved, a new table is appended to the end of the file and contains a pointer to the previous cross-ref table to trace back through earlier versions.

A PDF file contains a cross-reference table of objects which can be used to quickly find the data needed to display a page. The table allows different pages to share data. As annotations are created and erased, the table is updated.

Searchability

With the Acrobat software, it is possible to find information instantly. There is a full-text search tool which allows the user to retrieve exactly what they need. Hypertext links can be used to simplify browsing and navigation features such as bookmarks and cross-documentation links are also included to help the user move through numerous documents faster.

Repurposability

Adobe's PDF for some time has been marketed as a Web tool offering greater design richness over the HTML language constraints. PDFs can be downloaded to the World Wide Web and accessed through the free Acrobat Reader plug-in for the two popular Browsers. A document created for print output and distilled into a PDF can now, with virtually no changes, be used on a Website. Sites can now be created with all the design richness available in page layout applications such as QuarkXPress and Pagemaker. Open in Reader and print.

PDF and PostScript

Although PDF files require PostScript information to be created, the resulting PDF files are different from their PostScript counterpart. A PDF file is not a PostScript language program and cannot be directly interpreted by a PostScript interpreter. However, the page descriptions in a PDF file can be converted into a PostScript file.

How PDF Files Work

The PDF file format is not a programming language like PostScript. You cannot send a PDF file to a laser printer directly because the file format contains information that a current PostScript RIP would not understand. The PDF does contain PostScript code, but the extra PDF data would inhibit the RIP from processing the document. A PDF file must be sent to a RIP through the Acrobat Reader or Exchange application. When output by Reader, the PDF is converted into a PostScript file and sent to the RIP just like any other PostScript file.

Perhaps in the future, the PDF will become the basic file format and the very concept of RIPs will change. PDF and PostScript are highly interrelated at present.

Creating a PDF File

The two methods for creating PDF are:

- PDFWriter
- Acrobat Distiller

The PDFWriter, available on both Apple Macintosh computers and computers running the Microsoft Windows environment, acts as a printer driver. The PDFWriter shows up as a printer in the Macintosh Chooser window. The user needs to choose that "printer" to create a PDF file. The user then "prints" their file to the PDFWriter and an electronic file is produced. This is similar to "print to disk."

For more complex documents that involve special fonts, high resolution images and detailed illustrations, the PDF file must be created differently because of limitations of PDFWriter. Acrobat Distiller was developed for this situation. Distiller produces PDF files from PostScript files that have been "printed to disk." The Distiller application accepts any PostScript file, whether created by an application program or hand-coded. Distiller produces more efficient PDF files than PDFWriter for various reasons and it is recommended if you are going to print to film or plate or on high-end digital printers.

Viewing and Editing PDF files

You can view a PDF file with Acrobat Exchange and Acrobat Reader. Acrobat Reader is a free downloadable file available from Adobe at [www.adobe.com]. Copies of the Reader can be shared with others. These two applications contain the interface that allows users to easily navigate through a PDF document, even those that contain thousands of pages.

To improve performance for interactive viewing, a PDF defines a more structured format than that used by most PostScript language programs. PDF also includes objects, such as annotations and hypertext links, that are not part of the page itself but are useful for interactive viewing.

Compression

There is about a 10 to 1 compression factor between the original application file and the PDF file.

Differences between PostScript and PDF

- *A PDF file may contain objects such as hypertext links that are useful only for interactive viewing. Sorry, PostScript.*
- *To simplify the processing of page descriptions, PDF provides no programming language constructs. It is a list of objects.*
- *PDF enforces a strictly defined file structure that allows an application to access parts of a document randomly.*
- *PDF files contain information such as font metrics, to ensure viewing fidelity.*
- *PDF requires files to be represented in ASCII, to enhance document portability.*

Creating, Using & Distributing PDF

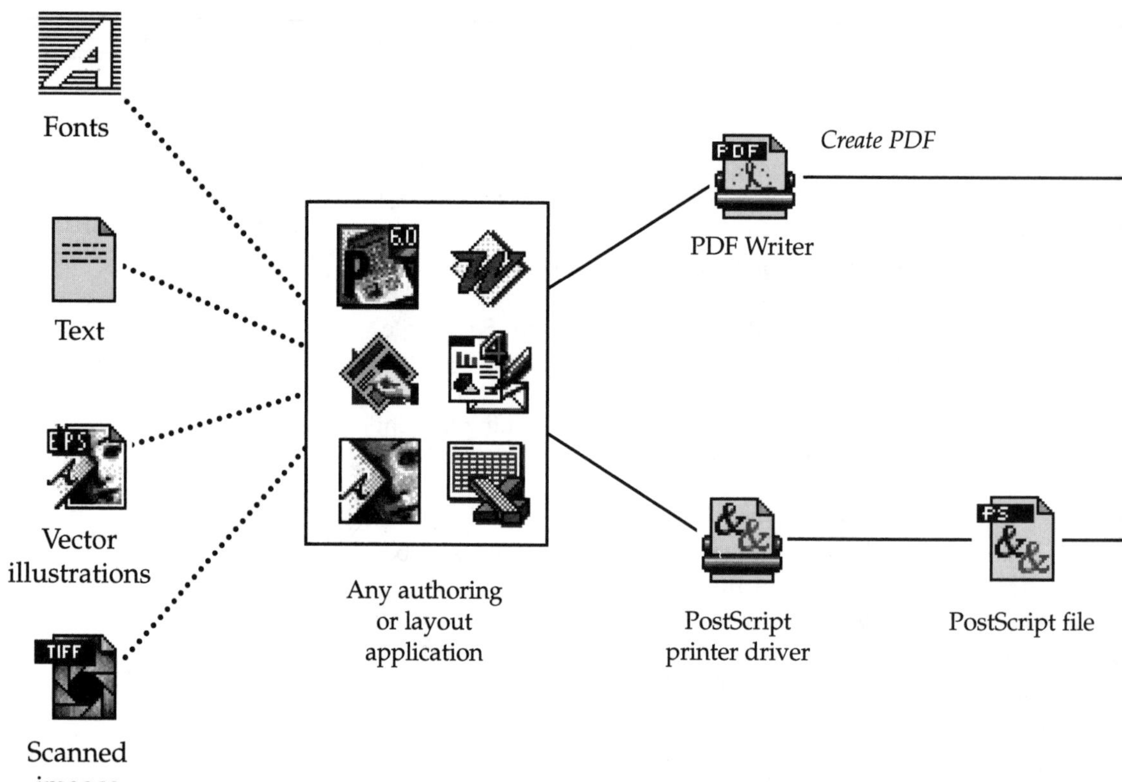

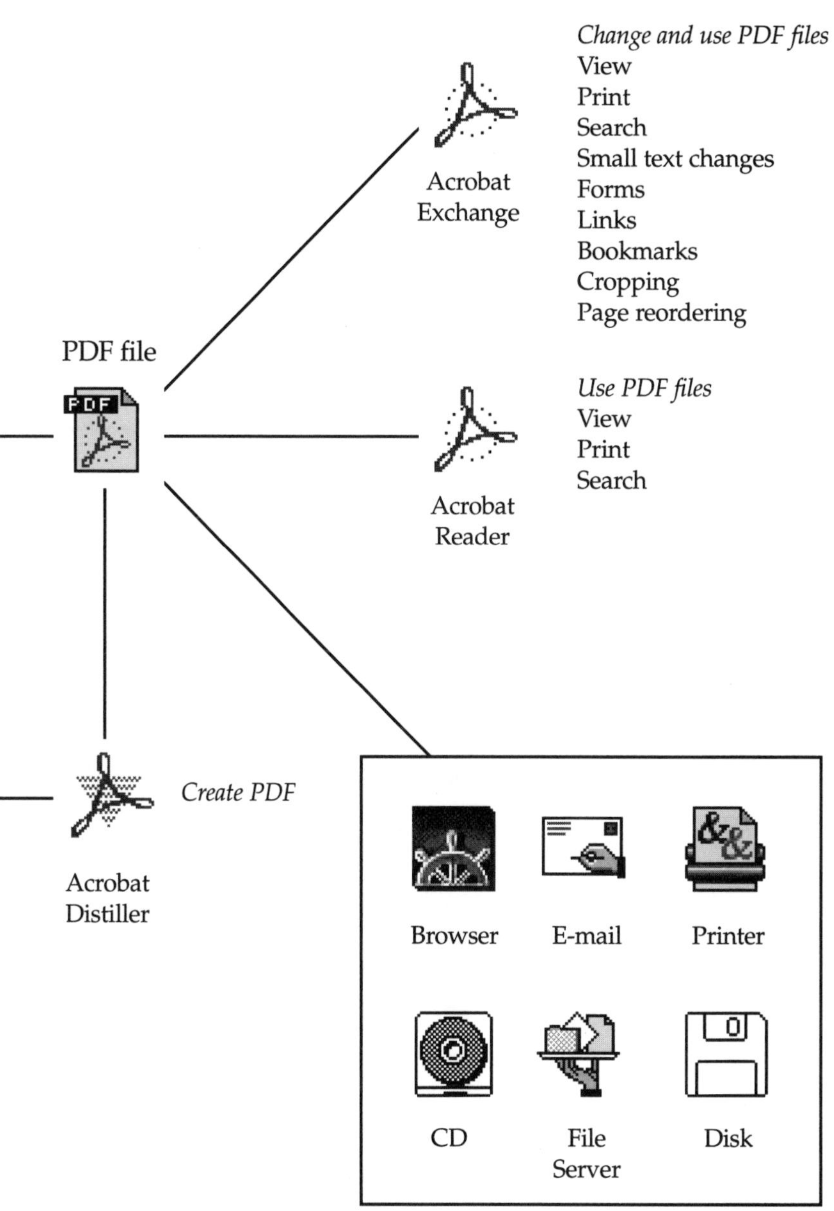
Change and use PDF files
View
Print
Search
Small text changes
Forms
Links
Bookmarks
Cropping
Page reordering
Acrobat Exchange
PDF file
Use PDF files
View
Print
Search
Acrobat Reader
Create PDF
Acrobat Distiller
Browser
E-mail
Printer
CD
File Server
Disk

Predictable in file integrity. *Missing fonts or PostScript resources used to mean long coffee breaks. In "high-end" PDF, all the font information is included in the file. No more need to have all the fonts available by all the players in the production process.*

Predictable in processing time. *In a modern workflow you want to predict the time it will take to process a file. When your digital platemaker has to supply printing plates for a press, you have to have a good idea how long it will take to produce your plates. Press downtime costs a small fortune. In a busy service bureau, you need to know how long a file will RIP so you can deliver it yesterday.*

In the Workplace

The PDF workflow has already been embraced by the printing and publishing industry with some very successful results. The Associated Press has developed AP Adsend. It lets you create a newspaper ad on a Macintosh or PC and save it as a PostScript file, distill it into a PDF file, fill out an on-screen delivery ticket specifying which newspapers are to run it and when, then transmit it in compressed form to the AP.

AP then distributes it directly to the designated newspaper or newspapers. The ad is received by the newspaper's computer looking just the way you created it. They can save it as an EPS and position it into their desktop layout file for the issue, or in most cases print it out and paste it onto a layout sheet. There is no ad film and no overnight delivery. Sorry, FedEx.

This technology goes beyond the transmission of newspaper ads. It allows access to entire electronic archives of information. The browsing, searching, and reading possibilities are extensive. It is a giant step for document independence, where software creates a giant electronic "manila envelope" filled with just about anything from pages to sound to video.

With cross-platform interoperability and sufficient bandwidth for video/audio transmission, an advertiser will be able to send ads and/or commercials directly to publications, broadcast media, or even directly to online service subscribers.

For newspaper and magazine publishers the digital distribution of advertising is a critical issue. They must have every part of the publication in digital form to take advantage of direct-to imposed film or plate. With Placed PDF functionality in PageMaker and expected in QuarkXPress, the digital distribution of ads is now a reality.

PlacePDF means that the PDF is treated like an EPS file and can be placed in a picture box in QuarkXPress or into a page layout in any other program.

The PDF format itself has no inherent print-device dependencies. Where print-device dependencies can get introduced is at the PDF-to-PostScript conversion step. This step may introduce dependencies because it has to take a position on what level of PostScript the print device supports.

- Level 1 does not support image compression; Level 2 does.
- Level 1 and "Red Book" Level 2 do not handle Type 42 (TrueType) fonts; more recent Level 2 implementations do.
- Levels 1 and 2 don't handle substitution of calibrated color for device color, LanguageLevel 3 does.

In each case, the PDF-to-PostScript conversion can work around limitations by converting the relevant construct to something acceptable to a lower implementation level: it can decompress compressed images, convert Type 42 fonts to Type 1 or Type 3 (almost certainly with some loss of hints), and substitute calibrated color for device color. The process of converting PDF to PostScript occurs when you open a PDF in Acrobat Reader or Exchange and click *Print*.

If a PDF file is going to be printed on printers of different levels, either it must be converted to the lowest supported level (which may produce a file much larger and slower to print than a higher-level file), or it must be converted multiple times. Fonts and graphics are still an issue with a PDF workflow because of printer RIPs being at diferent levels of capability.

If users import 72-dpi GIFs enlarged to 350 percent in their QuarkXPress layouts, the PDFs that are made aren't going to be any better. There are also two more places for them to make mistakes: when users write the PostScript file to disk, and when they set the Distiller preferences. In both cases the right decisions must be made. What makes us think that these files would be any cleaner had they been sent in native form? Hopefully, training and some automated scripts will help to get these files right.

	Reader	Reader +Search	MS Office Macros	Exchange	PDF Writer	Distiller	Catalog	Scan	Capture Plug-in	Import	Touch Up
Macintosh	•	•		•	•	•	•				•
Power Macintosh	•	•		•	•	•	•	•	•	•	•
Windows 3.1	•	•		•	•	•	•	•	•	•	•
Windows 95	•	•	•	•	•	•	•	•	•	•	•
Windows NT 3.51	•	•		•	•	•	•	•	•	•	•
Windows NT 4.0	•	•	•	•	•	•	•	•	•	•	•
SunOS	•	•		•		•					
Sun Solaris	•	•		•		•					
HP-UX	•	•		•		•					
AIX	•	•		•		•					
Silicon Graphics IRIX	•	•									
Digital UNIX	•	•									
Linux	•										
OS/2	•										

Acrobat is made up of several interrelated components. The chart above shows the present availability of those components for each of the computer platforms and operating systems.

This is why PDF is so popular—it runs on almost every major platform.

4

PRINT-RELATED PROCESSES & ISSUES

Now that we have reviewed how PDF becomes a predictable, platform-independent, page-independent entity which solves many of the limitations of PostScript, we must tackle other print-related workflow issues. PDF is the link for completely digital workflow for high-end printing and publishing. PDF alone is nice, but PDF in a digital workflow is nicer.

The very essence of digital workflow for printing and publishing involves the integration of many process steps. Workflow is a collection of functional processes. The most common processes include:

- Preflighting
- Trapping
- OPI serving
- Imposition

Each of these steps has evolved from manual techniques to computer operation with manual intervention, and now to totally automated approaches. For a long time each step often required a different computer server to perform a function or functions. The trend today is toward more comprehensive and cohesive systems that are transparent to the user.

Trapping

Trapping can take place at the application program level, at a separate computer with dedicated trapping software, or at the RIP equipped with trapping functionality.

Trapping Approaches

Automating the analysis process for a PostScript file has two approaches.

- The first approach parses the PostScript code to identify the logical objects on the page (text strings, tint blocks, contone images, line drawings, and other objects) and their relationships to each other. It works with geometric properties, and is called the vector method.
- The second approach rasterizes the file and then analyzes at the resulting raster image to determine where colors are adjacent—called the raster method.
- Hybrid systems use a combination of vector and raster technologies.

There is debate about placing device-dependent trapping within a PDF. If one wants to make a PDF that will be printed flexo, offset, and gravure, they would need three different trapping schemes, or three different PDF files, instead of one PDF file that could have the trapping applied in RIP.

Agfa showed an IRT (In-RIP Trapping) approach that keeps these device dependent process control "elements" outside of the PDF "digital master." Although one can represent traps within a PDF file, a better approach is to have these as comments that can be modified and applied for different printing requirements, keeping the PDF device independent. Agfa used the Adobe PJTF (Portable Job Ticket Format) to hold trapping and other device controling information (such as imposition).

Each approach works. Vector-based trapping is a mathematical masterpiece and works well with PostScript which is a geometric, vector-oriented method of describing a page. Analyzing the objects to be trapped should be simpler from a vector viewpoint. The output of a stand-alone trapping product (if it is also PostScript code) for most pages will be more compact if it is derived from an object description rather than a rasterized bitmap. That, in turn, reduces the transmission and processing time for the RIP that will receive the code.

Once the objects have been identified within the trapping program, sometimes relatively little mathematical manipulation is required to generate the chokes or spreads needed, just a matter of changing the width and depth of an object according to a set of formulas. (When objects cross over multiple colors, then a new PostScript trap object is generated with its own width and depth. Here, more arithmetic is required.) With complex object outlines, such as serif type, vector trapping is more effective in generating the smaller trap outlines for type without losing its defining shape. Part of this is because sharp corners can be regenerated mathematically with precision, which is better than a raster approach that might round off corners.

One type of PostScript data that resists vector analysis is scanned images. These are truly raster data, so vector-oriented trapping programs must look at the pixel values to determine the color value of the trap. To trap to a vignette or a photographic image, there are two approaches:

- determine an average value for the entire image
- figure the traps on a pixel-by-pixel basis (often known as sliding traps)

Anyone can convert a PDF to EPS and trap it and re-distill it. This is a valid workflow. One can even RIP a PDF (that is, output PDF from Reader or Exchange to a PostScript file and send it to a RIP) and into a raster file and trap it, and if they wish, Save as EPS *and distill this. Even TIFF/IT-P1 files can be sent through solutions by Total Integration or Shria and made into EPS and Distilled or one can represent pre-separated copydot scans of four-color film in PDF though it will be tough to trap the TIFF/IT and copydot files when in this state.*

Using either approach requires some level of analysis of the raster data. Vector approaches can bog down when there are lots of tiny objects on the page because of the need to generate and process the many tiny objects needed to create the trap areas.

Raster-based trapping algorithms have been refined to the point that they can be executed very quickly. A raster file is the least common denominator for any page once separated into plates, it is very easily converted into screened bitmaps, the ultimate form for any page when it goes to a raster output device. Raster-based algorithms should not have to redo the rasterization process and should find it equally easy to work with any number or combination of objects on the page. Raster approaches generate gobs of binary data. The interim data structures tend to need lots of RAM and disk space, and the results can take a long time to output. This is not quite the problem it used to be, as disks and chips get cheaper by the hour, and data compression techniques improve. High-end prepress systems have always done trapping by analyzing raster data.

Hybrid trapping uses combinations of vector and raster analysis. Some approaches rasterize the file at relatively low resolution to locate object boundaries and color combinations. They use this knowledge to create new objects containing the trap colors, which are then output as a series of PostScript objects These objects are then merged with the original EPS file and sent to be RIPed. Hybrid approaches sometimes end up rasterizing the file at two different resolutions in two different machines which could lead to noticeable trapping problems.

No mathematical program can anticipate all design situations and corrections, and some of these situations must be made at the source application, while others can be done in the trapping program. The more changes that can be made in an automatic trapping program, the more efficient the resulting workflow will be.

Some Trapping Functions:

- Trap color and placement based on components of adjacent colors.
- Trapping of blends with sliding traps for smooth transitions.
- On-screen preview of all trap locations and colors.
- Unlimited trap zones to confine a trap area or apply different parameters.
- Integrated batch-processing capability.
- Trap-conforming EPS files or multipage PostScript files, from anywhere, to anywhere.
- Correctly spread light into dark colors, and achieve optimal colors and placement.
- Increase productivity by outputting files immediately after trapping is complete.
- Maximum control trapping bitmap and continuous tone images against other objects.
- Evaluate and adjust the traps you want before you commit to page or imposed film.
- Trap only the areas that need it, or alter parameters based on custom requirements.
- Set parameters for each file to be trapped; leave file unattended during processing.

In-RIP Trapping

A while back, Mitch Bogart, the technical genius at Rampage, emphasized that trapping functionality should be moved to the RIP. Some people have argued against such a move, claiming that if the trapping took place in the RIP, you wouldn't be able to check the trapping before you have printed on the press. As long as a RIP takes input in a standard form (EPS files for example) and output is in standard form, a RIP should be considered open rather than closed and proprietary. Trapping may also be handled faster and better when integrated with the RIP. There are other functions such as screening that are also best left integrated. What about spot color separation, JPEG decompression, and OPI replacement? There is a technical synergy that comes from grouping functions together. It also removes the burden for many of these tasks from the originator.

OPI was born with Aldus and then became part of Adobe when the companies merged. Adobe eventually spun off all the prepress systems products as a separate company, called Luminous. Luminous was then acqiuired by Imation. Now Imation has done away with the Luminous name and integrated the product line into Imation.

Regarding proofing, the mistake lies in thinking of a RIP as an invisible black box that comes glued to each output device. Not only is this more expensive, since each output device, proofer, and printer must have its own RIP, but, as many have pointed out, the multiplicity of RIPs leads to inevitable visual fidelity problems. Different RIPings produce different results. This is especially true when dealing with OPI replacement, fonts, spot colors and other enhancements for high-quality, high-speed production RIPs. Instead one should view the RIP as a sort of central workstation, taking in files and outputting to the screen and multiple peripherals. Before, the RIP was part of a system; now, the RIP is the system. However, Extreme and PDF change the concept a tad. Visual fidelity is assured because the PDF captures the page with more data about the page and the same RIP architecture is used.

Adobe has a PostScript interpreter which incorporates built-in trapping of color pages with a patented, state-of-the-art in-RIP trapping technology. Trapping of color pages is the process of micro-adjusting images on multicolor output devices to compensate for physical limitations of printing presses and other reproduction systems. Adobe expects to license to OEM customers the Adobe PostScript interpreter software with built-in trapping capabilities. Two of Adobe's printing system manufacturer customers, Agfa Division of Bayer, Inc. and Crosfield Electronics Ltd., now part of Fuji, demonstrated in-RIP trapping technology in September 1996.

Imposition

One area in the prepress industry that has developed rapidly in the past couple of years is electronic imposition. Due to the prevalence of large-format imagesetters and platesetters, many users are turning to imposition programs for workflow automation. Some imposition functions:

- Standard and custom imposition layouts for sheet or Web press printing.
- Enhanced shingling and bottling controls.

The concept of Automatic Picture Replacement was born with Scitex when they sold a product called Visionary, based on QuarkXPress. OPI was intitially developed for PageMaker by Aldus using single-file TIFF images. DCS (Desktop Color System) was developed by Quark, Inc. and a prepress/ catalog company. DCS is a sort of extension to the EPS format. It consists of as many plates as you have colors plus a preview (on top of the preview that you have on a Mac for EPS files in their resource fork—this other preview is used if you print to a composite device such as a color printer).

In DCS 1.0 you had only multi-file DCS-EPS files, and you could only handle CMYK, so you always had files like _filename_.eps (the preview), _filename_.K (the black plate), _filename_.Y (the yellow plate), _filename_.M (the magenta plate), _filename_.C (the cyan plate).

In DCS 2.0 you can have the same thing as one single file, where internal indication of byte offsets lets a digesting software know where to find the respective pieces. And above that you can have any combination of plates, e.g. spot colors. The PlateMaker plug-in for Photoshop has been devloped by alap (www.alap.com) and should be available from any XTension/Plug-in distributor.

- Form, file, and page-level positioning and rotation, with verso/recto page controls.
- Customizable page and sheet marks, with the option to use EPS art as a mark.
- On-screen preview of press sheets, with all marks and pages in place and proportion.
- Support for pin-registration systems with full control over form and sheet position.
- Impose PostScript files from any application or platform, output them to any device.
- Accommodate all standard binding methods, as well as irregular layouts.
- Gain maximum control by applying parameters by the job, file, or page.
- Achieve highest degree of accuracy when compensating for folding discrepancies.
- Modify any printer's mark to meet particular production requirements.
- Check the accuracy and placement of all parts of a form before output.
- Accurate placement of imposition forms for plate-ready film or press-ready plates.
- Send, impose, and return pre-trapped files for separation without intervention.

OPI

Aldus' Open Prepress Interface (now under Imation) has become a generic term meaning automatic picture replacement. PageMaker users wanted a simple way to use high-res color photos that had been scanned on high-end scanners, without having the data burden that accompanies those images. Aldus decided it made more sense to use PageMaker to design the layout and compose the text, then add a few commands to tell the output system how to position the color files. They were right.

OPI is an extension of the PostScript language and was developed by Aldus Corporation. OPI workflows can improve prepress system performance by reducing the amount of data that workstations and networks must carry and process. An OPI Server keeps high resolution graphics stored until imagesetter or printer or platemaker output time, and creates a low resolution "View file" for applications to work with. The preview is sometimes called:

- a proxy image
- an FPO (For Position Only)
- a view file
- a screen viewfile
- a placement file

An OPI Server adds the ability to "OPI-Publish" TIFF images from the Server database. For each high resolution TIFF image which is "OPI-Published," a view file (a low resolution of the same image) is made available. When users of OPI-compatible applications need TIFF graphics, they can use these view files instead of the actual high resolution graphics. Since the view files may contain fewer than 75 pixels per inch (compared with high resolution TIFF contones with up to 300 samples per inch or line art with up to 1,000 samples per inch), much less data is transmitted and processed in the workstation.

The computer operates faster, since these view files contain much less graphic data, but users can still see each graphic on the screen and can scale, crop, rotate, etc., as if it were an actual high resolution graphic. These low-res "placement only" files contain information about where the high resolution file is located, how the image has been scaled, cropped, and rotated. This information is in the form of OPI comments within the low-resolution file. At output time, the application creates a PostScript file with image processing instructions (OPI Comments) substituted for each OPI view file. The OPI Server scales, crops, rotates, and merges the high resolution images with the PostScript file according to these instructions.

Macintosh users can access OPI features only via OPI-compatible applications such as QuarkXPress or Adobe PageMaker. OPI operation with these applications is identical to standard operation with two exceptions:

- Some functions are faster, due to the smaller quantity of graphic data that is being handled by the computer.
- To output an item containing OPI view files, or to place it in the Server database, a Macintosh user "saves" it as an EPS file in a Server folder, with TIFF images omitted.

It might be said that somewhere in the mists of time it was thought that EPS could do what PDFs do. But EPS did not embed font data (which it now does with PDF).

EPS wanted to be what PDF is: a viewable, editable PostScript file.

In a nutshell:

Format	***Images***	***View File***
OPI	*TIFF*	*Low-res TIFF*
DCS	*EPS*	*PICT*

Sometimes two Server folders are set up for this purpose—one for direct output and one for storage in the Server database. QuarkXPress also offers an alternate method for OPI output in which the user can "save as EPS" with TIFF omitted.

For direct output, the OPI merging function (part of the OPI Server) receives the PostScript file, integrates the high resolution image from the database, and performs scaling, cropping, and rotation as directed in the OPI comments before automatically outputting the entire job to the PostScript device. OPI resolves the problem of large image files and deals with the data burden that impedes productivity.

The OPI industry-standard convention defines how to embed instructions in a PostScript output file to tell the output device where and how to merge the various text and graphics components of a page. OPI enables users to work with low-res preview images in their page-makeup programs, and keep the high-res

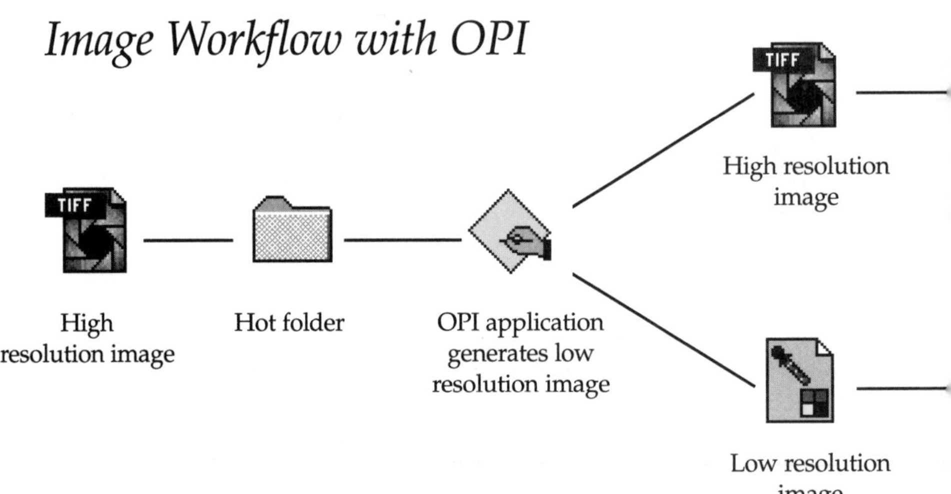

graphic images close to the imagesetter. This maximizes workstation productivity and minimizes network traffic.

Working with OPI

Pre-1: Send your images to a service bureau or printing service and have them scan them and provide you with the low-res screen images while they maintain the high-res print images on their OPI Server.

1. Make up pages using any of a variety of desktop publishing applications. Compose and assemble the editorial content, line art, charts, ads, and other page elements.
2. Place low-res OPI images on the page using a preview image, which is a low-resolution TIFF image.
3. Send the job to the service bureau or printing service for output.
4. The OPI server reads the path name, fetches the high-res image from the Server, and merges the image in position with the text and other elements.

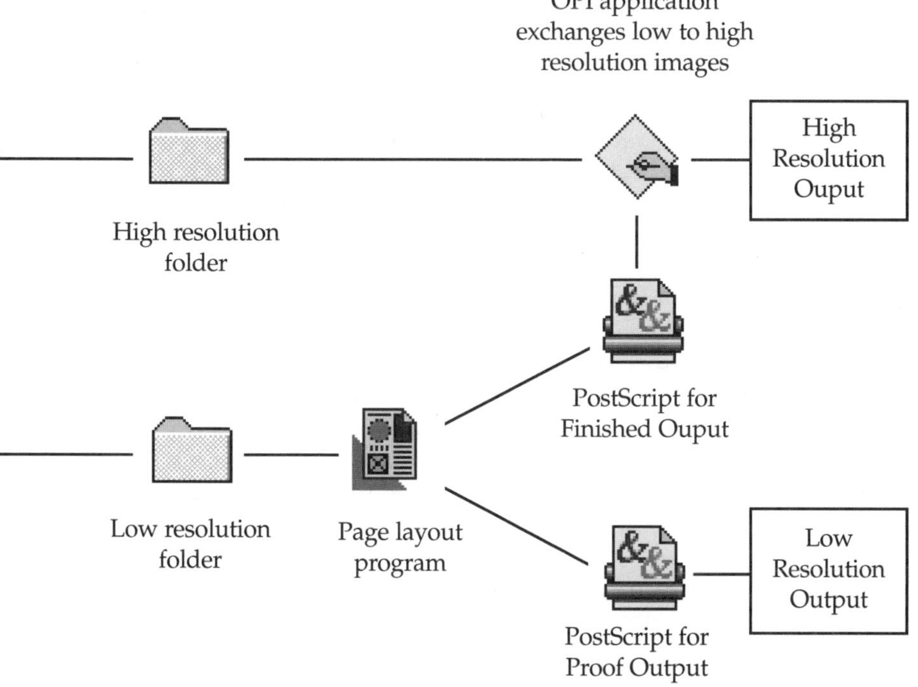

The high-res image resides at or near the RIP or RIP Server or the network Server, and its storage path and file name must match the storage path and file name on the Server. Many vendors offer OPI solutions that support TIFF, EPS, or DCS files. Most support all the cropping and sizing commands issued in the page makeup program. When the page makeup program creates a PostScript output file of the job for the printer, it appends these commands, along with the path name and file name, as PostScript comments in the job stream. When the OPI-compliant output device reads these comments, it acts upon them by retrieving and merging the high-res image.

DCS and OPI

Many OPI solutions also support DCS (Desktop Color System or Separation), another standardized convention for handling color separations created with desktop publishing programs. DCS originated with Quark Inc. as a way to manage color separation files. In general, DCS is a subset of the EPS file format. In producing color separations, DCS-compliant programs such as Photoshop generate a set of five EPS files. These five files include a main, or "composite" file, as well as a file for each color separation: cyan, magenta, yellow, and black. The composite file contains the names of the cyan, magenta, yellow, and black EPS files and the path name to their storage location, PostScript commands to print a nonseparated version of the image, and a 72-dpi PICT version of the image for viewing on the screen. DCS 2.0 offers easier maintenance by offering a single file format which contains all of this information.

In a typical DCS operation, the user places the composite image in the Quark file. When the user prints the job, Quark sends the color separations instead of the composite image. OPI systems that also support DCS enhance this operation by allowing the color separation files to be stored on the Server, so Quark does not have to transmit these large color files at print time. Quark sends only the callouts, containing the path name to the separation files, and the OPI Server fetches those files accordingly.

Encapsulated PostScript

PostScript was originally designed only to send files to a printer. But PostScript's ability to scale and translate (move the origin of) what follows makes it possible to embed pieces of PostScript and place them where you want on the page. These pieces are EPS files. EPS is considered a graphic file format.

The PostScript code in an EPS has to follow certain rules. For instance, it shouldn't erase the page since that would affect the whole page, not just its own part. It is forbidden to select a page size, because this would both change the size of, and erase, the whole page.

An EPS file includes a special header made up of PostScript comments (starting with %) which have no effect on a printer. The most important comment is %%Bounding Box. This gives the location of the EPS picture if it is not scaled or translated. A program uses this information to place the picture accurately within a page. The PostScript part of an EPS file is "stripped in" to the PostScript generated as the document is printed, preceded by PostScript "scale" and "translate" instructions.

If you send an EPS file to the printer it might print a copy of the graphic. Or it might print nothing at all. Or a blank page might exit the printer. EPS files aren't designed for printing, but sometimes you get lucky. At the very least, EPS files always print on a default page size since they must not include a page size.

When a desktop publishing program uses an EPS graphic, it isn't smart enough to interpret the PostScript in the EPS to show a picture. So, the EPS file is often accompanied by a preview. This is a low-resolution picture the application program does know how to show. There are several forms of preview. An EPS file without a preview is still usable but probably shows on screen as a gray box—people expect more than that!

There are three types of preview:

- Macintosh
- DOS
- System independent

The Macintosh preview is a PICT graphic in the EPS file's resource fork. This means the EPS file's data fork contains just PostScript. The DOS preview is embedded in the file, and there's a special header. A DOS EPS with preview cannot be printed until the header and preview are removed. In DOS, the preview is embedded as a TIFF or WMF graphic.

An EPS file with system independent preview is called EPSI. This adds a monochrome bitmap as comments inside the file. It isn't really system independent since in Macintosh and DOS many applications don't support it. They can use the file, but won't show the preview. Many Macintosh programs will read DOS format EPS files, and handle them OK if they contain a TIFF preview. DOS programs can read Macintosh EPS files but they can never see the preview hidden in the resource fork.

Other variations of EPS which may make a file unusable are binary and Level 2. Binary EPS files work well on a Macintosh, but most PCs can't print them, because any Control+D in the data will reset a typical PC PostScript printer. Most EPS files written on a Macintosh are binary and don't work on most PCs. Level 2 EPS files can only be printed on a Level 2 printer.

This little discussion on EPS and related forms was provided to help you understand that we, as an industry, have been struggling to find a universal, standardized format for moving files and documents around networks.

Placed PDF may replace EPS since it includes fonts. But applications must add code to accept PPDF files.

Quark, Inc. has stated that they will support PDF export and import capabilities in an eventual upgrade to QuarkXPress 4.0.

Placed PDF and Refined PDF Export

You now have the ability to place any page from an Adobe PDF file into a PageMaker publication. The Placed PDF feature enables PageMaker users to reuse and repurpose the millions of PDF pages that have been created with Adobe Acrobat. For example, using the Import PDF Filter, a user can select an individual page from a catalog saved as PDF and place it into an ad or brochure being created in PageMaker. In addition, the PDF import filter allows users to control the resolution of the PDF on-screen preview for faster performance.

With the rapid adoption of PDF for digital printing workflows, Adobe has improved the Export PDF interface to streamline the process of preparing PDFs for print production. Customers and service providers will find the controls for output color model (such as CMYK or CIE device independent color), OPI comments and font and file size optimizations easier to use.

PDF Import Filter Version 1.0 for PageMaker
The PDF Import Filter 1.0 works with Windows 95, Windows NT 4.0, and MacOS. The Placed PDF is similar to a placed EPS graphic. It appears in PageMaker as an on-screen preview, using the preferences from the filter preferences dialog box and cannot be edited. The PDF always prints at high resolution, but prints at the resolution of the screen preview when printed to a non-PostScript device. To import a PDF page:

- In PageMaker's layout view, choose File > Place. In Windows, PageMaker lists PDF documents with a .pdf extension. To see a valid file without that extension, choose All Files for Files of Type. In MacOS, PageMaker lists PDF files with file types of PDF<space> and TEXT.
- Double-click the file to place it, or select the file and click Open (Windows) or OK (MacOS). If prompted to select a file type in Windows, choose Portable Document Format from the list, and then click OK.
- In the filter preferences dialog box, select options for importing specific pages, and for including PostScript printing information and display settings.
- Position the graphic where you want and click.

You can also import a PDF directly from Netscape Navigator.

The PDF Import Filter dialog box provides options for PostScript printing and display settings. The dialogue box includes Navigation arrows beneath the thumbnail image to advance through the PDF document page by page. Thumbnail images of each page appear in the dialog box. One is the default page number. Specify a page number, and then click to select.

Once documents have made the transition to electronic form and have made their way through a pre-press or pre-publishing system one of the most important steps—and it occurs at various points—is proofing, or the verification of documents prior to printing.

Proofing
"Edging closer to dotlessness" as Seybold Publications describes it, may be the theme in the color proofing area. The contract proof (the verification proof that the client, service bureau, and printer agree will be the standard for color and quality)

Proof
The contractual prediction and verification, through simulation, of the expectation of eventual reproduction, that is legally defensible

The time to attach an output profile (a description of the behavior of the imagesetter or platesetter) is when sending a job to the output device. At that point, it does not matter if the profile is an ICC (International Color Consortium) profile or a PostScript CRD. The real issues:

- *Tools to calibrate the device and produce accurate profiles*
- *Attaching profiles to devices and/or jobs to honor calibration*
- *Coordinate rendering intent (a characteristic of each object in a job) with output device profiles*

PostScript 2 already has the mechanisms to provide the underlying data model. PDF has equivalents. Using Distiller to clean up PostScript is not possible when ICC information is embedded in the file.

ICC profiles cannot be embedded in a PostScript file. ICC profiles can be attached to (or embedded in) images (in a TIFF file), and appropriate CSAs and CRDs can be inserted into the PostScript file by the application or driver. When Distiller creates PDF, the CSAs are preserved and the CRDs are discarded. To "reattach" CRDs or otherwise honor output-specific ICC profiles in a PDF as part of the PDF language may be counter-productive, and device-dependent. Preserving transformation profiles might be useful.

If you want to honor an output ICC profile, you probably want specific behavior in Exchange, Reader, or some other PDF interpreter or printer, not in Distiller, which only "produces" the PDF. This would probably be handled using an Exchange plug-in.

issue is moving toward an uneasy acceptance. Most contract proofs have used film-based technology, but with the increasing move to all-digital workflows, and as computer-to-plate systems avoid film entirely, film-based proofing is being replaced by proofs from digital data. A contract proof has traditionally shown the exact halftone dot structure so that potential printing problems like moiré can be avoided. Some digital proofing systems reproduce halftone dots, and some do not. Print buyers are accepting contract proofs without halftone dots. Screening is now pretty much a non-issue since print buyers seem prepared for moiré passé. The contract proof market now appears to be a battle between proofers with and without dots.

Most vendors of CTP systems also offer imposition proofers to replicate blueline imposition proofs. These tend to be large-format monochrome plotters, although there are some in color and some that print on both sides of the sheet to show true imposition. Imposition printers, used in conjunction with inkjet, dye sublimation or other proofing engines, are looked at as the future course for digital proofing within new workflows. For people who still want traditional dot proofs (and are willing to pay for them) digital dot proofers are available. And some users may even keep an imagesetter around to produce film only for proofing purposes in a CTP environment.

Remote Proofing

A major trend is that of remote proofing, where an inkjet dye sublimation, or other color proofer is physically installed in a customer location. PDFs from the customer are sent to the prepress or printing service and processed. The Server system prepares a version of the PDF that calibrates to the eventual reproduction device and the files are returned to the customer for proofing printout. Since the PDF files are compressed, they can be sent via telecommunications lines to and from the customer.

New Servers and RIPs based on electronic job tickets will automatically direct PDFs to queues based on the customer, reproduction device (litho press, flexo press, digital color press, or whatever) and convert or modify files as required for each step in the workflow.

5

DIGITAL WORKFLOW ENVIRONMENTS

Face it—mechanicals are gone. Do you really feel bad about it? Workflow is digital. And discussions of digital workflow always seem to start with conventional workflows: scanning, assembly, film output, stripping, contacting exposure, duping, proofing, and plate exposure. Since most print-oriented organizations have moved into film imagesetting and imposetting, there are now more users with partial digital workflows than those without them.

Partial digital workflow refers to the fact that most users still have little islands of automation that are not integrated into a comprehensive system. Using network or sneaker-net, they are moving files to specialized servers for specialized operations. Too often digital workflows have been constructed around people rather than machines and software processes. The trend today—and the PDF is in the forefront of that movement—is to move workflow to totally automated systems. We cannot continue analog thinking in a digital world.

The benefits of PDF printing and publishing are most evident in a digital systems environment. Today, our perception of a system is a bunch of Macs and/or PCs cabled together to share various output devices. In reality, the network configuration and functionality are the most important issues in prepress and prepublishing productivity.

Before Networks

When computers were first introduced they were batch-processing oriented. All work was delivered to the computer for processing *en masse*. By the 1970s, typewriter and then video terminals were attached to the computer to provide access to files and CPU processing. This gave users increasing amounts of interactivity. There were limitations to the number of terminals that could be connected and users were limited in what they could do and when they could do it. This led to the development of local area networks as an alternative method of connecting computers… and people.

Network Basics

A network is everything that ties computers together and enables them to communicate, including hardware and cables (the physical things) and software (the stuff you can't see but does all the work). A network allows computers to be connected together, so that they may share common software, data, or devices. A network is the sum of all its parts.

Computers may be connected in a number of different ways. Apple Macintosh computers may be connected using either LocalTalk or Ethernet. Windows-based PC and compatible computers are typically connected using Ethernet. LocalTalk and Ethernet describe the physical aspects of connecting computers and additional software is needed to make the system operate.

In the Macintosh environment, this software is included—AppleTalk. In the Windows environment, it is necessary to add additional software such as Microsoft Windows for Workgroups, Artisoft Lantastic, Novell Netware, or others. Microsoft Windows 95 and 98 have network software built in.

Networking Macintosh Computers

In the Macintosh environment, the simplest and least expensive networking approach is LocalTalk, which is built into every Macintosh.

You can construct a simple network of two Macintosh computers using LocalTalk with PhoneNet-compatible connectors—common telephone wire that connect computers, and the same wire that is used to connect a telephone to the wall jack. You can also use the same connectors to connect computers to your printer and share it. Unfortunately, it is very slow.

A LocalTalk-based network can be as simple as two computers and a printer connected together. With LocalTalk, computers and printers may be over a thousand feet apart, depending on the quality of the cable used. Computers are strung together, or daisy chained, using the connectors. If additional computers or printers need to be added to the network, they can be daisy chained into the existing connections.

Bits per second
Kbps = kilo (thousands) of bits per second
Mbps = mega (millions) of bits per second

230,400 bps would be 230.4 Kbps.

Usually if the number is even thousands or millions we use kbps or mbps but if it is not, the whole number is presented.

This type of connection is inexpensive, but not very fast. The speed of the communication between computers is 230,400 bits per second. This may seem fast when compared to the fastest modems available, but it may not be fast enough.

Computer modems are now about 56.6Kbps or 56,600 bps. They started out at 300 bps—honest!

An alternative is to use Ethernet, a much faster networking technology—at least 43 times faster than LocalTalk. 10-Base-T Ethernet is at 10,000,000 bits per second; 100-Base-T is at 100,000,000 bits per second; and 1,000,000,000 bps Ethernet is not far away. Fiber optic connections are being applied by early adopters. With its high speed data transfer rates which can out perform copper wire, optical fiber will clearly become the new method for transmitting data.

Most printers for Apple computers are not directly compatible with Ethernet, so the use of a LocalTalk-to-Ethernet gateway is needed. The gateway converts the high speed Ethernet communications to the lower speed LocalTalk format so that existing printers can understand the information. Some high end printers, imagesetters, and platemakers will directly support Ethernet without a gateway.

A Macintosh-based network using Ethernet does not connect computers and printers together by daisy chaining them—they are connected into a Hub. A device known as an Ethernet Transceiver is used to connect the cabling to the computer. For the Macintosh to use an Ethernet network, it must have an Ethernet card installed. Most recent Macintosh computers are delivered with a built-in Ethernet card. Most computer stores or catalogs can supply the card and instructions for installing it. The Ethernet Transceiver connects the card in your computer to the cabling of the network. The maximum distance supported by Ethernet is 500 meters.

Two cabling types in use: 10-Base-T and 100-Base-T. The number comes from the speed of the network (10 or 100 megabits per second), "Base" refers to the communications technology (Baseband), and the "T" refers to Twisted Pair, the actual physical cabling type. Devices in a 10-Base-T network must be within 100 meters of one another.

Once the Ethernet network is physically set up, the Network Control Panel in the Macintosh is used to select Ethernet rather than built-in LocalTalk. With Ethernet in place, the only difference the user will notice is improved performance. One of the computers on the network is designated as the Server, and the other computers are its Clients. Usually, the fastest computer should be the Server.

Bits galore
Bit = 0 or 1

Byte = 8 bits

Kilobyte ≈ 1,000 (thousand) bytes or 8,000 bits

Megabyte ≈ 1,000,000 (million) bytes or 8,000,000 bits

Gigabyte ≈ 1,000,000,000 (billion) bytes or 8,000,000,000 bits

Terabyte ≈ 1,000,000,000,000 (trillion) bytes or 8,000,000,000,000 bits

Humungabyte ≈ A Whopper with large fries. About seven bits.

Networking Windows Computers
The networking picture in the Windows environment is more complex. The physical aspects of networking are almost the same as the Macintosh environment but LocalTalk is not used in the Windows environment. The networking method built into Windows for Workgroups or Windows 95 is known as the Microsoft Windows Network. This method is similar to AppleTalk in appearance and operation. The printer is connected directly to a computer, rather than to the hub itself. In the PC environment, the computer allows its directly connected printer to be shared. Any computer on the network can then connect to the shared printer and print. Most Ethernet cards for PCs come with a connection on the card, so a transceiver is not needed. Certain newer Macintoshes are also configured this way.

AppleTalk and the Microsoft Windows Network are known as peer-to-peer networks: any computer can be a Server, and any computer can be a Client. A computer can also be a Server to one computer and a Client to another at the same time.

Local Area Networks
A local area network (LAN) is a collection of hardware, software, and users brought together so as to allow them to cooperate in a fully integrated environment. A LAN typically covers a limited geographical area, measured in meters rather than in kilometers. LANs can cover the linking of two to several hundred users spanning a single office, to one or more departments spanning several floors of a building or spanning an entire site. LANs usually complement wide area networks (WANs) to extend this environment to interconnect or bridge LANs locally or across great distances to form larger networks. Local area networks encompass:

- Computers
- Workstations
- Peripherals, such as printers and fixed disks
- Cabling and associated components
- Software

Interconnection
There are three techniques for interconnection of computer and related equipment:

- *Centralized:* The system is a self-contained entity capable of autonomous operation. The units of communication in such cases are address and data blocks and work in a master-slave relationship. A stand-alone mainframe is a prime example.
- *Decentralized:* This is communication between systems. The units of communication in this case are byte and data blocks and work in a master-slave relationship. A mainframe computer with concentrator(s) attached to it falls in this category.
- *Distributed:* This is network communication among self-contained autonomous intelligent systems. Such a system works in a relationship of cooperation and not master-slave. A cluster of Macintoshes connected to a cluster of Sun workstations connected to a cluster of PCs is a good example of such a system. LANs fall in the category of distributed systems.

Sharing of Information and Resources

A distributed system should look transparent to the user. The whole system should appear as one large dedicated local system and all the remote resources should appear as if they were local to the user. The interface to such a system should be user friendly. People usually work in groups, and perform related tasks. Whatever information is presented on paper can also travel over a LAN in the form of data. This ability to transfer data throughout a department or an organization enables users to exchange messages, documents, forms, and graphic files. They also have access to common software packages on the LAN. Though information itself is a resource, the primary purpose of installing a LAN is to share system resources, like software and peripherals such as laser printers, optical disks, etc.

Disadvantages of a LAN

The disadvantages of a LAN are:

- General administration, backing up, adding new users, loading software, etc. have to be done by a competent person or staff, called the Network Administrator.
- If the file server fails in the middle of a session, sometimes it is not possible to salvage all user files, as some Servers do not provide for incremental back ups.

In a properly administered network, data stored on the file server would be regularly backed up and this would take the pain out of backing up files from the users' point of view. Also, the file server itself can be kept in a physically secure room, which means better security particularly for sensitive customer data.

- Security of Data: If the file server is not in a reasonably secure place, then unauthorized people may gain access. If user privileges and file protection mechanisms are not properly implemented, it becomes open to misuse.

LAN Concepts

The first component of a LAN is the Communication Channel, also called the transmission or the LAN medium, and typically should have the following characteristics:

- High speed bandwidth
- Flexible and extendible
- Reliable and maintainable

A LAN medium defines the nature of the physical path along which the data must travel, and allows a great number and wide variety of hardware devices to exchange large amounts of information at high speed over limited distances. A local area network is more than just the cables.

LAN Topologies

The physical medium may be arranged in a number of ways. The overall geometric shape, or topology, is very important in a LAN design. There are three basic practical topologies used in LANs: Star, Ring, and Bus.

Transceiver
To connect your network cable to a computer, you need an adapter. The transceiver converts the network signal into one that the computer can deal with (and vice versa for data going out from the computer).

Repeater
Network cables can only carry a signal so far before resistance degrades it. A repeater takes the signal at some point, pumps it up, and lets it travel a greater distance.

Hub
A number of computers may be clustered into a section of a network. That section is connected to a hub, which connects to other sections.

Star Networks

This topology usually forms the basis of a wide area network. In this type of network, each station is connected to a central switch by a dedicated physical link. The switch provides a path between any two devices wishing to communicate either physically in a circuit switch or logically in a packet switch.

Ring Networks

Stations are connected by a loop of cable and each connection point, called a repeater, is responsible for passing on each fragment of the data. Access is not under central control and the data is sent in packets. Within each station, there is a controller board which is responsible for:

- Recognizing packets addressed to that workstation
- Controlling access to the ring—deciding when it is clear to start transmitting.

Bus Networks
Bus networks are the most common LANs. They do not need any switches, and in their simplest form, no repeaters. They share a common, linear communication medium and each station requires a tap which must be capable of delivering the signal to all the stations on the bus. The data is sent in packets, and each station listens to all transmissions, picking up those addressed to it. Bus networks are passive, since all the active components are in the stations, and a failure affects only that one station. Stations on a bus network are limited in distance and only one station at a time can transmit.

Choice of a Server
On a network, a server is a computer with a large amount of disk storage that has shared software and information. Other computers on the network are clients and access the software or information as needed on the server. Choosing the right server and equipping it properly are the keys to the success of a LAN. A server is usually a computer that holds bulk of the LAN Operating System and shares its resources with workstations. In most LANs, a single server:

- Stores shared files
- Stores software
- Links to printers or other output devices
- Links to tape drives and storage media
- Links to modems
- Links to RIPs

As a rule of thumb, plan on 1 Tbyte of server storage—or at least 500 Gbytes.

You can boost performance further by using a disk controller that also incorporates a dedicated cache of high speed RAM.

Typically, a LAN outgrows a server at about 40 users, but the limit depends on the applications in use. A server can be used either as a Dedicated Server or as a Concurrent Server. Using the server as a Concurrent Server degrades network performance, and may even crash the network—so forget it.

These resources are shared by all connected users. As a LAN grows, these functions are spread over many servers and separate data management and communication servers may be needed.

One of the first decisions is whether to buy:

- a standard PC or Macintosh as a dedicated server and tailor it with third party add-ons
- a PC or Mac designed as a proprietary server unit
- a Sun Computer or Silicon Graphics workstation as a server
- An NT running on an Intel Pentium PC or DEC Alpha hardware

Dedicated Server
Networking methodologies use a dedicated server. In this case, one computer (typically a very fast one) is designated as a dedicated server. All other computers that attach to it are clients only. This technique is used for larger networks that demand higher performance than can be realized with peer-to-peer networks.

With a dedicated server, all shared files are on the server, and the client computers access it for their information. A server will usually have a network operating system installed on it (Novell, Lantastic, etc.) and the monitor and keyboard will be removed. The server will automatically start its software on power up, and only service requests from the network. Printing is shared as before, except that in very large networks, another computer is usually designated as a print server and will only service printing needs.

Proprietary Servers
Because proprietary server options are designed for a particular LAN operating system, you avoid incompatibilities that crop up with a standard PC. For example, some third-party back-up systems and power supplies do not work reliably with certain LAN operating systems. Proprietary units are optimized for their specific LAN operating system.

ms= millisecond
A meaure of disk access time. For instance, the amount of time from when data is requested by the CPU to when the drive returns the data.

Storage
A fast hard disk and disk controller are vital to server's performance. A disk with 40 ms average seek time is too slow for most LANs. If you expect a lot of traffic, consider a 16 ms or less system. How much storage you will need depends on applications. If you want to store a lot of shared files and programs on the server, think big. Get a disk controller that can daisy chain several drives together, so you can add storage as needed. You will certainly need more drives, especially if you plan to use the disk mirroring options available with LAN operating systems as a backup approach.

Cache RAM
The more memory available for a server's hard disk, the faster the server and LAN operating system will run. Think big

again—say 100 Mb of RAM. Since fetching data from the cache is much quicker than getting it from disk, disk caching can speed access to hard disk data. It stores the last data read from the drive plus the next few sectors in RAM, gambling that the software will request that data next.

Network Adapter Cards

No matter how fast the server, performance is limited by the speed of the server's LAN adapter card. Most vendors offer intelligent cards, equipped with RAM to speed throughput, but they are a bit more expensive.

CPU

Make sure the server uses a CPU with the fewest wait states. Zero is the best, and two are too many. If the network is really busy, use a server with a 100 MHz CPU or better.

Backup

A server should preferably be equipped with a tape backup unit that can hold all the files you want to store. The backup software should be compatible with your LAN operating system and should be capable of backing up all system files. It should also be capable of running while the server is online and perform while unattended.

Drivers

One adapter card will exchange packets over a shared cable with any other adapter, since they all conform to the same electrical signalling, physical connection, and media access specifications. But things are different on the software side of the card. Since each manufacturer designed and implemented its adapter using slightly different hardware components, each adapter needs customized software in order to address them and to move data through the system. This piece of software is known as the driver software.

Print Servers

A print server receives jobs from a user on a network, stores that job in a queue, and then forwards the job to an output device on the network—most networks have multiple output devices, from low-res laser printers to a high-res imagesetters and platemakers. Features such as queue management, statistics reporting, printer setup, and file storage for later printing are usually common. A typical scenario:

- Select *Print* from the application's menu.
- Your computer connects to the printer and asks if it is ready to accept a job.
- If the printer is busy with another job, the computer waits for the printer which may only need to finish somebody else's job or you may be the 7th person waiting.
- When the printer is ready, the computer sends the first packets of data which the printer receives and processes (while your computer waits) until the job has been completely sent to the printer.

If you're the ninth person waiting to print, the wait could be enormous. (You might show your college ID when you enter the queue and get a senior citizen discount before your computer is freed for use again. OK, we exaggerate.)

Most computers allow you to print in the background. Background printing means that when you select *Print*, the computer saves the job to a temporary file and a separate piece of software handles communicating that file to the printer, when the printer becomes available. You can continue working on the computer while the job prints. When the computer needs to send data to the printer, the application running in the foreground may have to pause, tieing up your computer. Within a few years, true multitasking will be available on most systems. In addition to releasing your workstation faster, a print server should also be able to:

- Manage multiple print queues
- Set up the printer
- Produce status reports

Queue Management

Queues are electronic "waiting lines" like the one at the checkout counter. Files are sent to a queue and then routed automatically to a particular device or function.

A print queue is a series of jobs waiting to print. A print server usually manages multiple queues, either for the same printer or for different printers. When combined with the setup feature, a print server can have different queues for a single output, each with an individual setup. The print server usually has different types of queues:

- Active—jobs print when the output device is available
- Hold—jobs print when the administrator releases them
- Completed—printed jobs remain stored on disk for archiving or reprinting
- Error—jobs that could not print are stored for review

The active queue is used when you have a job to print and you want to print it now. You can use a hold queue, for example, if you want to print jobs overnight. That way, jobs that need to get out during the day get sent to the active queue, and jobs waiting in the hold queue get sent when network load is lower, or when higher-priority jobs have finished printing. A completed queue lets you hold onto jobs for future printing; and an error queue holds the jobs that could not print because of either a printer error, a PostScript error, or a network error. Then, you can fix the error and resend the job. The hold queue, in particular, lets you manage the printing services on your network. Jobs can be sent to the print server computer, but don't print until the system administrator directs them to the appropriate active queue. This type of queue works for jobs requiring special attention, such as special media (film or plate) or switch settings. They can be held until the system administrator has the output device set up properly.

The ability to support multiple print queues allows you to designate queues for specific print devices, so you automate job routing and eliminate manual switching. For instance, you can have a queue for a plain-paper device and one for a film device. During the proofing stages of the job you send it to the plain-paper queue; for the final pass you send it to the film device. To manage all these queues, the print server should be able to:

- delete jobs in a queue
- redirect jobs from one queue to another
- change priority of jobs in an output queue
- view the status of jobs in the queue
- enable or disable any of the queues

In addition to managing the jobs within the queues, the print server should let you tie specific printer options to a queue. If you have a hi-res imagesetter, you might want to have different queues for low, medium, and high resolutions, depending on the job's requirements. Then, you only need to select the queue that is called "2400 dpi film" for example, and the job automatically goes to the correct output device and prints at the correct resolution. For plain-paper laser printers, you could have different queues for the different paper trays. For digital color presses like the Agfa Chromapress or Xerox Docucolor you could have multiple devices with certain types of paper in use.

By including a printer configuration in the print queue, jobs always print the way you want them to print. For an imagesetter, you can use printer setups to make sure all the RIP settings are set correctly. Settings such as page orientation, negative or mirror image modes, resolution selection, and page grouping can be set by the print server before a job is sent to the imagesetter. A print server should be able to set any of the options available from the RIP's software.

The print server also maintains statistics about each job, providing the user with a report on printing times, number of pages printed, source workstation name, date and time of job, and more. This report could be in a format that can be imported into IBM Lotus, Microsoft Excel, or other programs for billing or accounting. Prepress service bureaus charge by the minute for jobs that exceed expected runtimes and a print server's job log provides the exact runtime for each job.

Benefits of OPI
- *Higher prepress productivity.*
- *Fast workstation release lets you get back to work in seconds rather than minutes.*
- *High-speed fetches to the Server result in more efficient network usage.*
- *Efficient system management.*

OPI Servers

High-resolution scanned images are the largest consumers of disk space, processing time, and transmission time in a printing and publishing network. While larger disks, data compression, faster computers, and faster networks help to carry the load, better management of graphics data is one of the best ways to improve any system's performance.

When the image requires color correction, retouching, or special effects, it belongs at the workstation. When the image has been approved for use, it belongs either on a server or at the RIP. When the job is run, the system should be able to locate the image without tying up anybody's workstation. OPI lets you configure an efficient production cycle by performing tasks at appropriate locations on the network.

Color Separation Houses
Color separations are the largest files encountered in electronic prepress. When you add up all four separations, you could have files totalling 60 megabytes or more. Files of this size can impair productivity unless they are managed correctly. In color separation houses, OPI does just that:

1. Scan images into a color workstation.
2. Touch up images on that workstation, or move them to a workstation dedicated to image editing.
3. Make color separations and transfer them to the OPI server. For network efficiency, you can transfer the images to the server in a batch during periods of low network traffic or via "sneakernet" on appropriate media:
   - Tape cartridges
   - Zip or Jaz cartridges
   - SyQuest cartridges (remember them?)
   - Magneto-optical disks
   - CD-ROM disks

With the separations resident on the server, the output device can be fed a continuous stream of image data. At the same time, the workstations are freed of data transmission burdens and used as intended: page design, image retouching and separation. In this way, OPI allows color separation and outputting to run in parallel, with no time wasted for data transmission.

Prepress Service Bureaus
Service bureaus benefit from the same production flow as color separators. Service bureaus send not only color separations through their imagesetters, but also lots of monochrome pages or text pages that contain color images. The workstation operators making up the pages use only low-res EPS or TIFF callouts, so their layout files are easily managed. When they send the job to the imagesetter, their workstations release quickly and they can begin working on the next job.

After they have scanned and stored the high-res images, they can return only the preview file to customers. Customers can work with the preview file in their page layout program, and crop, scale, rotate, or any other manipulation. The preview file is generally small enough to be sent on diskettes or e-mail.

Improvements in workflow and automation of the communication between production processes are crucial success factors. Until today the choice for prepress automation has been:

- *the closed system approach with proprietary "big file" data formats including a proprietary workflow approach*
- *the open PostScript system, based on separate components—each the very best available for their specific functionality—but also with unpredictable production performance and an incremental step-by-step workflow approach.*

Newspapers

Newspapers use different production systems to create different types of work with one system for editorial text, another for charts and illustrations, and another for display ads. A single newspaper page may contain elements from all these systems. At deadline time, when the last element required for a page is approved, the page must be printed as fast as possible. Printing complex broadsheet pages containing many images without an OPI solution ties up a page layout station. OPI allows the storage of graphics in a central location on the network, so users can access them with low-res callouts.

Magazines

Magazines, like newspapers, use different production systems to create different types of work with systems for editorial text, charts and illustrations, and display ads. OPI enables the integration of these separate files at the output device. Magazine production operations accrue the same benefits as newspapers for display ad work, and many of the same benefits as a color house for color separations. For display ads, magazines have logos and clip art that are used repeatedly by advertisers. In addition, magazines use photos, graphics, and icons for section identifiers. Typical magazine color uses 133-line screen halftones. Higher line screens mean scanning at higher resolutions, resulting in larger file sizes. When a magazine brings its production work inhouse, they set up a color production cycle similar to a color separators.

Data management is now probably the biggest hurdle publications need to address. For a single publication produced direct to plate, there are huge volumes of data. Each full-page ad scanned on a copy dot scanner requires 180 Mb of storage (45 Mb for each single-color separation). The data management situation for ads is complicated by the requirement to handle scheduling, versioning, and sometimes split runs. There are composite editorial pages, which include low-resolution FPO view files and associated high-resolution scans of editorial images. Storage, both live and archival, becomes a major issue, as does management and tracking. In order to produce 100 of its periodicals using computer-to-plate technology, there will be the need to store and manage 2–2.5 terabytes of information.

Publishers

Because they follow a page model, PDF files are appealing to traditional publishers. One area receiving much attention is the capability to put newsletters or other publications online in PDF form and then have subscribers download the files and read them. To the subscriber, there is the appeal of timely information. To the publisher, there is the appeal of being able to distribute without the overhead of printing. Printers are not thrilled with this idea. This distribution method amounts to a site license to customers to print and distribute copies. Restricting the number of times a customer can download a file does not prevent thousands of copies being sent via e-mail or printed and distributed conventionally by the subscriber, all from a single download.

Image Server

The terms image server and OPI server are used interchangeably but there is an important distinction evolving. Graphic arts firms are storing all images for repurposing, from print to Web or CD-ROM and back again. These images can be in separate files or part of PDF documents. Since an OPI server only serves print, the term image server may now take on a broader connotation.

An image server can be any computer on the network with one or more large disks to store image files, whether they are high resolution for print, or Web screen images or both. You can use one or several computers as image servers. The RIP computer must be able to access a disk used to store the high-res graphics.

An efficient way to configure an OPI system is to use the same workstation running the RIP as the image or network server. The high-res image is then transferred to the server once. At output time, the RIP reads the image from its own disk. No matter how many times the image is output, it only needs to be transferred over the network once. In the real world of production, an image is usually used more than once in the publishing process. This does call for very large disk capacity.

The high-resolution images placed on the image server will usually be final images with all color correction, retouching,

You can use the network or any file sharing utility, or transportable disk to transfer the high-resolution file to or from the image server. Once you make a callout to a high-res file, do not move it or change its name. If you do, the OPI function cannot locate it to include in a job.

and separation done. If users need to make changes to the high-res image or perform a color correction they can do so if they replace the image on the image server with the new image. For such a change, the preview image does not need to be updated. But if a change is made that would affect the way the preview image interacts with the page makeup program, a resizing of the image, for example or the way the image is accessed on the server, like a name or location change, then the preview image must also be regenerated.

If the RIP computer is used as the image server, this function only needs to retrieve the high-res image from its own disk. RIP software with OPI functionality is available for Macintosh, Power Macintosh, Sun Computer and Silicon Graphics, and the growing prevalence of PC/NT computers.

OPI functions may be done at the RIP while some OPI solutions require a free-standing server for integration. You can configure an OPI system to suit your production needs with:

- Each component on a separate workstation
- RIP and image server on the same workstation

When printing to a print server (a server that spools jobs for an output device), the workstation program releases within seconds and the operator goes back to work. Without a spooling capability, the workstation is not released until the job is printed. When you send a job containing an OPI callout to the proper queue on the print server, it routes it to the appropriate OPI server for output.

One Workflow Model

1. Workstations running OPI-capable application programs place images on the OPI or image server over the network for use by any workstation.
2. Any workstation on the network sends the job to the appropriate print server queue.
3. The print server spools the job, releases the workstation, and transmits the job to the appropriate output device.

Transmission time is quick because the job contains only a low-res callout of the image. The RIP with the OPI integrating function reads the callout in the job, and connects to the image server as directed. Because the same workstation may be used as the image server and the RIP, the integrator only needs to retrieve the image from its disk. The integrator merges the high-res image into the job stream with the other page elements and the page is printed.

Once the publication is output, what happens to the images? In the old days, they were archived to tape. Today, publishers and service firms are interested in the future of their images. That means they want to store them in such a way that they can be found quickly, accessed rapidly, and converted (re-purposed) to various file formats for print or presentation.

Prepress systems are also linking OPI Servers to image archives. An image database becomes important because users cannot find images based only on their file names. Some production pros can retrieve images on this basis, but designers may not. Without reliable image pattern-recognition technology, we have to rely on keywords, indexed fields, and full-text queries of captions or description files. These are typically stored in a database (relational or fixed-field) and searched by a full-text indexing engine.

Server Evolution and Integration

It all started with one PC connected to one printer. Add more PCs and more printers and you have a system. A prepress networked system usually consists of multiple workstations, a file server and a printer or printers connected by network cables.

Sometimes a print spooler is added so that files destined for the printer are accepted by the spooler to release the workstation's application. The spooler then queues the job or jobs based on prioritization and sends them to the printer. The difference between a print spooler and a print server is based on the amount of time files remain on the disk. A spooler may delete files sooner than a server.

Servers galore

A Server is any device with information shared by client workstations on a network. Every network must have a server and it is simply a network server.

A network server stores centralized files that are shared by clients. It can also be called a file server.

A network could have multiple servers, one of which could be used to store large image files. It would be called an image server.

With large volumes of image and data files, some servers could support a database capability for searching and retrieving the stored data more efficiently. This would make it a database server.

Another server common to networks supports a shared printer or other output device. It has its own disk so that jobs are transferred to the disk and the client workstation does not have to wait until the printer is finished. It is called a print server. *The print server retains files for future runs or archiving.*

All PostScript output systems must have a RIP, a raster image processor. The RIP usually has a large disk to store software and pre- and post-RIPed files. It is called a RIP server.

The RIP should be equipped with OPI functionality. The disk and system associated with the RIP is then also called an OPI server.

The server could encompass multiple functions, such as trapping, imposition and ripping. It might be called a super server.

Lastly, the server could fully support Adobe Acrobat 3.0 with its superb collection of high-end printing functions. PDF files can be trapped, imposed and color managed. That gives us a PDF server.

Thus, a network could have all of the above functionality, or some combination, or like most, it could integrate the server (for the network, image storage, OPI, and RIPing) and the RIP into one server. Or the server into one RIP.

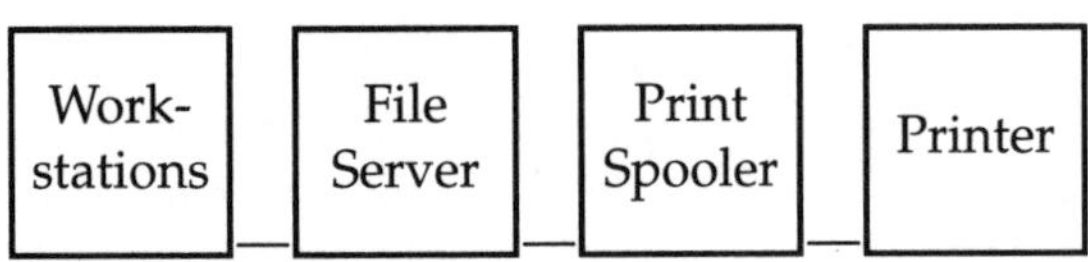

The printer on a prepress network is usually a PostScript-based printer and therefore has a RIP. Most desktop printers have the RIP inside the printer…

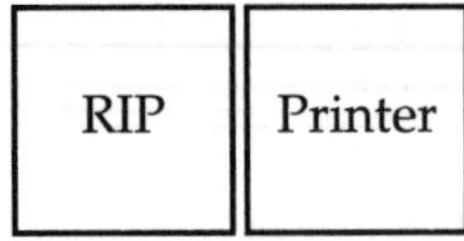

…while imagesetters and platesetters and proofers have the RIP as a separate unit, connected by a cable. Today, every raster-based output device must have a raster image processor.

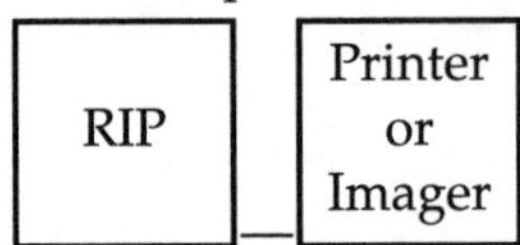

A server may be added to the output function to store RIPed files for later printout of the entire file of one or more of the color separations. This may be called a print server or a print spooler. We are going to call it a RIP server because it serves the RIP. At one time there was a RIP for each and every output device. Today, the trend is to try to RIP-once-and output-many-times. So the RIP server functions as a print spooler/server, holding files for later printout or archiving.

The RIP server and the RIP may be integrated into one unit.

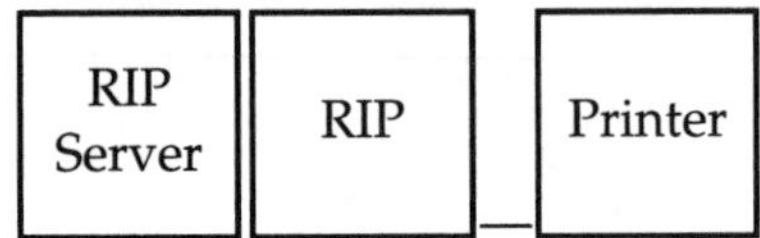

An OPI server could be added to the system for automatic picture replacement.

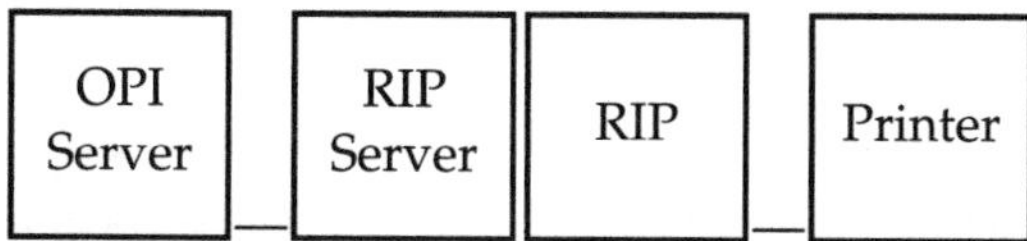

Or the OPI server and the RIP server could be integrated while the RIP is a separate unit . . .

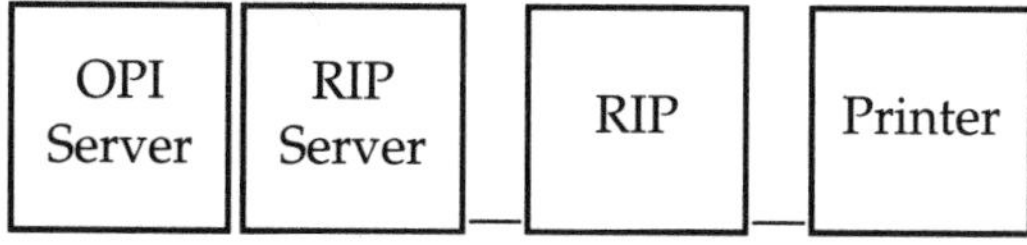

. . . or the OPI server, RIP server and RIP could be integrated into one unit.

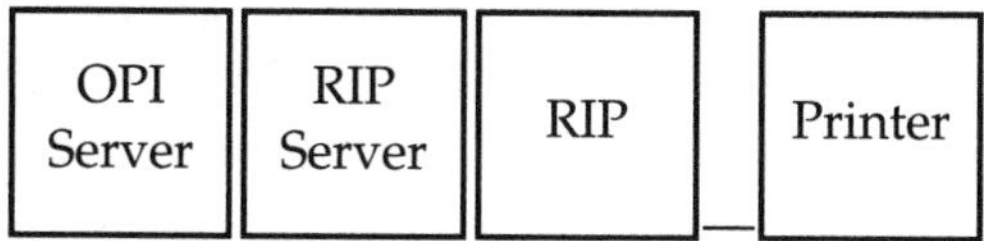

At various levels there could be more than one printer, proofer, imagesetter, digital color press, platemaker, or other output alternatives.

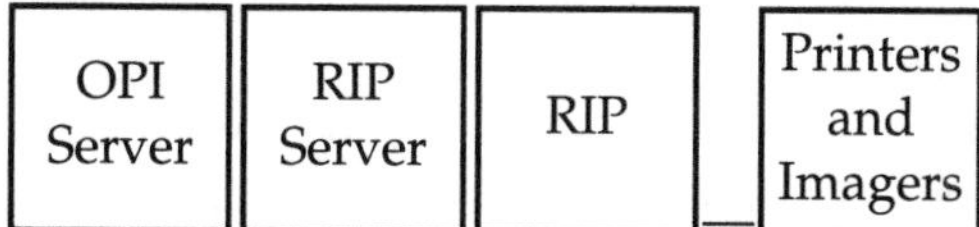

When the functions of OPI, RIP, and print server are integrated into one server, we are going to call it a *super server*. It then is networked with the file server and the printer or imagers.

File Server
Super Server
Printers

To the super server we add the final ingredients of PDF handling, trapping, and imposition. The final system now takes form as a *PDF server*.

The RIPs and systems described in this section are only for illustration. It was not our goal to provide a comprehensive review of all available workflows, but rather to provide a sort of overview of some of the products and trends. Those trends which we have observed are:

- *Multivendor systems evolving to single-vendor systems.*
- *Totally automated workflows—the mouse is in charge.*
- *Industry-standard hardware platforms.*
- *Industry-standard networking.*
- *Integrating RIP functions at multiple stages in the process.*
- *The use of the Web as a business tool.*

Job Tickets are just the ticket
There is workflow server software that handles the queueing and job management of all jobs in process. It has some extra features such as load balancing, preflight, filmsaving, and more. It can also automate trapping and imposition using standard desktop applications such as TrapWise and Presswise. It uses the concept of "hot folders." This concept came from:

- *the need to define and indicate up front the steps the job must go through*
- *the need to have the full "processing" information available at any moment by anyone involved in completing the process*
- *the need to control and "post calculate" a job*

The Adobe PDF will change the very nature of networks and servers and systems and prepress. With scripts or plug-ins many routine tasks can be automated. For instance, a script might take a QuarkXPress file, open it, distill it, open Acrobat Exchange, perform a function, save it, then server functions would trap the PDF, impose it based on the electronic work order, direct it to a proofer, and prioritize it to a print queue.

Server Schizophrenia: RIPs Trap, Impose, Serve, and Print
OPI servers, workflow servers, database servers, file management, and image servers. Servers are migrating to RIPing and archiving, archive image databases are expanding to handle work in-process. Print servers, once limited to spooling, now perform trapping and imposition and promise to automate workflow, as database-driven workflow software makes similar claims. RIPs once only RIPed; now they serve. Servers only served; now they RIP. The result is that almost every server and almost every RIP system do almost the same thing.

Workflow is changing. Workflow software has migrated from text-based systems to prepress document production that helps route jobs to the required queue or invoke processes when work is dropped in a queue or hot folder. The server is simply a central (network) function that can run background tasks like automatic trapping, or rasterizing (RIPing) a file for output to a printer, imagesetter, platemaker, or whatever. File servers are based on UNIX or Novell networks, with Macintosh, PC/NT ,and UNIX workstations handling processing. Workflow may simply mean setting up "hot folders" to perform prepress functions and letting the super server do the rest.

The server approach shifts the processing burden from individual workstations to a central server for more efficient printing and job handling. Sending files to the server takes seconds, even for pages with gigabytes of images. Software directs where and when each job is to print, inserts high-resolution scans precisely where they belong in the layout, monitors print progress, and maintains statistics. Queued jobs can be rearranged, placed on hold, deleted, or moved among queues with ease. Some server functions are:

- Unattended management of a number of printers through multiple queues
- Image substitution through OPI
- User-definable printer setups
- Queuing controls
- Device, application, and platform-independence
- Control over a job from the server or a workstation
- Centralized image and print processing
- Security for printing resources
- Fast spooling to a central server
- Storage and retrieval of images on the network
- Multiple projects moving and numerous devices working without intervention
- Accurate replacement and positioning of high-resolution scans before imaging
- Configure any output device to the resolution, line screen, and screen angle preferred
- Assign multiple queues to the same device, or multiple devices to the same queue
- Spool PostScript files from any source, output them to any PostScript device
- Manage files from anywhere on the network, and re-queue without respooling
- Share images and manage printers through one server, even if computer types vary
- Network-based job management
- Enhanced queue monitoring
- Workflow optimization and job load balancing
- PostScript 2 or 3 resource management
- Preflight job verification
- Support for in-RIP separation
- Film optimization
- RIP and output device management
- Integrated RIP
- OPI image replacement
- Image File Conversion (for PhotoCD, TIFF/IT, CEPS data formats)

Scitex developments
Brisque is the Scitex line of digital front ends which integrates and automates virtually all prepress production output operations.The Brisque DFE seamlessly coordinates the essential prepress production tools and processes: preflight checking, automated job tickets, picture replacement schemes (Scitex APR, OPI), soft proofing, trapping, queuing and job management, imposition, screening, and RIPing. The Brisque's architecture accommodates PDF in a comprehensive way, from RIPing all the way to print. The company has already integrated PDF into the Brisque infrastructure to allow Brisque DFEs to seamlessly accept both PostScript and PDF files in a single workflow. Implementing PDF RIPing involves the same drag and drop process as PostScript RIPing. When PDF is enabled, users can choose which type of file they want to RIP and, using the icon-based Graphical User Interface, drag and drop the file onto the RIP icon, define RIP parameters as they would with PostScript files, then select PDF parameters, and define the page or pages to RIP. The selective RIPing option is only possible in PDF because of the page-independent nature of the format.

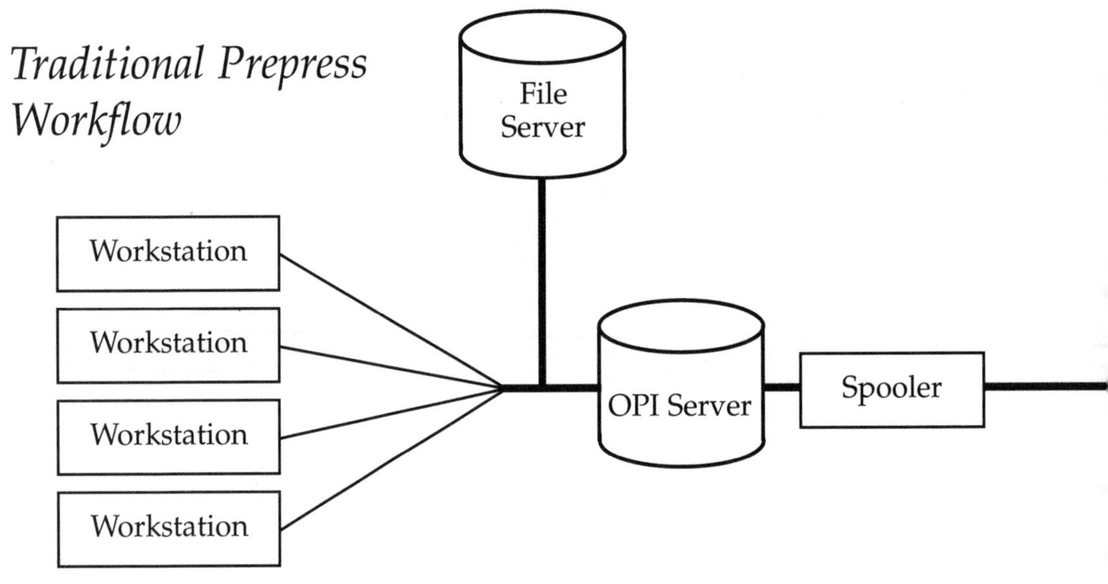
Traditional Prepress Workflow
File Server
Workstation
Workstation
Workstation
Workstation
OPI Server
Spooler

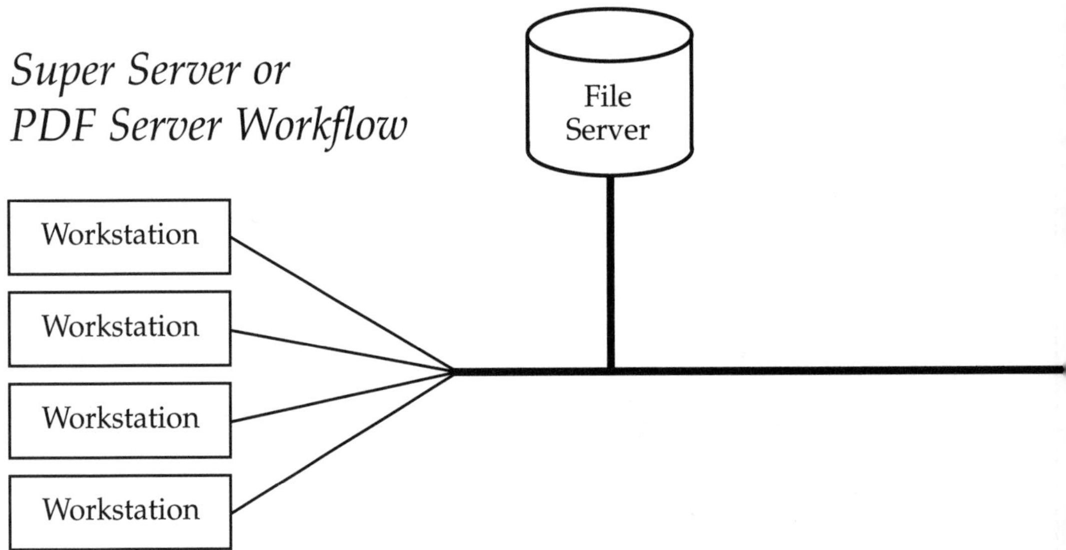
Super Server or PDF Server Workflow
File Server
Workstation
Workstation
Workstation
Workstation

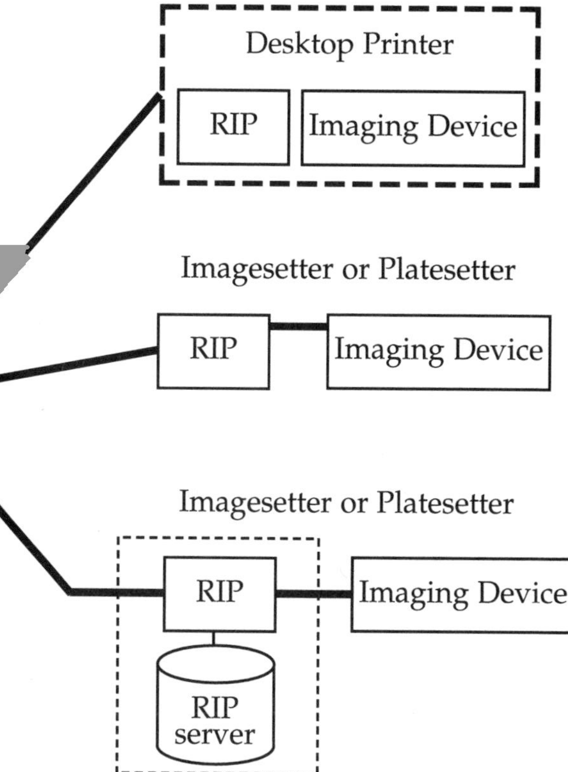

One Workflow

The designer creates content using standard desktop publishing applications and converts it to PDF. This PDF digital master maintains the capability for viewing, proofing, and adding notes and edits to the file until it is RIPed. Finally the content creator gets more control right from the start and well beyond delivering the application file. The service bureau gets a self-contained PDF file including all fonts and resources. Using Job Ticket mechanisms, the service bureau can add settings for advanced resource checking, imposition, OPI, etc. The system then fully automatically moves the job through the required processes. The final result is a PDF or PostScript file that can be sent to a platesetter or proofer or used for CD-ROM or Internet publishing. The benefits—and business opportunities—of being able to repurpose the same content, are obvious.

The printer checks or adapts the imposition templates and trapping settings in the PDF file, sends it to an imposition proofer, and outputs the job to the PDF RIP. He stores the raster files or "print files" on the PrintDrive Output Manager, where he can preview them on the dot level, proof, them to an imposition proofer, manage them, and output them to an imagesetter or platesetter. The PrintDrive controller even opens up PostScript workflows to take in and output legacy CEPS systems' proprietary bitmap formats (CT/LW).

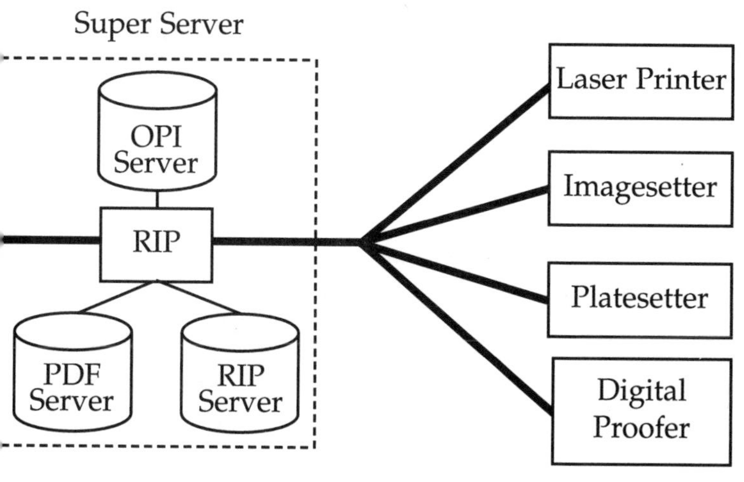

The high-end PDF format is very flexible

The PDF format brings all the functionality needed in the next generation workflow. PDF is a self-contained format that includes job data and job ticket information. You can view and print or proof it whenever and wherever you want, from any major platform and operating system, it is really device independent.

In contrast with the bitmap or vector formats, the object-based PDF is slim and smart. "Slim" because, unlike the complex, continuous datastream in a PostScript file, it consists of a compact—or distilled—object-oriented database of imaging operations that can immediately represent the document, on a page by page level. "Smart" as in editable—long the dream of PostScript workflows—since you can find and change elements on the page and data level. Smart, too, because of the Job Ticket information, part of the PDF file, that lets you store and manage device-dependent information, independent from job content.

Workflow Solutions Aplenty

In 1995 Linotype-Hell (now Heidelberg) pioneered RIP operation, building on the early work done by Monotype with the Lasercomp in the late 1970s. In 1995 the company developed Delta Technology, which essentially splits the RIP process into two steps: PostScript interpretation and the Delta list. PostScript processing takes place in the DeltaWorkstation; screening takes place in the DeltaTower. This whole process is controlled by DeltaSoftware, which includes capabilities such as print spooling and OPI. The DeltaWorkstation multiprocessing capabilities enable several processors to work in parallel, increasing throughput. It produces the DeltaList, a single layer file identical to what will appear in the final output. The file is transferred to the DeltaTower for screening. The entire system concept allows functions to be handled by separate components: PostScript processing by the DeltaWorkstation, screening by the DeltaTower. All are controlled by DeltaSoftware, including DeltaImagemanager and DeltaPrintmanager.

Delta workflow was as follows: Send single Quark pages to Delta1. RIP, trap, and scatter proof on Iris. Once proofs are checked, the DeltaLists are transferred to Delta2. The low-res bitmaps that are created with the DeltaLists are then imposed on the Signastation. The Signature is then printed to Delta2, the DeltaLists are picked up (similar to OPI). The print queue on Delta2 is set up to proof the signatures to the forms proofer first. If the proofs are OK, the same signature is forwarded to the CTP system. After plates are imaged, CIP3 files are automatically generated. In this workflow the pages are only RIPed once. The created DeltaLists are used for exposure of plates, color proofs, formproofs, imposition, and CIP3 file generation.

Delta Technology allows pre-ripped files (DeltaLists) to be trapped, proofed (digital blueline or Iris), and imposed before committing to plate or film. As screening is done in a separate box attached to the output device, the operator has control of the output parameters. They are not locked in at RIP time. Delta runs on Windows NT and is configurable with offline RIPs, trapping stations, etc. CIP3 files can be generated automatically from the DeltaLists. Color management (ColorSync profiles) can also be applied to the Delta data.

Scitex Solutions

The Scitex Brisque RIP system is an output controller for prepress production. Brisque automates production processes with "job ticket" templates. Each job ticket describes a workflow consisting of operations to be finished in a particular order according to specific parameters. It will not work with non-Scitex output devices, either for final output or proofs (except an HP printer). Brisque now supports OPI on a Scitex device, as well as DCS. It works with CT and New Linework formats, which handle 65,000 unique colors in linework and 32 color channels.

It RIPs data into the internal Scitex CT and linework formats. Both the CT and New Linework formats can be edited. CTs can be edited in Photoshop. Screening is done on the fly by the screening controller built into the Scitex imagesetters. For continuous tone proofers, the Brisque combines CT and Linework files into a single high-resolution format and will trap CT to LW, LW to CT, and CT to CT. Scitex prefers to rasterize first and work on the rasterized file after. Brisque can drive three different types of output from one RIP.

Harlequin Solutions

Harlequin provides workflow management and a facility for editing the data in a "late-binding" fashion that includes trapping. Harlequin has multitasking and multiprocessing but doesn't offer OPI within the RIP, but its OEM customer implementations provide this support. Harlequin also supports a PCI card screening accelerator. Harlequin Display List Technology allows for editability of the PostScript display list, providing a hook for customization between interpretation and rendering.

This option lets OEMs and other third-party vendors write tailored applications that add customized features to ScriptWorks. Applications include PostScript verification and previewing; object editing; integration of trapping and/or imposition capabilities; conversion from PostScript into other languages or formats like TIFF/IT; the detection and rendering of vignettes using alternative processing; and enhanced image processing capabilities. Harlequin is taking advantage of this access to the display list for an integrated automatic RIP-based trapping solution, called EasyTrap.

Harlequin PDF developments

Harlequin is developing its own extensions to the PDF 1.2 specification. They see some issues and opportunities with the current PDF specification and feel the need to address these. Their "PDF+" plan includes:

Plate Colors*—All PDF jobs are assumed to be composite (or gray). This extension would allow marking of plates as cyan, magenta, etc. for easy recognition by film or plate processors.*

Vignettes*—This extension quickly recognizes and optimizes inline vignettes for circles and rectangles for improved performance and reduced file sizes.*

Encapsulated Functions*—This extension handles required procedures that are specified in PS definitions of colorspaces to provide more precise color representation.*

Imation Corp. changed the name of its subsidiary, Luminous Technology Corporation, to Imation Publishing Software—a developer of software products, services, and technologies for the prepress, print production, and graphic arts industries, which was acquired by Imation in October, 1996. Software solutions within the Imation Publishing Software business portfolio include Color Central, Media Manager, OPEN, PressWise, PrintersWeb, TrapWise, Virtual Network, and Virtual Network Pro.

APX (now LPX). The name changed from APX to LPX when Luminous spun out of Adobe in early 1996. The goal of LPX from the beginning has been to support PressWise, TrapWise, Color Central, and PrePrint Pro workflows, by allowing users to produce DSC 3.0-conformant PS directly from QuarkXPress 3.x. APX is a QuarkXTension that is designed to smooth the process of creating QuarkXPress 3.x PostScript files for use with Adobe prepress products. Using this XTension ensures that the resulting PostScript file conforms to the Adobe Document Structuring Conventions (DSC) so that they can be post-processed by Color Central, PrePrint, PressWise, TrapWise, and OPEN.

When the PostScript job draws an object, instead of simply adding the object to the display list and continuing as usual, HDLT (Harlequin Display List Technology) will first invoke a procedure. That procedure may be written by an OEM or a third-party vendor. It can use PostScript to do any computation necessary. HDLT is available as a layered option for ScriptWorks running on all industry-standard platforms.

ScriptWorks is a high-performance software RIP management system configured with all the necessary features and functions to run in a wide variety of commercial printing and publishing environments. It is also a universal interpreter able to process a wide variety of file formats such as PostScript, EPS, PDF 1.2, TIFF 6, and TIFF/IT-P1. ScriptWorks was designed from the ground up to meet the varied and demanding needs of its OEM partners and their end users and to run on the OEM's choice of hardware platforms and operating systems. ScriptWorks includes a complete and functional user interface that provides extensive controls for page setup, output device calibration, media management, etc.

Harlequin ScriptWorks 5.0 is a software RIP management system that implements PostScript LanguageLevel 3 operators. It is a multi-language RIP management system that lets users follow whatever workflow they prefer—a PDF workflow; PostScript 1, 2 and LanguageLevel 3 files; TIFF 6.0, TIFF/IT-P1, EPS; and more. ScriptWorks is a hardware-independent software RIP. It can process files produced by applications that are LanguageLevel 3-compatible and which contain the new extensions and changes to the PostScript language as specified in the recently published update to the PostScript Language Reference Manual entitled "LanguageLevel 3 Specification." New LanguageLevel 3 features in ScriptWorks 5.0 include:

- Hi-Fi Color—Harlequin's new N-Color capability allows an arbitrary number of colors to be correctly processed and printed from virtually any color system, including CMYK and spot color systems as well as Hi-Fi color systems such as Hexachrome. In addition, Harlequin N-Color is fully integrated with screening, calibration, rendering, raster formats, and page buffers, trapping, separations, and all Harlequin color management options.

- Smooth Shading—Reduces printing time and improves output quality by rendering gradient fills at the resolution of the target device using a series of designated pattern libraries.
- Masked Images—Enables printing of composite images clipped to a raster mask.
- PDF direct processing—ScriptWorks 5.0 continues to support native printing of PDF v1.2 (and earlier) files.
- Job Ticket Format (JTF)—Initially ScriptWorks 5.0 will be able to read an Adobe Job Ticket and use information contained therein to build page set-ups. Additional functionality will follow as the JTF becomes more widely implemented in the industry.
- Embedded ICC Profiles—ScriptWorks 5.0 recognizes an ICC format device profile embedded in the PS/ PDF/TIFF input stream and uses it to remap file output to the target device.
- Remote RIP operation—Harlequin's new RIP remote feature is a Java applet that allows the use of a standard Internet Web browser to select, input, submit, and control job processing to ScriptWorks RIPs located in virtually any location in the world.
- Remote proofing of color-managed files.
- The ability to handle Photoshop duotones.
- The ability to control spot color separations at any point in the process.
- User-programmable screening extensions.
- Symmetric multiprocessing (SMP) support.
- "Extra Grays" (over 4000 gray levels).
- "In-RIP" color management with Harlequin Color Production Solutions.
- Full ICC 3 support, including "device-link" profiles.
- TIFF/IT-P1 processing.
- Display list access with Harlequin Display List Technology (HDLT).
- "In-RIP" trapping with EasyTrap.
- Native processing of TrueType fonts and storage in compressed formats.
- Support for internationalized user interface.

Many suppliers have provided RIP systems that maximize off-the-shelf workstations. Thus, Agfa, for example, has software RIPs for Sun, Mac, PC/NT, and other computer hardware platforms.

The phrase "PostScript 3" is used in different ways, which has led to much confusion. Adobe now uses PostScript 3 as its trademarked brand name referring to its product implementations as in the phrase, "Adobe PostScript 3 Version 3010 Product Supplement." The PostScript 3 name or "brand" refers to Adobe-based products and not to the PostScript language specification which Adobe now calls "LanguageLevel 3." What does "PostScript 3 compatibility" mean? PostScript 3 products can interpret files containing PostScript LanguageLevel 3 operators that have been prepared by compliant applications. In addition, PostScript 3 products have other functions that are new but not necessarily part of the PostScript PDL. For example, the ability to accept PDF files is widely accepted as a PostScript 3 product feature as is the ability to perform in-RIP trapping. Other PostScript 3 product features in various levels of availability include WebReady Printing, PlanetReady Printing, etc., yet none of these features are operators within the LanguageLevel 3 specification.

Platforms supported include Power Macintosh; all Intel-based Pentium PCs (supporting Windows 95 and Windows NT); Digital Alpha workstations and servers (supporting Windows NT) and UNIX platforms, including Sun Solaris and SGI IRIX. Symmetrical multiprocessing (SMP) systems and all popular network environments are supported.

What is "PostScript LanguageLevel 3" and how does it differ from "PostScript 3"? And, how does ScriptWorks 5.0 compare with Adobe PostScript 3 products? The terminology and distinctions between language and product are subtle and have been a source of substantial confusion in the marketplace. This confusion has tended to mask the fact that Adobe PostScript 3 products and Harlequin ScriptWorks are significantly different products developed for and suited to significantly different printing and publishing applications. LanguageLevel 3 is the name of the latest version of the PostScript page description language (PDL). It includes a series of extensions and/or changes to the language documented in the supplement issued on October 10, 1997 to the PostScript Language Reference Manual entitled "LanguageLevel 3 Specification."

Helios PDF for OPI

Helios PDF Handshake allows PDF documents to be integrated into prepress workflows, including those incorporating OPI file and print servers. The OPI server reduces the resolution of images, but also generates standard EPS or TIFF low-res images which are supported by QuarkXPress or PageMaker from hi-res original images which are not suitable for those layout applications; like images in Photoshop native or CIE Lab JPEG format. Helios PDF Handshake goes one step further by supporting PDF originals as input for the OPI process. The OPI server now becomes an OPI/color management/PDF workflow server. You can use PDFs—whether a single drawing or a logo, or a fully designed advertisement—with QuarkXPress and PageMaker applications. By using the EPS low-res representations of PDF originals, customers can now work with PDF input as they do with EPS or TIFF. PDF workflow is a reality from layout to output including automatic color management for documents with raster images,vector illustrations, logos, colorized text, backgrounds, etc. Final output can be separated for device-specific CMYK, as well as transformed to RGB or CIE Lab.

AII Solutions

Autologic Information International (AII) has streamlined its RIP capabilities by enabling some key functions to be performed after a job has been rasterized and before it is output to an imaging device. Among these functions are imposition, step-and-repeat processing, proofing, and outputting a job multiple times without having to rasterize the file again. This capability, which AII is marketing as Post-RIP Assembly among its commercial customers, is similar to the Bitmap Stitching feature offered to its newspaper customers. For label production and other applications involving step-and-repeat operation, Post-RIP Assembly requires only that an element be rasterized once, after which it can be repeated horizontally and vertically any number of times without re-rasterizing.

What is the relationship between PostScript 3 and LanguageLevel 3? Adobe PostScript 3 product implementations include the ability to interpret the extensions to the PostScript language known as LanguageLevel 3 plus selected additional features that have been described in peripheral documentation. However, not all PostScript 3 products include the same feature set, other than the fact they conform (or will conform) to the new PostScript LanguageLevel 3 specification.

For color proofing, AII recombines the rasterized CMYK data and prints them on a color proofer. A software algorithm downsamples the resolution of the raster data for the 300-dpi printer, without having to rasterize again for the different resolution. It is possible also to replace part of a page by substituting one rasterized block for another one based on *x, y* coordinate positioning. Other post-RIP capabilities include rotating pages 180 degrees and replacing an entire page within an imposed job. The program includes facilities for tracking elements of a publication being output, including reporting where each element resides (with filters available to limit the display to items conforming to certain criteria), which publication and edition each one belongs to, the output device each was sent to, etc. It also provides an error queue for jobs that fail to output and an option to specify how long finished jobs are held before purging.

Rampage Solutions

The Rampage RIPing system is a comprehensive solution for film or plate output. It uses an open-architecture design and lets you connect multiple RIPs to one output device. The RIP runs on industry-standard hardware. Additional productivity features include: automatic trapping, CEPS format support, OPI server functions, imposition, step & repeat, and Ramproof, a function that allows a RIPed file to be output to a proofing device or monitor and then to an imagesetter (RIP once, plot twice). Rampage's TrapIt1 rasterizes an incoming file at low resolution to do its analysis of what kinds of traps are needed, based on the relative luminance values of each pixel.

Noun: RIP
Plural: RIPs
Verb: RIP, RIPs
Past Tense: RIPed
Gerund: RIPing
Comparative: RIPable
Believe It Or Not: RIPley

But at the same time it generates a display list of the objects on the page in drawing order, taking into account the order in which they are layered on top of each other. Traps are then computed for each object relative to the others that are below it in the display list and have intersecting boundaries. The output, new PostScript-like instructions, is generated from the trap decisions and combined with the original PostScript file. Object formats allow layering objects with transparency values, generally impossible in normal PostScript. Another is the ability to select and modify trap areas or other attributes easily because each object is its own element rather than a set of colored pixels. RIP enhancements include:

- Automatic vignette detection, which treats all objects in a vignette as one object at high resolution. Support for gravure output, with antialiasing from high resolution down to gravure resolution, eliminating the need to output film and scan it to accommodate gravure printing.
- Facilities for adjusting press compensation, replacing one set of values with another when switching from a sheetfed press to a web-based printing press.
- "Smart shadows," which puts shadows over areas outside a clippath, regardless of what is underneath them.
- "Automatic touchplates" to replace one to four inks each with a different transfer curve of that ink plus add a special spot color with its transfer curve. This works like a duotone to change the curve of one or more of the CMYK inks and add a spot color based on the same data.
- Expansion of blends to 256 elements, regardless of the original input.

Agfa RIP Solutions

Agfa's Cobra software raster image processor combines a Sun SPARCstation with PostScript Level 2 software RIP. Cobra is based on Adobe's Configurable PostScript Interpreter (CPSI) and is not tied to dedicated RIP hardware in order to migrate to other platforms. Cobra technology offers the synergy of the Sun SPARC processor chips, the advanced Solaris operating system, and the Cobra multithreaded architecture. Users benefit from improved capabilities of the optional PixelBurst coprocessor. Cobra is also available with optional Agfa CristalRaster stochastic screening and Agfa Balanced Screening Options software to address special halftoning requirements.

Agfa's MultiStar RIP multiplexers are Agfa's solution to the high level of RIP performance needed for intensive production of hi-res TIFF environments. Each MultiStar contains a two-channel RIP multiplexer and can house one to two Emerald-based Star hardware RIPs in one enclosure. Users can combine Agfa hardware and software RIPs for maximum performance and flexibility. A MultiStar-based system can improve the performance of an Agfa imagesetter and RIP by doubling processing capabilities and eliminating RIP bottlenecks.

Agfa's Taipan exploits the multitasking and multiprocessing capabilities of the Windows NT operating system and the latest Adobe CPSI PostScript Level 2 software. It runs Taipan on a dual CPU workstation and it is easy to add a server with OPI capability to the same platform, or perform two tasks such as outputting one file and start RIPing the next simultaneously. It also provides the NT-print spooling functions that help you produce more jobs per shift. Taipan runs under the standard Windows NT operating system and can be integrated into an existing network of PCs, Macintoshes, and UNIX workstations. The network simultaneously accommodates AppleTalk, Hot Folder, TCP/IP, and Windows Named Pipe input channels—further enhancing connectivity. The Taipan RIP separates the RIPing process from the output process. Files may first be RIPed to disk for preview and approval before they are sent to the imagesetter or platesetter. Agfa's Preview software allows you to preview jobs on a video monitor.

Taipan Pilot is an interactive networked user interface on any PC or Mac workstation on the network that lets you monitor RIP information such as resolution and job status, and output settings such as media type and punch configuration. You can check print spooling, job log information, and previews. Taipan is not tied to dedicated RIP hardware and can be upgraded to the latest software and to more powerful platforms in the future. AX exploits all Adobe PostScript 3 features such as 16-bit screening and smooth shading. Both support the new set of 16-bit Agfa Balanced Screens, for more gray levels and soft blends.

Taipan AX's multithreading software design allows it to take advantage of the multitasking and multiprocessing capabilities of the Windows NT operating system and Adobe's CPSI software. Taipan AX is designed to simultaneously perform different tasks such as outputting one job and RIPing the next. It also provides NT spooling functions, allowing you to produce even more jobs per shift. You can separate the RIPing process from the output process. Files may first be RIPed to disk allowing you to preview and approve them before they are sent to the imagesetter.

Preview software allows you to preview single and multiple pages of the same job from any Mac or PC in your network by connecting to the RIP to see the RIPed pages. You can zoom, pan and request any combination of the color separations as well as view spot colors, screen angles, and ink coverage. Taipan AX runs under the standard Windows NT operating system (for DEC Alpha). The network simultaneously accommodates AppleTalk, TCP/IP, and Windows Named Pipe input channels as well as a Hot Folder system for both PostScript jobs and PDF input. Taipan AX is a PostScript 3 RIP, upgradable to the latest software features and compatible with PDF-based workflow systems. The interactive user interface is available on all Windows 95, NT, and Macintosh front-end workstations on the network.

Agfa PDF Workflow

In 1997, the Agfa Division of Bayer advanced RIP and server architecture to a higher level by establishing the Acrobat 3.0 PDF as the standard for moving document files around a prepress network. Agfa designed a digital workflow that re-engineers preflight checking, automated job tickets, automatic picture replacement, soft proofing, trapping, queuing, imposition, screening, and rasterization.

Agfa Apogee is a PDF-based Publishing Production System including the PDF Pilot Production Manager, the PDF RIP, and the PrintDrive Output Manager. Agfa has been developing new workflows based on the high-end PDF file format standard from Adobe Systems. PDF is a flexible, editable, predictable, compact file format that works on a page-independent level and is device independent. Agfa's new Apogee system will use PDF to allow highly automated and efficient connection of prepress functionality such as creation, trapping, imposition, RIPing, OPI, job tracking, color management, etc. Apogee is based on the use of PDF as a "digital master" and consists of: the PDF Pilot Production Manager, the PDF RIP, and the PrintDrive Output Manager. The PDF Pilot Production Manager combines PDF-based workflow automation technology for preflighting, imposition, OPI, etc. with systemwide implementation of PDF-based job tickets. The PDF format allows viewing, editing, and processing from any workstation on the network, local or over the Internet. The PDF RIP rasterizes PDF, as well as PostScript Level 2 and PostScript 3 files. The PrintDrive Output Manager automatically stores, manages, and queues the rasterized jobs for imagesetter, proofer, and platesetter output.

It allows immediate plate remakes and intelligent backups for digital platemaking, as well as a Preview feature. You can disconnect the RIPing process from the imaging process by grouping similar jobs together. To the RIP, the Apogee PrintDrive acts as a fast "writing engine," allowing you to process more jobs. Preview software allows you to preview single and multiple pages of the same job by connecting to the RIP and view the RIPed pages from any Macintosh or PC on your network. You can zoom, pan, and request any combination of color separations, as well as view spot colors, screen angles, and ink coverage. Taipan 2.0 and Taipan AX RIPs directly connect to the PrintDrive through TCP/IP. The output of the RIPs is automatically compressed and sent to the PrintDrive.

A graphical user interface allows you to view the status of the RIPed jobs, as well as manipulate and control the timing and priorities of the output. You can control the PrintDrive from any Macintosh or PC in your network and determine a preferred set of parameters, selectable at print time. Previewing of raster files, as with Agfa's Taipan or Taipan AX RIPs, is also possible on the Apogee PrintDrive, regardless of the number of connected

ROOAOOAOA
Rip Only Once And Output Over And Over Again

Theoretically, this is not possible. The end result of the RIP process is a rasterized bitmap with screening and other information specific to a particular output device.

Thus, one bitmap cannot drive multiple different outputs. Even those platesetters that can image new proofing materials must do an additional RIPing. Rampage downsamples the bitmap for proofing. Screen RIPS to the display list and then sends that file to a platesetter and a digital color proofer, each with its own hardware rasterizer. Scitex and Heidelberg RIP to an intermediate raster file and then RIP to a bitmap.

If the end result of the RIP process is a rasterized, screened file, then ROOAOOAOA is impossible. If you wish to move the rasterization to the output device and call the production of the display list or some intermediate file, RIPing, so be it.

RIPs. Apogee PrintDrive acts as a file buffer in digital workflows, offering digital imposition proofing capabilities—in B&W and color—for a large format proofer, and directly from the bitmaps stored for final output.

Adobe Solutions
Extreme is a RIP technology that can process both PostScript and PDF streams. Files first enter the "Coordinator" which determines whether the file is PS or PDF by its inherent page independence. The PS files go to the "Normalizer" and the PDF files go to the "Page Store." The "Normalizer" acts as Acrobat's Distiller and converts the PS file to a PDF. These distilled files then continue on to the "Page Store" where all documents are stored as PDFs. Pages are processed through the RIP and finally passed on to the "Assembler" which dictates the flow of information to the marking engine. In addition to digital presses, Extreme's technology is applicable to large-format imagesetters, proofers, and platemakers, as well as digital printers. Below is a schematic of the internal flow of data from PostScript file to processed pages stored for output to the imaging engine.

Inside Adobe PostScript Extreme
Since Adobe PostScript Extreme is all about high-speed printing, the key to understanding it is knowing what determines printing speed. The two main factors that determine this are rasterization speed (how fast a printing system can turn a

Adobe Extreme Architecture

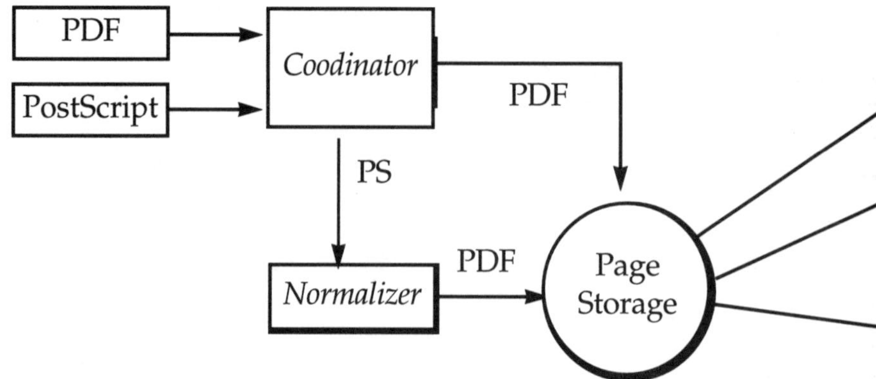

document into a series of dots) and the printer's engine speed (how quickly it can pass paper through its system and transfer a rasterized image onto the paper).

The new class of high-speed production printers have extremely fast engine speeds, so the only thing that tends to slow them down is the rasterization process. Most professional printing systems today use PostScript RIPs to rasterize documents. While PostScript RIPs can be very fast, they're not as fast as the engine speeds of high-end production printers.

The initial idea behind Adobe PostScript Extreme was to design a system that could quickly "feed" rasterized pages to a high-speed printing engine by using several RIPs, each simultaneously rasterizing various pages of a document. But that design wouldn't have worked with PostScript print jobs, because they usually can't be split into separate pages before they're rasterized. A PostScript file is typically a single, complex program that describes an entire document.

What it takes to rasterize a certain page can depend on information or a graphic state that was defined within the description of an earlier page. The Adobe PostScript Extreme architecture needed to be able to process page-independent print files, that is, print files that consist of discrete page units that can be processed separately.

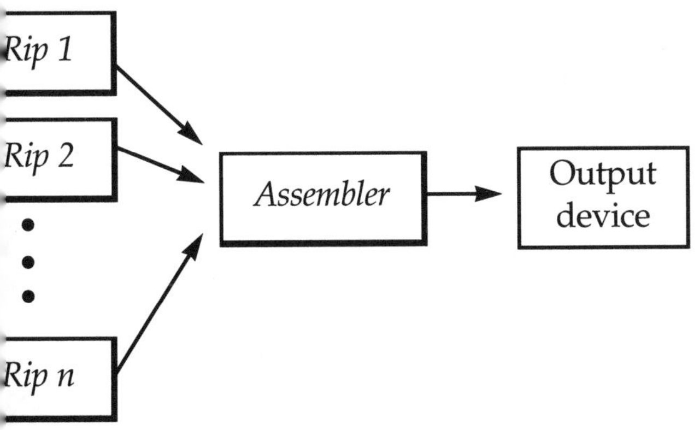

A PostScript Extreme system takes PostScript or PDF files. A "Coordinator" evaluates the file for format. If a PDF file, the Coordinator sends it to a "PDF Page Store" device (disk or file system). If a PostScript file, the Coordinator sends it to a "Normalizer" component that converts it to PDF, and then sends it to the "PDF Page Store" device. PostScript Extreme then feeds individual pages to up to ten PostScript RIPs (which convert the PDF pages back to PostScript to rasterize), staggering them for duplexing and other needs. Once rasterized, Extreme sends pages to an Assembler and print engine.

PostScript print files can be page-independent if they conform to a standard set of document structuring conventions (DSC). But few applications create PostScript files that are DSC-compliant, so this wasn't a very practical way to provide the page-independent files required by Adobe PostScript Extreme. That's where PDF comes in. Adobe's portable document format is by definition page-independent, and far more standardized than PostScript. Adobe enhanced PDF so it could include certain types of information required for high-end printing—OPI comments, halftone settings, and the like. PDF files created by Acrobat 3.0 can include this high-end information.

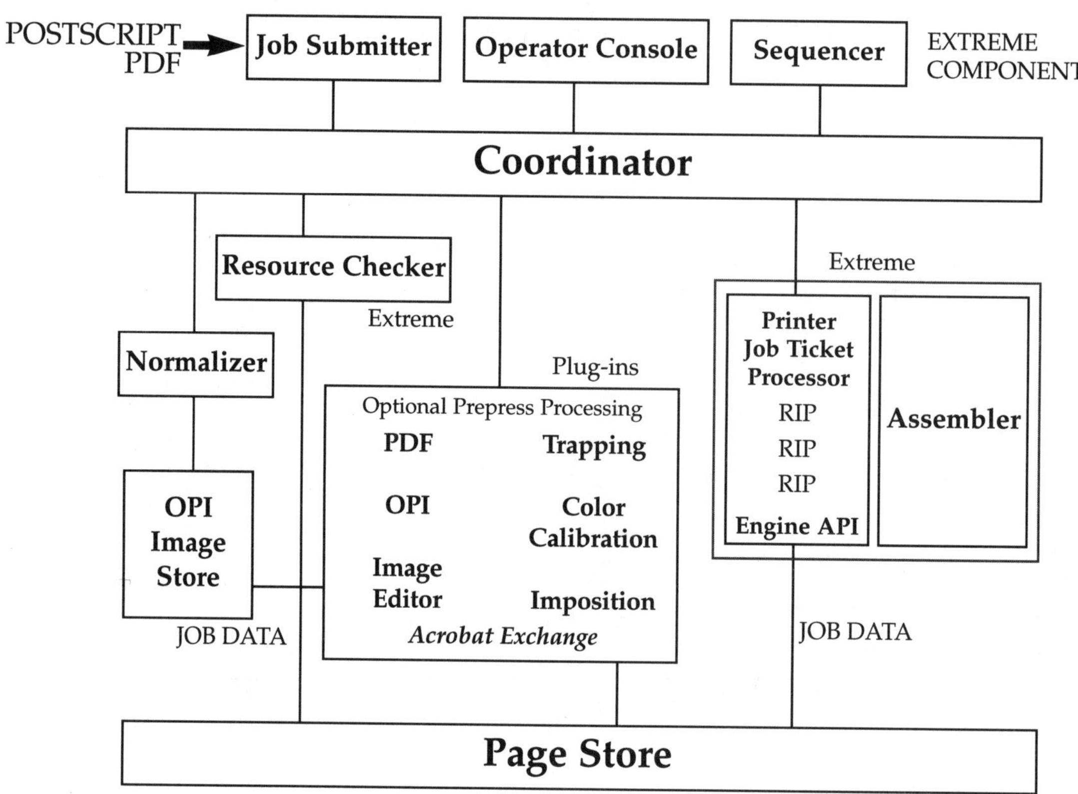

6

Creating PDF Files

The first step in any information distribution system involves how the document will be used and who will use it. An end-use evaluation for the PDF focuses on distribution and usage concerns. How will the PDF be distributed and used? If the intended distribution is Web-based and on-screen viewing, then portability and small file size are more important than quality. However, if the end-use is high-end output to an imagesetter or platesetter, then image integrity becomes the overriding factor. An analogy is that of a scale. On one side of the scale is image integrity and on the other side is file compression.

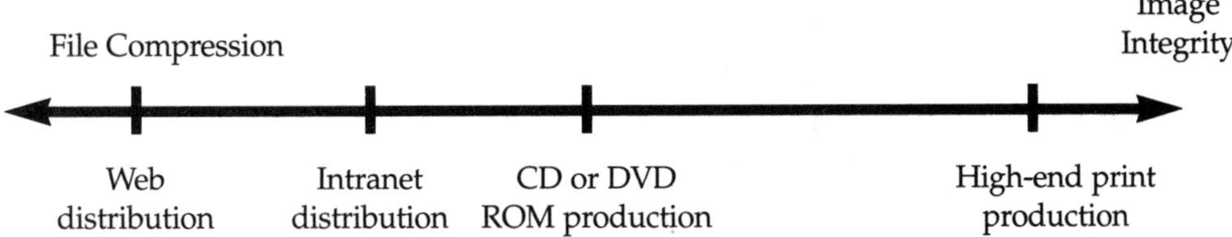

Currently there are two ways (actually 2.5 ways) to create PDF files—PDFWriter and Acrobat Distiller. Depending on end-use, one or the other will best suit your needs. The choice is actually very simple. When producing text documents with small amounts of graphics that are not intended to be printed for professional production purposes, PDFWriter is a good choice. If high-end production is the goal and proper reproduction of graphics is essential, then use Distiller. The growing repurposability of documents and intense needs of high-end printing requires the use of Distiller.

PDFWriter is found in the Macintosh Chooser as a special printer driver.

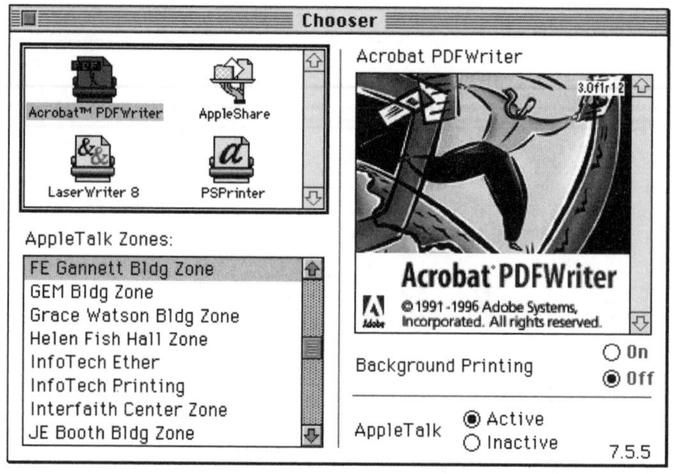

Please note:

PDFWriter creates the PDF using the screen image (QuickDraw or GDI) to create the PDF.

Distiller uses the Print Driver and PostScript to create the PDF.

PDFWriter is faster, but Distiller is more reliable.

Acrobat PDFWriter

The PDFWriter appears as a printer choice in the Chooser. PDF files are created by accessing the Page Setup and Print dialogue boxes of the document-creating application.

Compared to regular printer drivers, there are two buttons in the Page Setup dialogue box that are special for PDFWriter: *Compression* and *Fonts*. With these functions the user can control how the PDF file will be created. Only use the PDFWriter for simple text or Web projects.

Compatibility

There are different base compression schemes used by Acrobat 2.1 and 3.0. Acrobat 2.1 base compression is LZW and Acrobat 3.0 uses a ZIP-like base compression. ZIP compression is approximately 20 percent more effective than LZW. Acrobat 3.0 compatibility also preserves halftone information which used to be discarded by Acrobat 2.1. Acrobat 3.0 also compresses fonts more efficiently than 2.1.

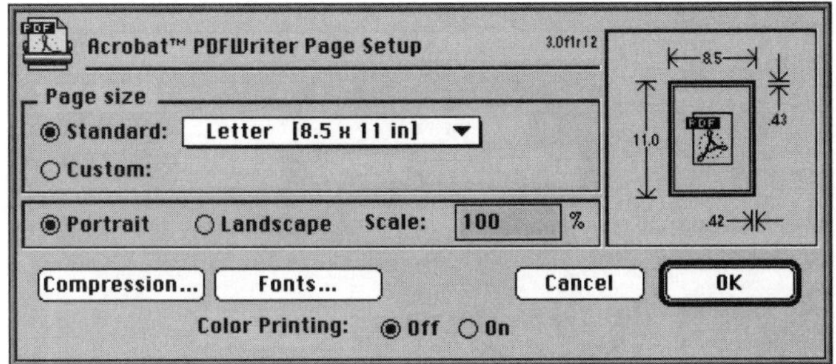

Compared to regular printer drivers, there are two buttons in the "Page Setup" dialogue box that are special for PDFWriter: Compression and Fonts. With these functions the user can control how the PDF file will be saved.

To ensure that your PDF document can be read by everyone, Acrobat 2.1 compatibility is a safe choice. However, if you'd like the added benefits of ZIP compression, use Acrobat 3.0 compatibility. This also makes sense because the Acrobat 3.0 Reader is available for free download at www.adobe.com.

ASCII Format vs. Binary Format

PDFWriter's default setting is binary which makes the PDF files about 20 percent smaller than saving them in ASCII format.

Compression

The most common reason for generating a PDF file is to enhance its transportation capabilities on digital media, either over a network or on storage devices. File size is often critical in order to best utilize storage space. Both PDFWriter and Distiller offer several types of compression which fall into two main categories, *lossy* and *lossless*.

Lossy Compression

The compression technique most used for contone images is called Joint Photographic Engineering Group (JPEG). JPEG falls into the category of lossy compression methods. This sounds worse than it actually is. Even though some information is taken away from the image to reduce the file size, the lost information is such that is not detectable in the image. There are five JPEG compression options:

- *High compression*
- *Medium-high compression*
- *Medium compression*
- *Medium-low compression*
- *Low compression*

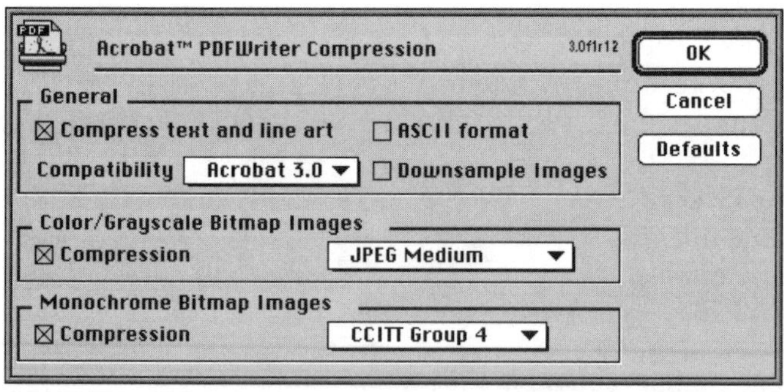

The compression dialog box for PDFWriter lets the user choose between the amount of JPEG compression or if a lossless method should be used.

Remember the balanced scale analogy? JPEG compression options are not the same as in Photoshop. Acrobat's "High" setting refers to compression and Photoshop's "Maximum" JPEG setting refers to image quality.

Remember, in Acrobat:
High Compression = Low Image Quality

And in Photoshop:
Maximum = High Image Quality

JPEG-High yields high compression rates with noticeable loss in image quality while *JPEG-Low* compresses little but preserves image quality. PDFWriter's default setting for JPEG compression is *Medium* which results in acceptable image quality for most images, depending on what you consider to be acceptable. To see the differences, print photos out at the different settings and compare them.

The compression ratio is not the same for each picture. It depends on the amount of compressible data. Images with smooth changes between tones will be compressed more than images with sharp edges and large changes in color and lightness. The JPEG algorithm is designed to compress continuous tone images, like photos. JPEG is not the best choice for compressing images with sharp changes in tone like screen captures or computer-generated line drawings.

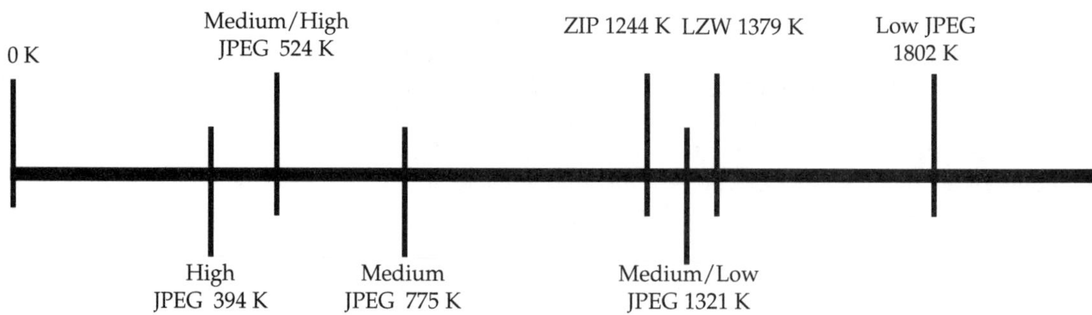

Lossless Compression
Lossless compression schemes do not suffer the same data loss that JPEG compression does. LZW/ZIP, CCITT Groups 3 & 4, and Run Length Encoded (RLE) are all lossless compressions.

Only LZW/ZIP can compress color, grayscale, and monochrome images. The Compatibility setting (Acrobat 2.1 or 3.0) will determine whether LZW or ZIP compression will be used. LZW/ZIP works well on the color/grayscale images with sharp changes in tone like the screen captures in this book.

Monochrome Compression
The final type of lossless compression offered by PDFWriter is for *Monochrome Bitmap Images*. The four compression techniques are:

- *CCITT Group 3*
- *CCITT Group 4*
- *LZW/ZIP*
- *RLE*

The basic compression idea of these methods is that if a picture has 5,000 pixels of black in a row, the file does not define the color of each pixel. For example, *pixel 1 is black, pixel 2 is black, pixel 3 is black,... pixel 4,999 is black and pixel 5,000 is black.* Rather it is defined as: *the following 5,000 pixels are black.* In PDFWriter this compression scheme is also used for text.

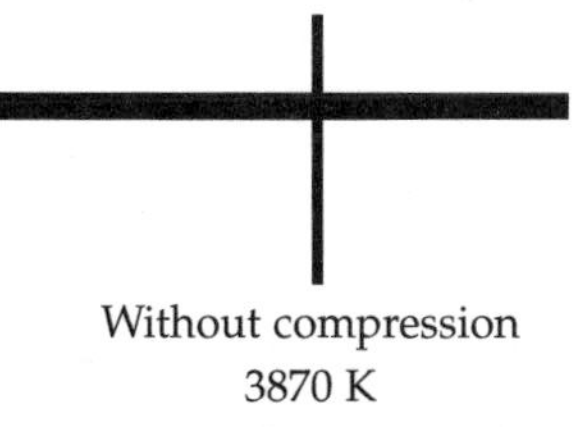

A visual comparison between the different compression rates that was accomplished on the picture on the proceeding pages

Without compression
3870 K

Uncompressed TIFF file

File size: 377 K
Compression ratio: 1

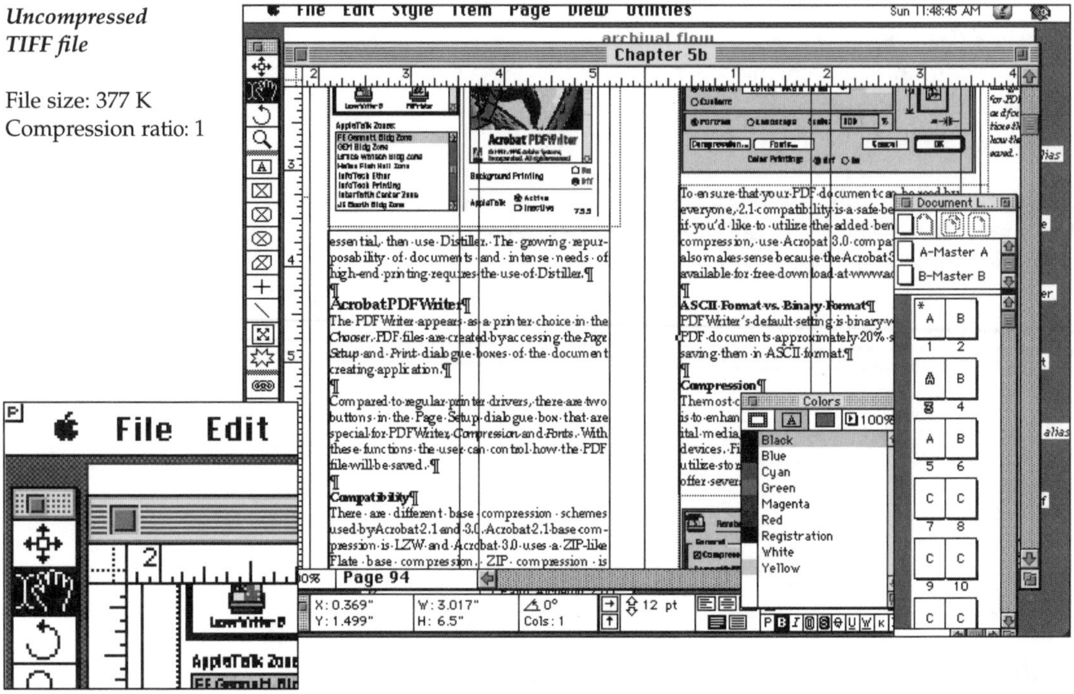

Low JPEG compression

File size: 259 K
Compression ratio: 1.45

Note the noise in the white areas. This is due to the compression techniques used in JPEG.

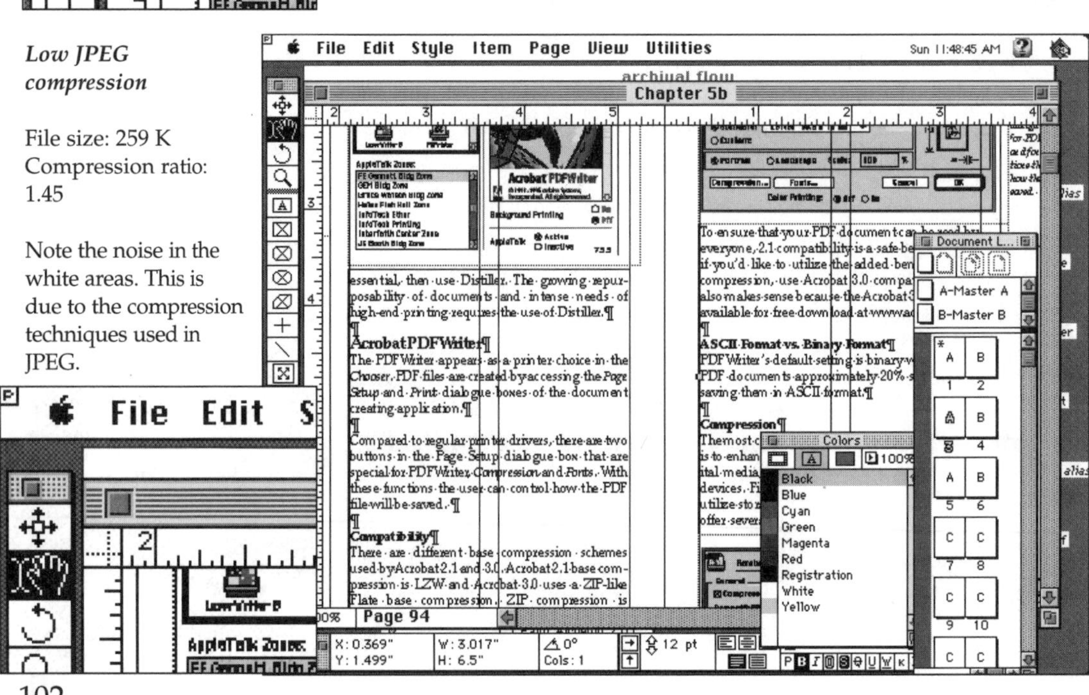

Medium JPEG compression

File size: 166 K
Compression ratio: 2.27

The compression is higher but the noise is becoming more noticeable.

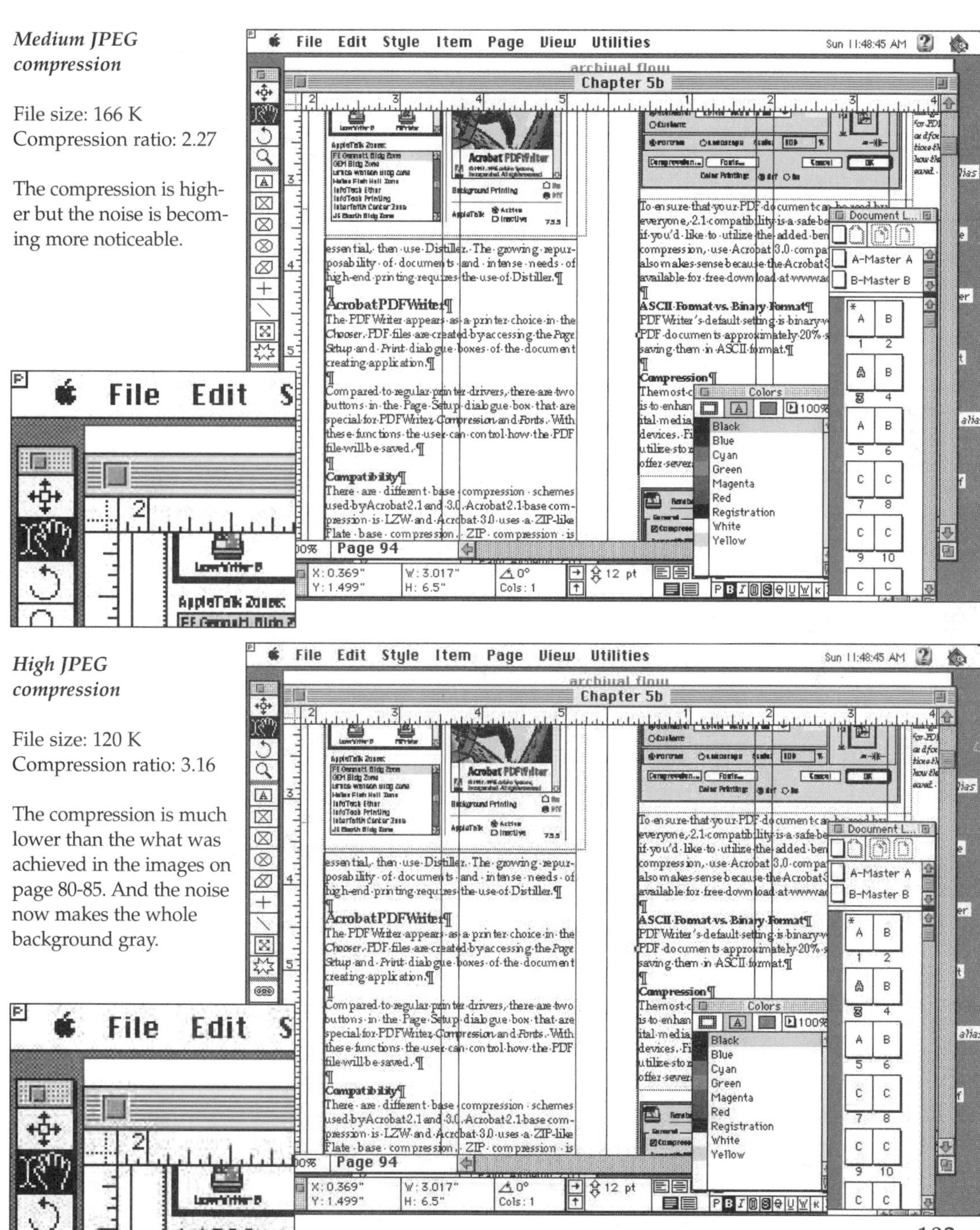

High JPEG compression

File size: 120 K
Compression ratio: 3.16

The compression is much lower than the what was achieved in the images on page 80-85. And the noise now makes the whole background gray.

ZIP 4-bit compression

File size: 28 K
Compression ratio: 13.6

As ZIP is a lossless compression. The quality is the same as the original, and because this compression is optimal for line art and artificial pictures the compression is very high.

ZIP-8 bit compression

File size: 31 K
Compression ratio: 12.1

As for the ZIP 4-bit the compression is high and the quality is excellent.

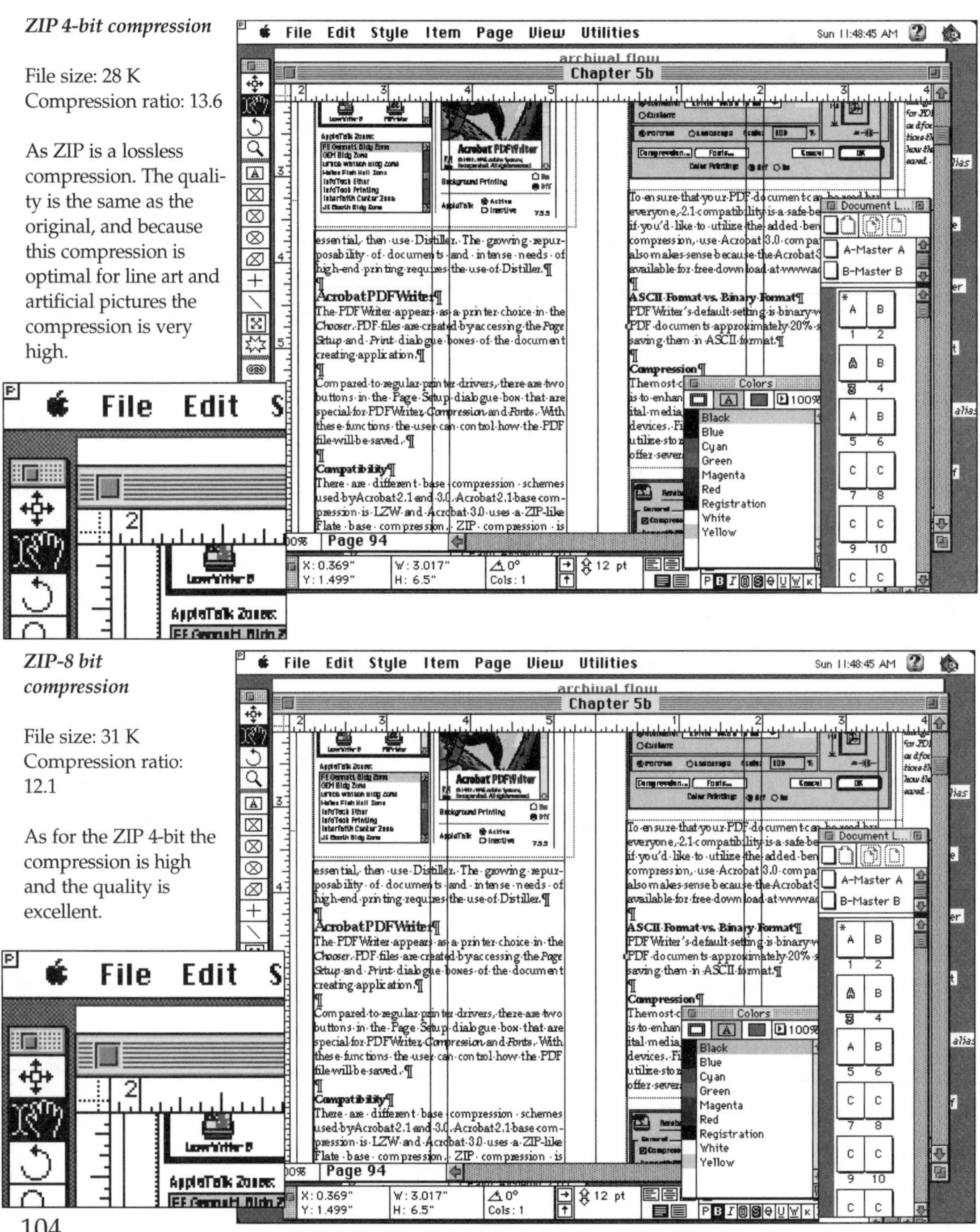

The font embedding samples on pages 108-109 were scanned and compressed using the above methods. The resulting sizes were:

Original File	*4.7 MB*
CCITT Group 4	*87 times smaller*
ZIP	*41 times smaller*
LZW	*32 times smaller*
CCITT Group 3	*29 times smaller*
RLE	*13 times smaller*

Downsampling Images
Downsampling reduces the resolution of images within a document. This results in smaller PDF file size. If the *Downsample Images* box is checked, PDFWriter will reduce the resolution of all monochrome, grayscale, and color images with the nearest integral factor that will result in a resolution as close as possible to 72 dpi. For instance, a 300 dpi image would be downsampled to 75 dpi—reducing the image file size by a factor of 16. Why downsample to 72 dpi? Because PDFWriter should be used primarily to produce PDFs for on-screen viewing and most monitors are 72–96 dpi devices.

Font Embedding
The marvel of Acrobat is its ability to retain all document font information—kerning, character shape, and scaling—while keeping the formatted information in a semi-editable text format. This is essential to maintain the look and feel of the document. PDFWriter can embed the fonts used in a document to ensure that the required font data is present when the document is displayed or printed on another computer which may not have the particular fonts installed. The receiving computer may not even use the same font format (Mac vs. PC fonts).

PDFWriter handles font inclusion in two different ways:
1. Embeds the entire font or a subset of the font.
2. Uses substitute fonts based on original font metrics and style.

Embedding Fonts
If selected in *Font* options in the Page Setup window, PDFWriter will embed the fonts used in the original document in the resulting PDF document. Each font embedded will be approximately 20K in the final PDF file size. In order to keep PDF documents

Compression
A 24-bit image is 3 x 8 bit channels. CMYK is 32-bit or 4 x 8-bit. 4-bit ZIP is lossy. It loses the four least significant bits in each channel, then compresses. ZIP means LZW compression which is not related to JPEG. ZIP is typically 10% better than LZW and is still lossless. (PK-ZIP or StuffIt do ZIP compression.)

Distiller has two ZIP options—4-bit and 8-bit. This suggests some loss of image data since it implies subsampling. Both of these job options set LZWEncode as the image compression filter, but set ColorImageDepth to 4 or 8 respectively. Adobe's document on Distiller parameters says that this parameter only takes effect when image subsampling is on, the "Downsample to" box is checked, and DownsampleGrayImages/ DownsampleColorImages is true.

For the best compression with no possibility of loss (for high-end work), uncheck "Downsample to" and "Automatic Compression," check "Manual Compression" and choose "ZIP (4-bit)" or "ZIP (8-bit)"—both will have the same effect.

Someone took a 300 ppi, CMYK image, placed it on a page and made eight different PDFs, one for each compression setting. They then ouput on film (150 lpi, 2400 dpi) and made proofs which were shown to 200 graphics professionals. Only two could identify both the best and the worst, and only because they could compare them. Often the page with the highest compression was identified as the best quality. The largest file was 37Mb, the smallest 2Mb.

PDFWriter and Distiller can handle Type 1, TrueType, or Bitmap fonts. Here is a brief description of each type:

PostScript or Type 1 Fonts
Type 1 fonts are scalable outline fonts which are defined using PostScript's bezier curves. Created by Adobe, oftentimes these fonts work best with RIPs because they do not need to be converted to be RIPed.

TrueType Fonts
TrueType fonts are also scalable outline fonts but they are based on quadratic curves, not bezier curves. Created by Apple and Microsoft, these fonts must either be converted to Type 1 before being RIPed or a TrueType Rasterizer must be used to create the bitmap for the output device. This conversion to Type 1 or rasterizing is often invisible to the user.

Bitmap Fonts
Bitmap fonts are non-scalable pixel maps of a given typeface. To use bitmap fonts, a separate font file must be used for each size or the "jaggies" will appear on type.

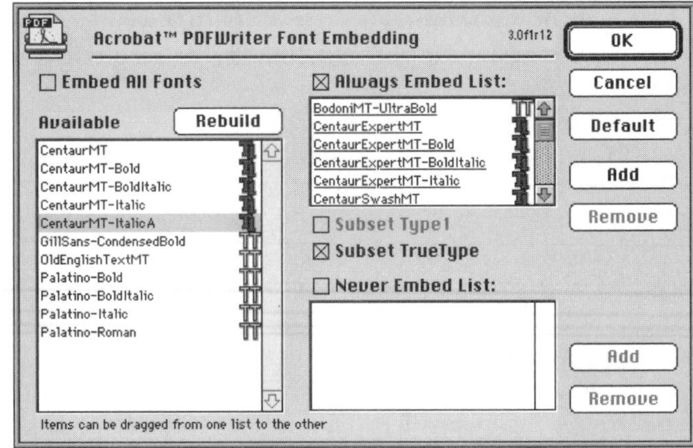

portable, font subsets can be embedded. Subsets include only the font characters used in the document which offers on average a file savings of 10K per font in the final PDF file size. If *Subset fonts* is selected and less than 35% of the characters of a font are used, PDFWriter will embed a subset of that font. If over 35% of the font characters are used, PDFWriter will automatically embed the entire font.

PDFWriter can embed Type 1 PostScript fonts (indicated by the icon) as well as TrueType fonts (indicated by a icon). The

PDFWriter's Handling of Fonts

best way to insure typographic integrity is to select *Embed All Fonts*. All fonts used in the document will be embedded in the resulting PDF file ensuring correct display and printing.

Another option is to specify a list of fonts to *Always Embed* and fonts to *Never Embed*. If working in a closed Intranet system, an office where all fonts are standardized, you could place all fonts in the *Never Embed* list. This will reduce the file size by approximately 20K for each font used in the document.

Simulated Fonts

If the fonts are not embedded, PDFWriter will gather information about the font relating to its style (bold, italic), metrics (character shape), and font name. This information will be saved with the PDF file and will only require about one kilobyte of storage space. When the PDF document is used later, and the original font is available, it will be used. If the font is not available, Acrobat will use the saved font metric and style information to create an "approximate" simulation font that resembles the original, as good as possible. The *Adobe Sans Multiple Master* and the *Adobe Serif Multiple Master* are used to make these simulated fonts "on the fly."

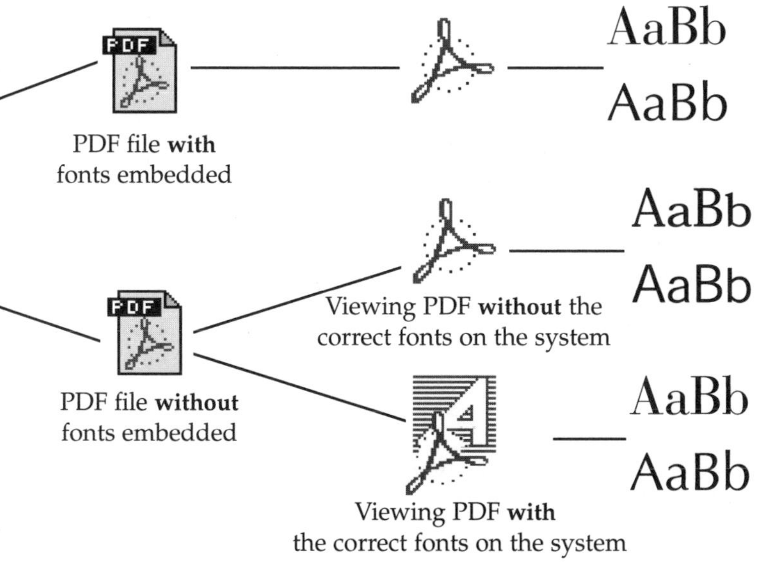

Fonts

If Distiller runs into a needed font while distilling and the font is

- *neither an active Type 1 font*
- *nor embedded in PostScript*
- *nor accessible to Distiller*

then Distiller tries to look it up in the superatm.db (SuperATM Database, though we'll never know why the Acrobat team chose to name the same file 'distsadb.dos' for the Wintel version) to retrieve the metric information needed to convert the PostScript pages into PDF (the font outline is not needed, as Distiller does not do any rasterizing).

The advantage is—if you are ok with Adobe's font substitution, you'll get a file with properly measured fonts (characters sitting where they should sit). If on the target machine Reader or Exchange have the respective original font available, they will use that original font, and you'll see perfect character shapes, etc. If the target machine does not have the respective original font loaded, Adobe's font substitution will simulate the font fairly well—good enough for tech docs, etc.

The disadvantage is—if you are creating PDF files for prepress production, font substitution definitely is not your preferred option. In this case it is better to force Distiller to not use substitution information, but at least issue a message "Font not found—using Courier" (in the log window, log file, and message file) and also arrive at a file that has Courier instead of whatever font was missing. If you remove superatm.db, Distiller won't complain, but will also not be able to retrieve font metrics for otherwise missing fonts.

Font Substitution

The PDF Language manages fonts through the use of a font descriptor, a small object including enough information to allow a PDF-based application to find or simulate a font needed in the document. PDF also allows an actual font (either a complete or subset font) to be included in the document.

PDF defines a base set of 13 fonts for which no font descriptor is required in a PDF document. These fonts are treated as universal, because they are guaranteed to be available with the Reader and other Adobe-produced PDF-based applications. The base 13 fonts are never included in a PDF document.

Although the PDF Reference Manual discusses font substitution, and identifies font descriptors as the means to accomplish font substitution, substitution is really a feature of applications attempting to generate, display, or print PDF, not of the language itself. Substitution is a behavior, rather than a language feature. Different applications implement different behaviors when handling a PDF font descriptor when they cannot find the original font.

In Acrobat Distiller, font substitution may be managed through use of a font database. This font database is essentially the PDF font descriptors for several thousand commercially available fonts. Distiller uses the font database to construct font descriptors and manage metrics for fonts referenced but not available when creating a PDF document from a PostScript file. ("Available"

Helvetica light	AaBbCcDdEeFfGgHh
Gill Sans	***AaBbCcDdEeFfGgHh***
Cochin	AaBbCcDdEeFfGgHh
Garamond	*AaBbCcDdEeFfGgHh*
Bodoni	AaBbCcDdEeFfGgHh
Optima	AaBbCcDdEeFfGgHh
Stone Serif	*AaBbCcDdEeFfGgHh*
Minion	AaBbCcDdEeFfGgHh

Gill Sans

There is very little known about Nicholas Jenson especially before he in 1470 is operating as printer in Venice.The best source of information that is available about him as person is his own testament from 1480. From here it have been derived that Jenson came from southern France and that he was born at Sommevoire. It is quite certain that he had worked in the royal mint of Toryes and later Paris and that he was very successful in diemaking for coin manufacturing. King Charles VII had learned about the invention of the printing press and thought that this was a good

Minion

There is very little known about Nicholas Jenson especially before he in 1470 is operating as printer in Venice. The best source of information that is available about him as person is his own testament from 1480. From here it have been derived that Jenson came from southern France and that he was born at Sommevoire. It is quite certain that he had worked in the royal mint of Toryes and later Paris and that he wa very successful in diemaking for coin manufacturing.
King Charles VII had learned about the invention of the printing press and thought that this was a good

The above illustration shows how the PDF file views/prints if the fonts were embedded in the file.

Helvetica light	AaBbCcDdEeFfGgHh
Gill Sans	AaBbCcDdEeFf GgHh
Cochin	AaBbCcDdEeFfGgHh
Garamond	AaBbCcDdEeFf GgHh
Bodoni	AaBbCcDdEeFfGgHh
Optima	AaBbCcDdEeFfGgHh
Stone Serif	AaBbCcDdEeFfGgHh
Minion	AaBbCcDdEeFfGgHh

Gill Sans

There is very little known about Nicholas Jenson especially before he in 1470 is operating as printer in Venice. The best source of information that is available about him as person is his own testament from 1480. From here it have been derived that Jenson came from southern France and that he was born at Sommevoire. It is quite certain that he had worked in the royal mint of Toryes and later Paris and that he was very successful in diemaking for coin manufacturing. King Charles VII had learned about the invention of the printing press and thought that this was a good

Minion

There is very little known about Nicholas Jenson especially before h in 1470 is operating as printer in Venice. The best source of information that is available about him as person is his own testament from 1480. From here it have been derive that Jenson came from southern France and that he was born at Sommevoire. It is quite certain that he had worked in the royal mint of Toryes and later Paris and that he w very successful in diemaking for coi manufacturing.
King Charles VII had learned about the invention of the printing press and thought that this was a good

The above illustration shows how the PDF file views/prints if the fonts were simulated by Acrobat.

means included in the PostScript file in such a way as to be defined in Distiller, or available externally through ATM, or in the usual places on the system.)

If, while converting a PostScript file, Distiller encounters a reference to a font which is not available, Distiller will attempt to look the font up in the font database in order to correctly place characters on the page. If Distiller finds the font in the database, it will insert the font's descriptor into the document. The resulting PDF file will be identical to what Distiller produces when the font is present, but not embedded.

If Distiller does not have the font database available when it is converting, and a font is not available, Distiller will produce an error message, and will use Courier instead of the font. This will usually result in incorrect page appearance when the resulting PDF document is viewed or printed, even if the system used to view or print the file has the originally missing font available.

The above is why some users do not recommend removing superatm.db. One can discover the missing font and correct it, but once the file has been distilled with a missing db, there is no fix except redistilling.

The average reader, not including professionals in the graphic arts industry, will probably not notice that the text typeface is a simulated typeface, but as the size of the type increases, so will the chance for detection. For instance, where predominantly text-based documents contain titles or headlines of a larger type size, subsetting only the few characters that are included in the title of the document will be your best option.

The subsetting of this font will ensure the proper reproduction and maintain the look and feel of the document. If small file size is more important than typographic integrity, font simulation works reasonably well on most standard sans serif and serif typefaces. For fancy fonts, beware.

Nonstandard typefaces including symbolic and ornamental typefaces are a little trickier. PDFWriter and Distiller should automatically embed any fonts which they consider "non-standard" but this is not always done. Nonstandard fonts could include expert sets, swash characters, or any font which does not conform to the standard glyph names described in the Post-Script handbook. PDFWriter and Distiller will embed these nonstandard fonts because a simulation can not be made using the Serif MM and Sans Serif MM. In the font dialogue box these typefaces are underlined. If the default button is clicked, they will automatically be moved to the *Always Embed* list.

Acrobat Reader and Exchange use the font descriptors in a PDF file, both for viewing and printing, in much the same way as Distiller uses the font database. This only happens when a font is not available at the time of viewing/printing ("available" here meaning the font [full or subset] is included as a resource in the PDF or is found on the computer system where Reader is running).

If a font is available, Reader/Exchange will use the font for viewing and printing. If a font is not available, Reader/Exchange will use the PDF font descriptor in conjunction with ATM to simulate the appearance of the font on-screen. When printing, Reader will use a printer-resident font in preference to a simulated font, but will use an included subset or full font in preference to a printer-resident font.

Reader/Exchange provides the facility, through the "Fonts..." subselection of the "Document Info" menu item" to get a list of all fonts, including substituted fonts, in a document. If a missing font is subsequently loaded onto the system where Reader is running and Reader (and the system itself, in the case of the Macintosh) is restarted, the Reader will no longer substitute, but will use the real font for viewing and printing.

PDF Creation

Acrobat™ PDFWriter 3.0f1r12 OK
Page Range: ◉ All ○ From: [ ] To: [ ] Cancel
☒ View PDF File
☒ Short (DOS) File Names ☐ Prompt for Document Info
Page Sequence: All ☐ Collate ☐ Back to Front
Output: Normal ☐ Spreads ☐ Thumbnails
Tiling: Off Overlap: 3"
Separation: Off Plate: All Plates
Registration: Off OPI:
Options: ☐ Calibrated Output ☐ Print Colors as Grays
☐ Include Blank Pages

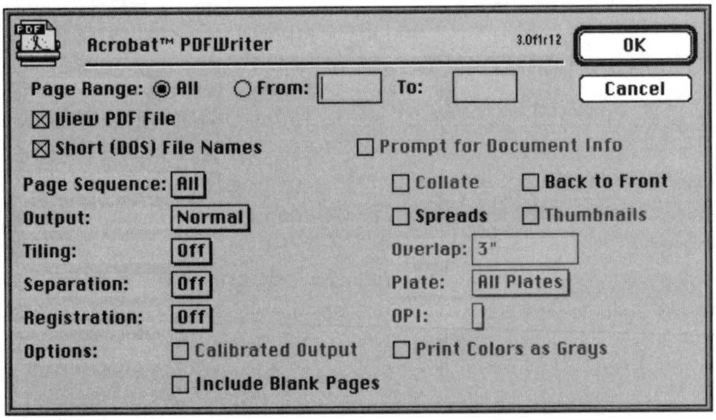

The PDFWriter Print dialogue box (QuarkXPress).

Once options for font embedding and compression have been chosen, creating a PDF is as simple as hitting the *Print* button.

1. Select *Print* from the *File* Menu
2. Name the resulting PDF file
3. Determine where the file is to be saved
4. PDFWriter handles the rest

PDFWriter Overview

Even though PDFWriter is extremely convenient and is the easiest way to prepare PDF files, it is not without drawbacks. First, applications do not "see" the PDFWriter as a PostScript printer, which means Encapsulated PostScript (EPS) images will be sent to PDFWriter as low-resolution rough screen versions. Also, PDFWriter cannot be used with Apple's page display and description format, *QuickDraw GX*. If QuickDraw GX is installed, PDFWriter will not be displayed in the Chooser.

"Silent simulation" should only be used for screen-based applications. For print applications, we suggest you embed all fonts. You can disable silent simulation by removing the superatm.db file from the Fonts folder in the Acrobat folder.

As a general rule, if your document contains EPS images or you would like more control over the compression and font embedding options, Acrobat Distiller should be used to create the PDF.

PDFWriter does not support all controls that are supported in a PDF file. And as mentioned above, PDFWriter is a non-PostScript printer driver, and the information will not be treated the same way as if the file was printed to a PostScript printer. To solve this problem, Acrobat Distiller must be used.

Acrobat Distiller

What Distiller lacks in ease of use is more than made up in its reliability and extended capabilities over PDFWriter. Distiller can be seen as a software RIP, where the PostScript codes are interpreted and an object list is generated. But instead of generating a raster representation of the page, it is formatted into a PDF document. In version 3.0/3.0x of Distiller, version 1.2 of PDF is used. The major difference from the previous PDF versions, 1.0 and 1.1, is that PostScript commands for professional print production are included. Some of these features are accessed in Acrobat Distiller, and for other functions, third-party plug-ins must be developed to take full advantage of the possibilities of PDF 1.2. PDF version 1.5 is imminent and it extends many of the PDF features.

Creating a PDF with Distiller requires first "saving" the document to a PostScript file (the data that would have been sent to a printer is instead saved in a file) and then opening that file in Distiller. The advantage of creating a PDF this way is that all of the data necessary to render the page is described in the PostScript file. As a result, Distiller can also act as a preflight tool to ensure that jobs are "RIP-able." Chances are that if it distills, it will print. Another advantage of Distiller is that it offers more control over compression and font opts than PDFWriter. High-end printing controls are also available through Distiller.

Now that we have told you how to use PDFWriter—don't use it! PDFWriter is good for "fast" PDF creation. It is almost as simple as printing a document to a printer. However, it does not allow the control and quality available using Distiller. And this will have a terrible impact on your files.

Creating PDF with Distiller

Why use Distiller instead of PDFWriter?

1. For more control over compression and font embedding options.
2. Your document contains EPS images.
3. To distill PostScript files from another platform.
4. You encounter problems using PDFWriter.
5. You do not want to go on medication to deal with stress.

Distiller can create PDF documents from both EPS and PostScript files.

The first step in creating PDF documents with Distiller is to produce a PostScript file. Because the PostScript file is going to be used to generate the PDF document, the correct page setup options must be set here. If the page orientation is not correct at this point, it cannot be corrected in Distiller.

When using QuarkXPress, it is also important to use the Acrobat Distiller printer description in the Page Setup menu. If a black & white printer description (most laser printers) is selected, the resulting PDF will be in black and white. This is also helpful if you choose to use a Custom Page size not supported by the selected printer description.

After the correct Page Setup options have been chosen, select *Print* under the File menu.

1. Choose the radio button *File* in the *Destination* box.
2. With this selected, the *Print* button will change to *Save*.

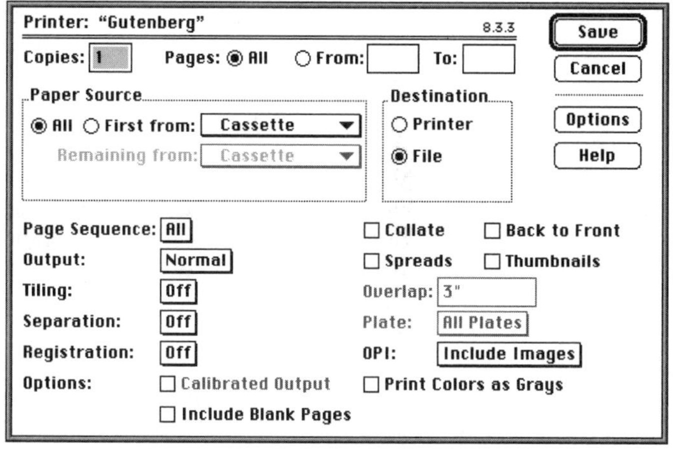

When making a PDF with Distiller you must have a PostScript file first. This is created by choosing a PostScript printer driver in the Chooser and when in the print dialogue box making sure that File is chosen as destination. Notice that the Print *button changes to* "Save."

If you are creating a PDF file with colors, it is crucial to choose a color PPD (like the Acrobat Distiller PPD) when creating the PostScript. If this is not done, the result will be a black-and-white PDF document.

3. Click on Save.
4. Name the PostScript file and designate the location where it will be saved.

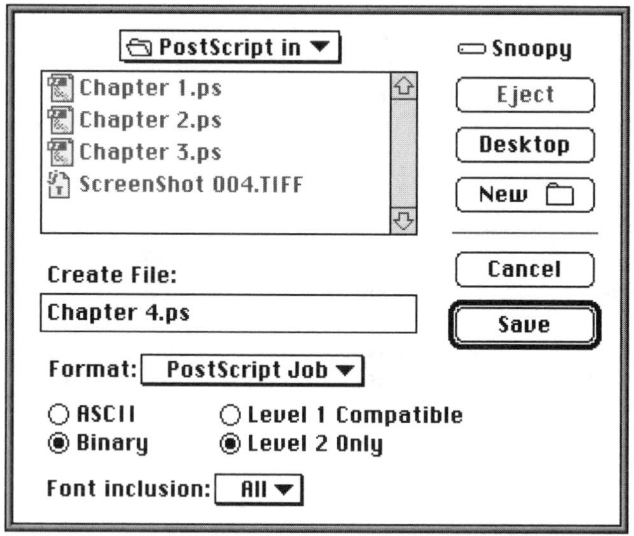

Do not use the ASCII option when creating PDF files. This is left over from an old version, and only Binary should be used.

Some users feel that ASCII encoding is desirable if the file may pass through some 7-bit communications channel that may mess up binary data. For example, if a PDF is attached to a mail message, or placed on an FTP server that you expect will be used by a wide range of people, then ASCII encoding might be a good idea.

But, it turns out that many e-mail gateways merrily insert hard returns into 7-bit ASCII files when a line is more than 60 characters long, hopelessly corrupting PDF files which may have lines longer than that, as it is allowed in the format definition. Besides which, 7-bit encoded compressed streams (images, pages) are 20 percent larger than 8-bit.

5. Select either PostScript Level 1 or Level 2. Since Distiller is a Level 2 RIP, it's best to select Level 2. If you have problems distilling the file, try using Level 1.

6. Determine the font inclusion—None, All, All but the standard thirteen, All but those in the PPD file.

All: All typefaces that are used in the file will be embedded in the PostScript file.

All but Standard 13: There are thirteen fonts that always are included in a PostScript printer (Courier, Courier bold, Courier italic, Courier bold italic, Helvetica, Helvetica bold, Helvetica italic, Helvetica bold italic, Times, Times bold, Times italic, Times bold italic, and the Symbol font).

All but Fonts in PPD File: This will send all fonts not included in the PostScript Printer Description (PPD). The PPD file contains information about the fonts installed on the output device. If the Distiller PPD is being used, there should be no problem. But if you are using a PPD for a printer with installed fonts not available to Distiller, you could get Courier in your PDF file.

To ensure that Distiller has all of the font information necessary to properly produce the PDF document, be sure to select include All, All but Standard 13 *under the font inclusion menu when saving the PostScript file. Although this will add to the overall size of the PostScript file, PostScript is only an intermediary step to the PDF creation. It can be discarded once the PDF document has been created. Acrobat Distiller will NEVER embed the standard Base 14 PostScript fonts, even when* Embed all Fonts *is chosen. This may be addressed in future versions. In a perfect world, this would be okay, since all PostScript RIPS ship with the Base 13 installed. However, if a customer has chosen to edit one of the Base 13 fonts without renaming it, a PDF workflow will result currently in the modified font being replaced at output time by the original font installed at the RIP.*

Including vs. Embedding Fonts
Including fonts in a PostScript file is not the same thing as embedding them in a PDF document. Including them with the PostScript file ensures that Distiller will have access to them when it creates the PDF. Only Distiller and PDFWriter can embed fonts in PDF documents.

The best advice is to include *All* fonts in the PostScript file. It is possible to *not* include the fonts but you must then make sure that Distiller knows where to find them for PDF creation. However, the foolproof method is to include them in the PostScript.

Remember, you need a PostScript file for Distiller and that PostScript file can either have all fonts embedded or Distiller must know where to look to find them on the local computer (the one where the job was created usually). Since the latter approach is fraught with peril, embed the fonts when you save the PostScript file to disk. Then there is no question that they are available. Now, you must also set Distiller job options to embed all fonts.

After all options for the PostScript file have been chosen, click on the *Save* button and the PostScript file will be generated.

Distilling PostScript Files

Creating PDF files from PostScript is as simple as opening Distiller, selecting *Open* from the *File,* menu and naming the resulting PDF document. Although the actual process is easy, setting up how the PostScript file will be distilled into a PDF document requires a little preparation.

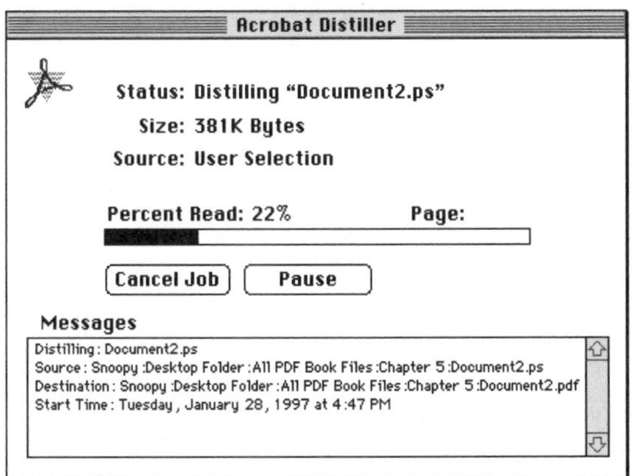

Understating the power of the software engine underneath, the Distiller opening window is deceivingly simple. The Cancel Job *button can be used to flush a job in the middle of processing. The* Pause *button prevents Distiller from accepting any new jobs until the* Resume *button is pushed (just like taking a RIP offline). If the* Pause *button is pushed in the middle of processing a job, it will finish the job and then pause. It cannot pause in the middle of a job.*

Distiller Job Options

This is the heart of customizing PDF documents within Distiller and is available in the Distiller menu. There are four sections to *Job Options*:

1. *General*
2. *Compression*
3. *Font embedding*
4. *Advanced*

General

Most of the General settings resemble those available within PDFWriter. However, there are added controls for Default resolution and Default page size. If the page size is not specified within the PostScript file, the page size will be set by the value placed here.

This is useful for distilling EPS files which do not contain any page size information. If the page size is specified within the PostScript file, Distiller will use the specified size not Distiller's default.

Resolution in Distiller

When creating a PS file from Quark using the Distiller PPD, you have the choice of setting a resolution (300, 600, 1200, or 2400). Then Distiller's Job Options *asks again. Do these settings affect the final resolution of the images in the PDF?*

These settings do not affect the resolution of images in PDF files, unless they cause QuarkXPress to subsample before "printing." But disable subsampling in Distiller anyway. These settings affect the "reported resolution" of Distiller. This can affect the number of steps in a blend. It's useful to make it match your final device, though it isn't critical if you use a large value.

Distiller Job Options—under the Compression *tab, uncheck the box next to* Downsample *in both* Color Bitmap Images *and* Grayscale Bitmap.

If you set up resolutions lower than the actual resolution of your images in page setup prior to making the PostScript of a page with images "downsampling" can occur when the PostScript is created, which no Distiller setting can "undo."

Resolution setting in Distiller's Job Options *affects some application-generated blends, but not images. Dpi settings in Distiller's Subsampling dialog affect raster images.*

Resolution setting in Quark's Page Setup *affects placed TIFF images in Quark pages, and possibly blends, so choose a resolution related to the target printer and the halftone screening of the job. Quark setup will not affect embedded EPS files.*

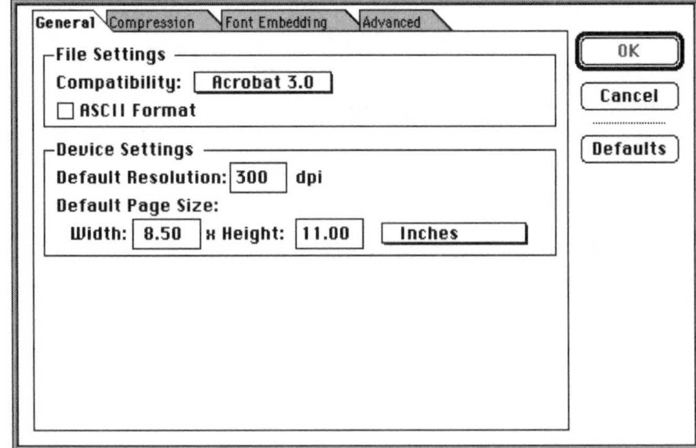

Distiller General Options

Compression

Distiller offers more control over compression options than PDFWriter. The *Automatic Compression* option in Distiller evaluates images in a file and applies the "best" compression scheme. If the image consists of many gradual tone changes, JPEG is used, as in a photograph, but if sharp edges are present, such as in screen dumps and line art graphics, LZW/ZIP (depending on the Compatibility setting chosen in General options) is used. The user can specify which level of JPEG compression should be used.

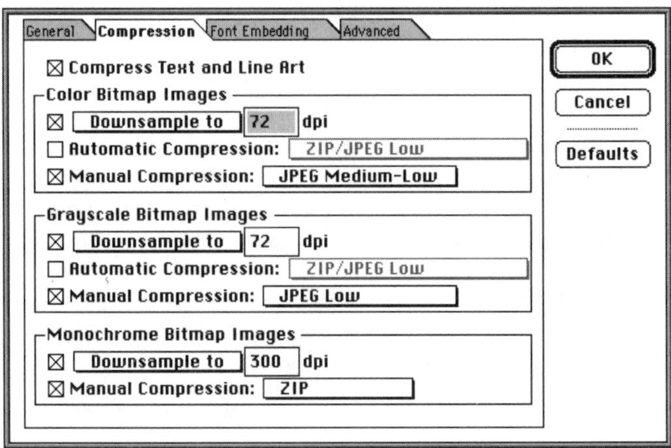

If individual control over the compression is desired, click *Automatic Compression* off and select *Manual Compression*. This lets the user specify exactly which type of compression should be used for color, grayscale, and monochrome bitmap images.

Using compression can cause problems with images, depending on the level of JPEG compression used. For Windows documents, switch to ZIP 8-bit compression, and switch off subsampling, to ensure that the PDF contains exactly the images that went in to it—and still have a healthy compression. Never use "subsample;" always use "downsample."

Also new to Distiller, and not available in PDFWriter, is the *Subsample to* option. Both downsampling and subsampling reduce the resolution of images and overall file size, however, they use different approaches. Downsampling evaluates the pixels in an array, averages those values into a larger remaining pixel that covers the same area. Subsampling selects the value of the center pixel in an array, discards the remaining pixels, and creates a pixel with the center value covering the same area as the array. Basically, downsampling averages pixel data and subsampling selects the center pixel and discards the other pixel data. Both subsampling and downsampling can be set to specific resolutions as low as 9 dpi.

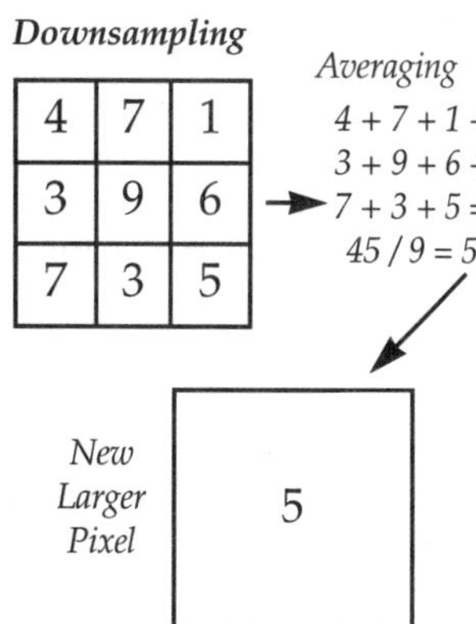

Downsampling can be used efficiently for production printing. For example; a PostScript stream made from a 400 dpi file for an advertisement can be distilled into a PDF downsampled to 350 dpi for use with a 175 lpi screen in a magazine. That same stream can be distilled into a PDF downsampled to 170 dpi so it can be repurposed to print in a newspaper where the screen ruling is 80 lpi. This repurposing using downsampling can be done without alteration to the original file or original scans.

Font Embedding

Font embedding controls are similar to PDFWriter but with finer control over when fonts are subsetted. As more entire fonts are embedded you are increasing the overall file size of the PostScript file but the PDF file is still pretty compressd. Distiller allows the subsetting threshold to be set by the user. Instead of PDFWriter's default of 35 percent, the user can specify any value from 1 to 99 percent and we recommend the latter.

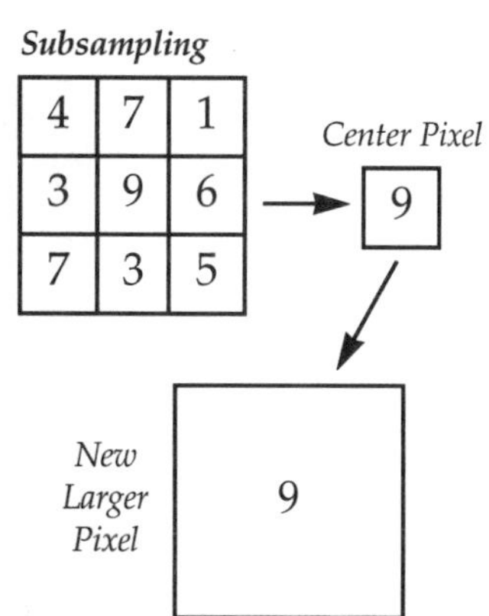

Please make sure you read the sidebars on pages 107 through 110 for explanations on embedding fonts within the Acrobat PDF. Once you learn it and set it, you will not have to worry about it again.

Downsampling

Downsampled to 150 dpi.
Distilling time: 13 seconds.

Downsampled to 72 dpi.
Distilling time: 13 seconds.

Full resolution 300 dpi.
Distilling time: 22 seconds.

Downsampling averages tone values from surrounding pixels and reproduces the average tone using one larger pixel. This is a method that takes more computing power and is slower than subsampling, although the quality is better.

Because downsampling averages pixels, the picture becomes more fuzzy, but looks better compared to subsampling especially with big reductions in resolution.

If Downsample Images *is selected in PDFWriter, it will automatically downsample images to 72 dpi or the closest possible value. Distiller allows you to specify the downsample resolution.*

Subsampling

Subsampled to 150 dpi.
Distilling time: 12 seconds.

Subsampled to 72 dpi.
Distilling time: 10 seconds.

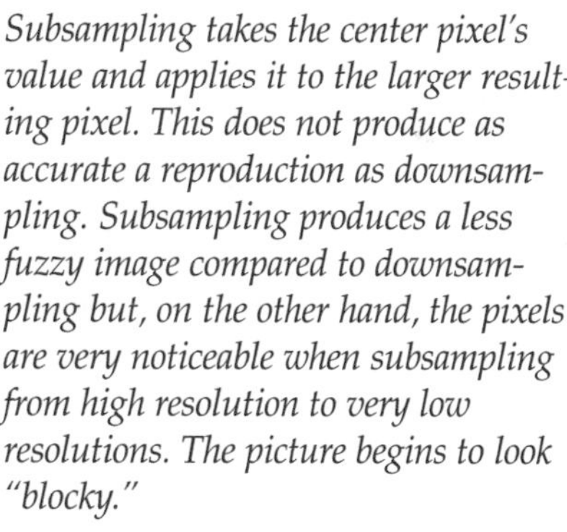

Subsampling takes the center pixel's value and applies it to the larger resulting pixel. This does not produce as accurate a reproduction as downsampling. Subsampling produces a less fuzzy image compared to downsampling but, on the other hand, the pixels are very noticeable when subsampling from high resolution to very low resolutions. The picture begins to look "blocky."

Subsampling can only be accomplished using Distiller. Because subsampling requires less computing power, sßubsampling takes less time to distill than does downsampling.

Full resolution 300 dpi.
Distilling time: 22 seconds.

Distiller Font Embedding Options

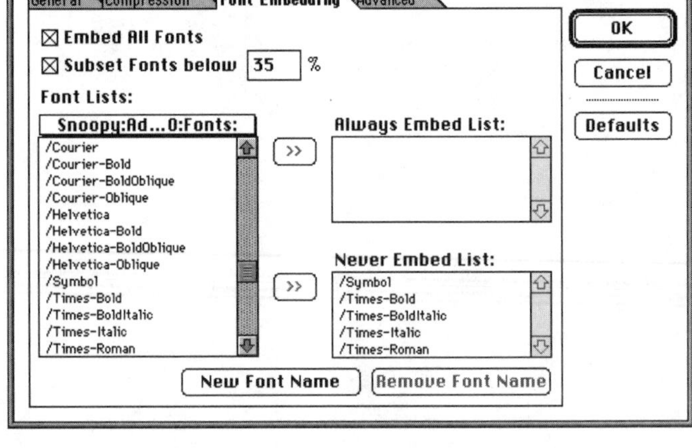

To ensure that proper fonts have been embedded you can open the PDF document in Reader or Exchange on a computer which does not have the fonts. Select File—Document Info—Fonts. *Under the* Used Font *category, the listings should read* Embedded *or* Embedded Subset.

Acrobat Distiller will never embed the standard Base 13 PostScript fonts even when Embed all Fonts *is chosen. There are actually 14 fonts in the* Never Embed *list: the base 13 plus Zapf Dingbats. Although none of these will ever be embedded in a PDF, Exchange will include Symbol and Zapf Dingbats in PS files that it exports (on a Mac). It will not include any of the other twelve. Making the choice in Distiller setup of* Subsetting below 99% *means subsetting whenever there are less than 99 percent of the full complement of glyphs.*

Another difference between PDFWriter and Distiller is font availability. Since PDFWriter creates PDF documents directly from the layout application, all fonts used in the document are available for embedding or substitution information. Because Distiller can be run either on the local computer that generated the PostScript file or on a network server, the fonts may not be available. If Distiller cannot reference the fonts, there is a risk that fonts will be missing and possibly not even simulated. To be certain that this does not happen, two methods are possible. The easiest way is to include the fonts in the PostScript file prior to distilling. The second method is to tell Distiller where the fonts can be found. To do this, select *Font Locations* under the *Distiller* menu. Although there is always a risk that the font used in the file may not be available in the font location and then `Courier` will be used.

The *Font Embedding* section of *Job Options* lists available fonts. If the *Embed All Fonts* box is checked, all fonts used in the document will be embedded. If a font is not to be embedded, Distiller will retrieve the font metrics so that a simulation using the Serif MM or Sans Serif MM can be made.

When creating PDF files, Distiller looks for fonts or font metric information in the following manner:

- In the PostScript file
- In the *Font Locations* menu (which by default includes

system folder locations as well as Acrobat's font folder). Distiller also looks in locations specified by a font management utility like *Suitcase.*
- The font database that is installed with Acrobat. This database contains the information necessary to produce simulation fonts for Adobe's Type 1 font library. However, since new fonts are released every day, and not all by Adobe, you have yet another reason to include the fonts in the PostScript file.

If after searching all of these locations, Distiller still cannot find the required font information, our old friend `Courier` will be used as a substitute font.

Advanced Options

With the release of Acrobat 3.0, Adobe has addressed some of the needs of the high-end printing market. Probably the most important for printing applications is the ability to include overprint settings and preserve halftone screen information.

See the Crackerjack description in Chapter 10.

Prologue & Epilogue Comments

The check box *Distill with prologue.ps/epilogue.ps* is important when you want to retain spot colors (defined as separation color spaces in PostScript) when creating a PDF file. If you do not use these epilogue/prologue files then spot colors will get mapped to process colors during the conversion to PDF.

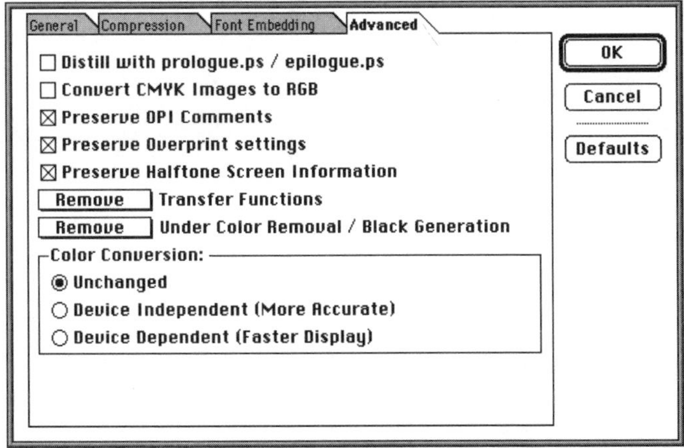

Distiller's Advanced Options

Distiller's Handling of Fonts

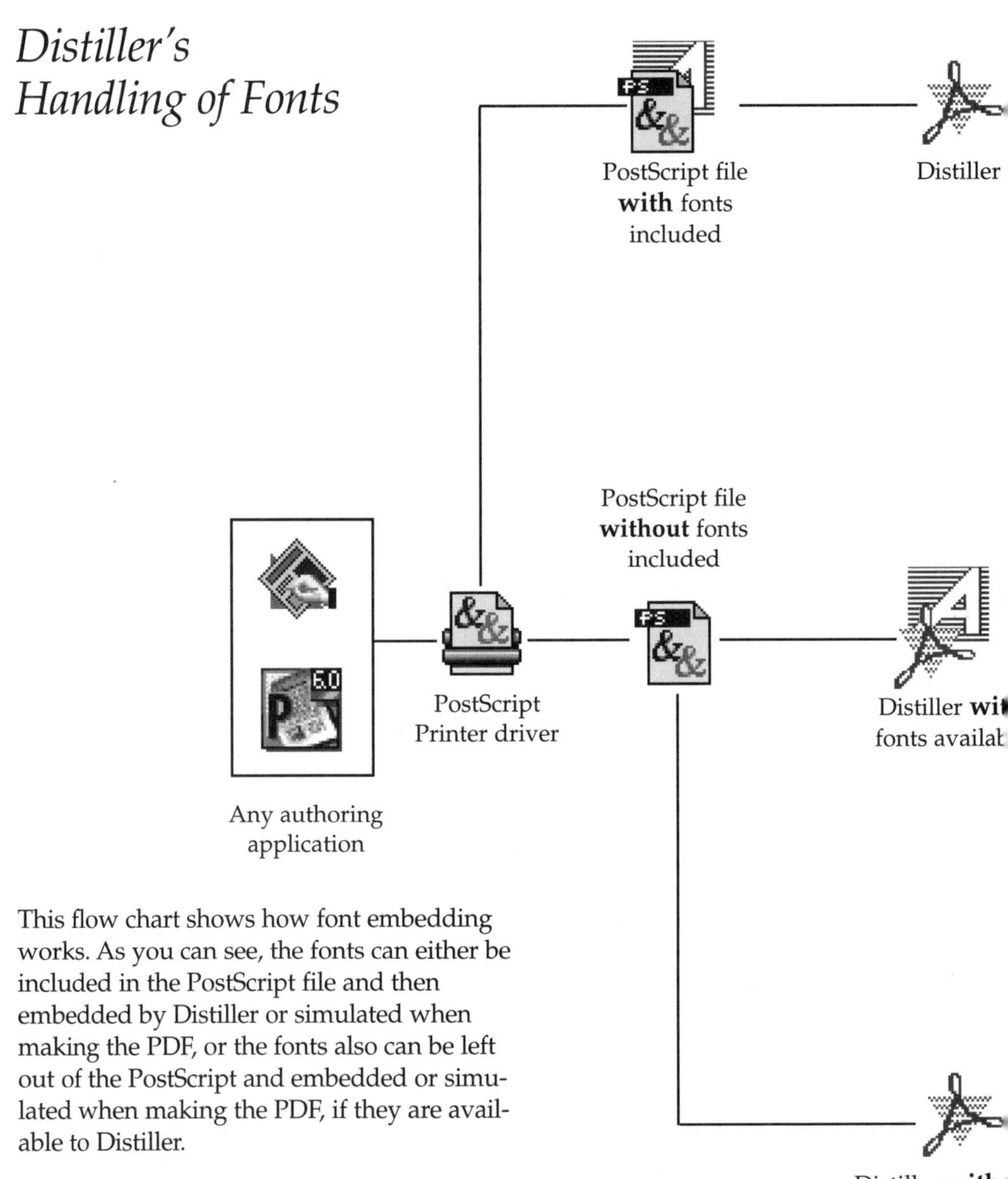

This flow chart shows how font embedding works. As you can see, the fonts can either be included in the PostScript file and then embedded by Distiller or simulated when making the PDF, or the fonts also can be left out of the PostScript and embedded or simulated when making the PDF, if they are available to Distiller.

When a PDF that does not have embedded fonts is viewed on a system that has the fonts installed, these will be used, otherwise the simulation will take place.

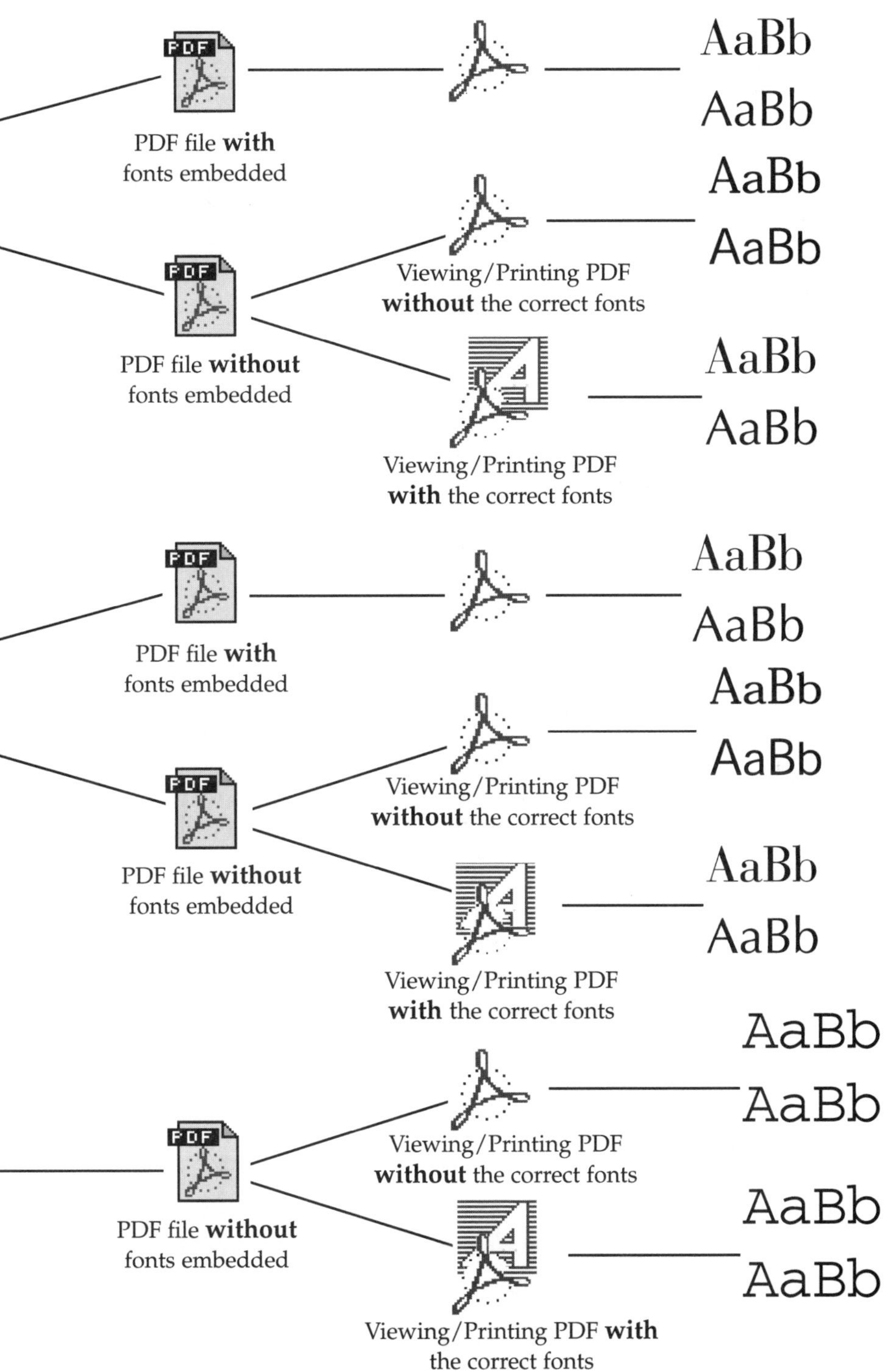
PDF
AaBb
AaBb
PDF file **with** fonts embedded
AaBb
AaBb
PDF
Viewing/Printing PDF **without** the correct fonts
PDF file **without** fonts embedded
AaBb
AaBb
Viewing/Printing PDF **with** the correct fonts
PDF
AaBb
AaBb
PDF file **with** fonts embedded
AaBb
AaBb
PDF
Viewing/Printing PDF **without** the correct fonts
PDF file **without** fonts embedded
AaBb
AaBb
Viewing/Printing PDF **with** the correct fonts
AaBb
AaBb
PDF
Viewing/Printing PDF **without** the correct fonts
PDF file **without** fonts embedded
AaBb
AaBb
Viewing/Printing PDF **with** the correct fonts

Creating spot color separations
Distiller will encode spot color information into the PDF, and Exchange will export PostScript for subsequent processing and output, using a Level 1 PostScript, resulting in the conversion of spot color information into CMYK equivalents. You will not be able to make them spot colors again.

To avoid this, read the instructions in the highend.pdf file and the readme file in the Acrobat folder Xtras/ high_end. Move the two files prologue .ps and epilogue .ps from the Xtras/ high-end folder into the folder in which the Distiller is located. This will convert the default of the PostScript operator from convert-to-process to preserve spot colors.

To output spot color seps, users either utilize a third-party tool for separation of composite, Level 2 PostScript at the RIP, or export PostScript which is capable of separation by desktop tools. For the majority of desktop separation tools, this means creating Level 1 PostScript. This is achieved in Exchange for the Mac by using Export/PostScript with a setting of Level 1 Compatible. There are significant side effects, such as the loss of internal compression of images which can result in a PostScript file larger than those using Level 2 compression filters.

Separation of Level 2-compatible PostScript can be achieved in the RIP, using third-party tools and RIPs that support in-RIP separation.

The default prologue.ps and epilogue.ps files included in the High-End folder of Acrobat will preserve spot colors as they are defined. To be used the prologue.ps and epilogue.ps files must be located in the same root folder as the Distiller application.

In a way, the functionality of the prologue/epilogue is similar to a PPD file. PPDs can contain snippets of PostScript that get included in a PostScript file. In the case of PPDs, a driver parses the PPD and determines where in the PostScript file being created to insert that PostScript code. The prologue/epilogue are PostScript files themselves that are specific to the context of the Distiller. The functionality would be the same as inserting additional PostScript code at the front or back of a PostScript file to be distilled.

Convert CMYK Images to RGB
Also offered is the option of converting CMYK files to RGB during PDF creation. RGB files are smaller than CMYK files, making the PDF file more compact. This is also helpful for Web distribution since monitors display RGB and not CMYK.

However, if the goal is to send the PDF file to a digital press or high-end output device, leave this box unchecked. Color transforms back and forth between CMYK and RGB degrade color quality in images. To convert images to RGB, click on the *Convert CMYK Images to RGB.*

You would never use this function in real-world print applications, yet the default is to convert CMYK to RGB. So remember to change it.

Preserve OPI Comments
Distiller can also preserve Open Prepress Interface (OPI) comments allowing for low-resolution FPO images to be placed into a PDF reducing overall file size. The PDF can then be sent to the OPI server and the low resolution FPO images will be replaced with their high-resolution counterparts.

The idea is that large image files do not have to be moved around on storage devices or on the network. When the composite page is produced, the FPO images are placed in the document. When printed to the OPI server, the low-resolution information will be exchanged for the high-resolution images. To preserve OPI comments when Distilling, make sure that the *Preserve OPI Comments* box is checked.

Preserve Overprint Settings
Another new function in 3.0 is that overprint and choke/spread information can be preserved. Often called trapping, choking/spreading is used to make press misregister less apparent when two colors butt against one another. Overprints can also be used for black type on a colored background. With this box checked, Distiller will retain the overprint, otherwise the underlying layer will be "knocked out."

Preserve Halftone Screen Information
Screening information can be preserved from the initial PostScript file so when output from Acrobat Exchange, the screening information is retained. Now images with various screen angles, line screen rulings, and dot shapes can be output at the desired settings, not the imagesetter's default setting. To preserve preselected screens, make sure that the *Preserve Halftone Screen Information* box is checked.

Although Distiller can preserve trapping settings, some page layout programs do not send trapping information with composite PostScript files. For instance, Quark XPress traps are only sent in the PostScript file when output to separations. The end result is no trapping. If traps are set within illustration programs like Illustrator or Freehand, Distiller will preserve the trap information.

Transfer Functions
Transfer functions are used to adjust the reproduction of an image on a specific output device. Acrobat 3.0 allows transfer functions, sometimes called transfer curves, to be applied, preserved, or removed.

PostScript comments regarding transfer functions can also be handled by Distiller. If *Preserve* is selected, any transfer curves will be saved along with the PDF document. The curves can later be applied to the image when the PDF is printed to a RIP that supports transfer functions. This is the equivalent of what Photoshop does when it saves transfer functions—it saves the curve but does not change the actual data of the image file.

Preserve Halftone Screen Information *passes "screen sets" from PostScript into the PDF document. With no other influences (such as Crackerjack), these screen sets will be passed into the PostScript code that is sent to the RIP. Since the screen sets are "tuned" for resolution, if the file gets redirected to a different device with different resolutions, the screen sets can fail—PostScript errors.*

Why is this in PostScript? If the halftones are to achieve a specific artistic effect, or if this is the only way that you can select halftones, then select Preserve. *Otherwise remove them since you can always make your halftone selections on the back end of Exchange using Crackerjack to create the PostScript for output or downstream process.*

Preserve Transfer Functions *passes transfer functions from the PostScript to the PDF document. If left in the PDF, these transfer functions will be passed into the PostScript that is sent to the RIP. Transfer functions provide a different output value for a given input value. Used for adjusting shades of gray, i.e., device or process calibration. If the file is redirected to a different device with different characteristics, then calibration will be thrown off.*

Why is this in PostScript? If it is to compensate for the characteristics of the scanner or for an artistic effect, then apply it. If it is to compensate for the characteristics of the output device, remove it, unless you are certain of your output device and this is your only means of calibration, in which case "preserve" it.

UCR
Preserve Under Color Removal/ Black Generation *passes UCR/ Black generation commands from PostScript into PDF. Without some other influence (like Crackerjack), this would be included in the PS code that goes to the RIP. These are instructions on how much black to generate when converting RGB to CMYK. This is print-specific and may confuse processes that are not print-aware. The scope of these commands may be limited to individual EPS images, with some images with UCR/GCR, and some without.*

Duotones
Photoshop duotones are made using a single grayscale B&W TIFF and embedding two transfer curves inside the header; it assumes that you incorporate a preseparated workflow—you will print PostScript plates from Quark before you send this preseparated PostScript to a RIP. The first time that Quark "prints" this TIFF (i.e. black plate) it uses a normal linear transfer curve: 0=0, 20=20, 50=50, and so on. When Quark prints the 2nd plate (Pantone xxx) it uses the same TIFF, prints it using a 2nd transfer curve (0=0, 20=5, 50=30, and so on.) This PostScript "transfer function" can be represented in PostScript, and either preserved or applied with Distiller, but only one transfer fuction can be applied or preserved per image. It is not that PDF cannot represent a duotone; Distiller can only apply one transfer function to one image. Even if this was not the case, Quark tries to "simulate" duotone in composite, and does not create a two-channel image in composite mode, because there are no PostScript Level 2 separation tools in the RIP to

If *Apply* is selected, the actual data of the image file will be changed when saved in the PDF document. This means that the image on screen, as well as when printed, will be changed. Selecting *Remove* will delete the transfer function from the PDF document. Since transfer curves are designed to adjust image reproduction on a specific output device, PDF documents for general distribution should remove any transfer curves.

Under Color Removal/Black Generation
Distiller 3.0 also allows for *Under Color Removal/Black Generation* to be preserved or removed in a PDF document. This information is used in the RGB-to-CMYK conversion process and is generally output device-specific. If the PDF document is intended for general distribution, this information should be removed.

With Crackerjack you want global control of UCR/GCR; "remove" UCR/Black generation since Crackerjack provides more control.

Color Conversions
Distiller also allows users to specify how color images in the file are defined in terms of color space and device-dependency. The default *Unchanged* option leaves color images in the color space in which they are defined.

With the *Device Independent* option selected, color objects not already mapped to calibrated spaces are converted to device-independent spaces like LAB. Device-dependent CMYK images are also converted into LAB space while device-dependent RGB files are converted to a Calibrated RGB space.

Selecting the *Device Dependent* option in Distiller will convert device independent images to device dependent RGB space. If on-screen display speed is an issue, as it is in Web-publishing, this is the best option to choose.

The Remaining Half of Creating PDF
It was mentioned in the beginning of the chapter that there are actually two and a half ways to create PDF files. The other half is to use Distiller Assistant and the Adobe PSPrinter Printer Driver.

There is a new plug-in for Export PS on the Adobe Web site. The new plug-in also accompanies the Acrobat 3.01 update.

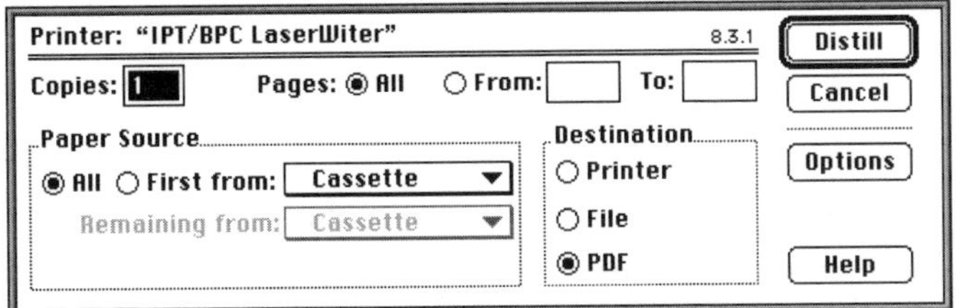

The wonder of it is really scripting. Using the *Virtual Printer* option of PSPrinter, *PDF* shows up as a third way to send PostScript files in the *Print* dialog box of most applications. When this button is selected, the PostScript is saved, Distiller is opened, and the PostScript file is distilled. After the PDF file is created the PostScript file is optionally discarded.

Now it is primarily an automation tool for a user, the potential for extended capabilities is evident. For example, in Adobe PageMaker 6.0, the user can decide if the table of contents should be made into a bookmark file, index words can be made into links, and the text flow can be defined as an article so that reading on screen is easier. (For definitions on Acrobat bookmarks, links, and articles, continue on to the next chapter.)

A disadvantage is that you have to set up Distiller options in advance as PSPrinter 8.3.1 does not offer the font embedding and compression options.

Distilling on a Network

In a production setting, Distiller can be set up on a dedicated network computer where a number of users can drop PostScript files into a *Watched Folder*. When Distiller encounters a PostScript file in this folder, it will create the PDF and place the file into an "out" folder where network users can then move or use the files.

In the Acrobat folder, there is a "startup" folder, which preconfigures Distiller. It is possible to customize the startup so Distiller is preconfigured correctly. It is also possible to create preconfigured hot folders which Distiller watches.

"separate" it. This is the same for CEPS RIPs. Representing duotones is not very good in Quark or Photoshop in a composite workflow, thus preseparated workflows.

Duotone approaches

1. *Start with Photoshop Duotone.*
2. *Note values in spot color curve.*
3. *Change the Mode to Grayscale.*
4. *Select* All *and* Copy.
5. *Change the Mode to CMYK.*
6. *Select* All *and delete the Cyan, Magenta, and Yellow Plates.*
7. *Select* Black channel *and* Paste.
8. *Create a new channel.*
9. *Select* New channel *and* Paste.
10. *With* New channel *selected, go to* Curves *and enter the same curve that was noted from Duotone.*
11. *Export Black and New Channel via PlateMaker (a QuarkXTension) into a DCS 2 file.*
12. *Bring the picture into Quark.*
13. *Print to PS Level 2, Binary.*
14. *Distill with spot files in place.*
15. *The result is a two-page PDF file, the 1st page the Black plate, the 2nd page the Spot color plate.*

Here is another way in Photoshop:

1. *Start with Duotone Mode.*
2. *Note plate order: Black 1st, PMS 2nd, etc.*
3. *Change to Multi-channel.*
4. *Use add channel option (background=white) to add 2 channels for duotone (1 for tritone; 0 for quadtone).*
5. *Arrange seps so that channel 1 = Cyan plate, channel 2 = Magenta, channel 3 = Yellow, channel 4 = Black, channel 5 = PMS, etc.*
6. *Convert mode to CMYK.*
7. *Export your DCS.*

You will retain curves that were set in the duotone mode.

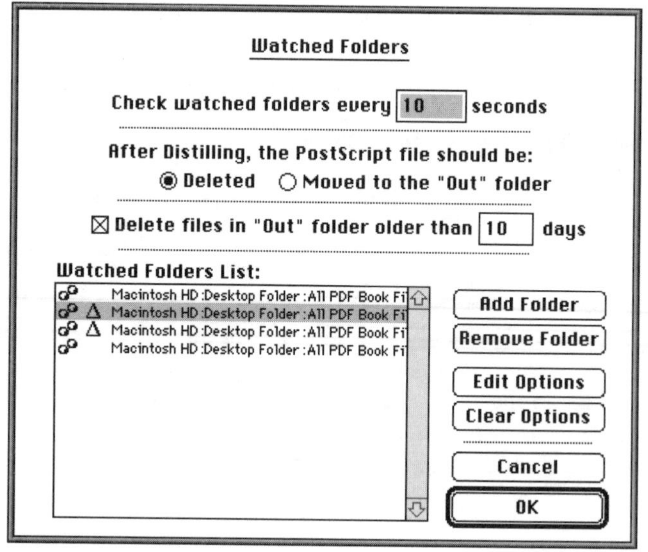

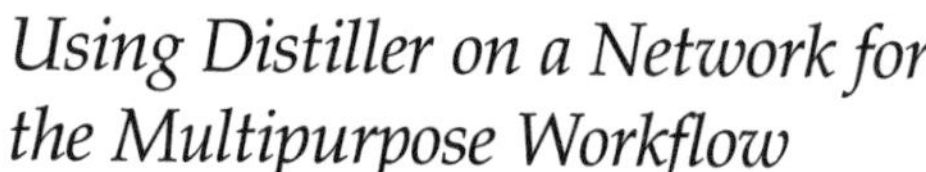

Using Distiller on a Network for the Multipurpose Workflow

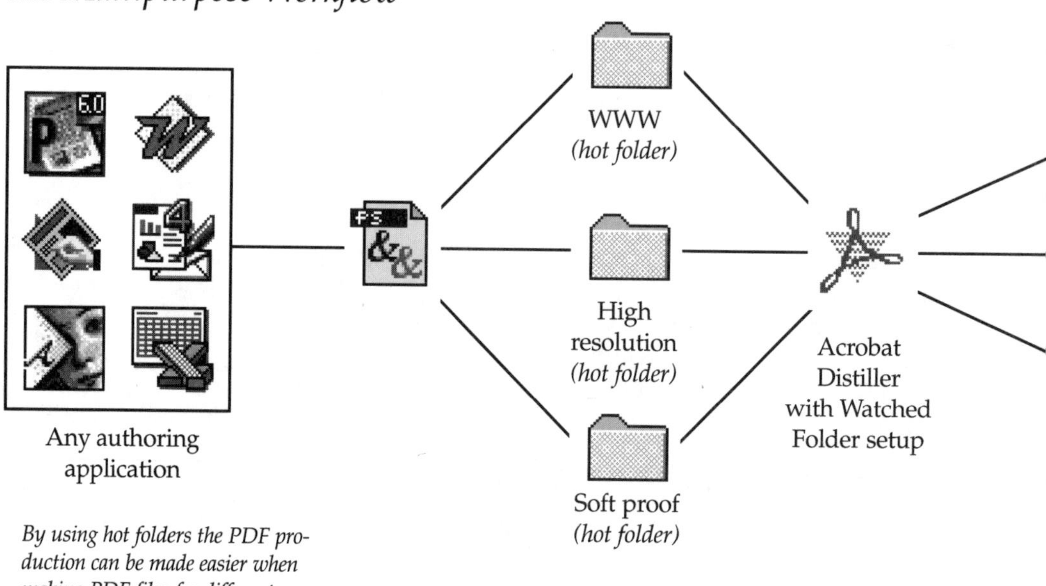

By using hot folders the PDF production can be made easier when making PDF files for different purposes.

Each of these Watched folders can be set to provide different compression and font embedding options. One folder could be designated for interoffice distribution with no font embedding. Another folder could be set for distilling PDFs for Web distribution by downsampling the images. This allows for the multi-purpose workflow.

To set up a folder, select the *Watched Folders* selection under the Distiller menu. Options can be set for when and where Distiller looks for PostScript files as well as what is done with the original PostScript file.

End Comments

Acrobat 3.x and the PDF format offer great versatility for Web-based publishing and high-end publishing applications. Choosing the right options reverts back to an end-use analysis.

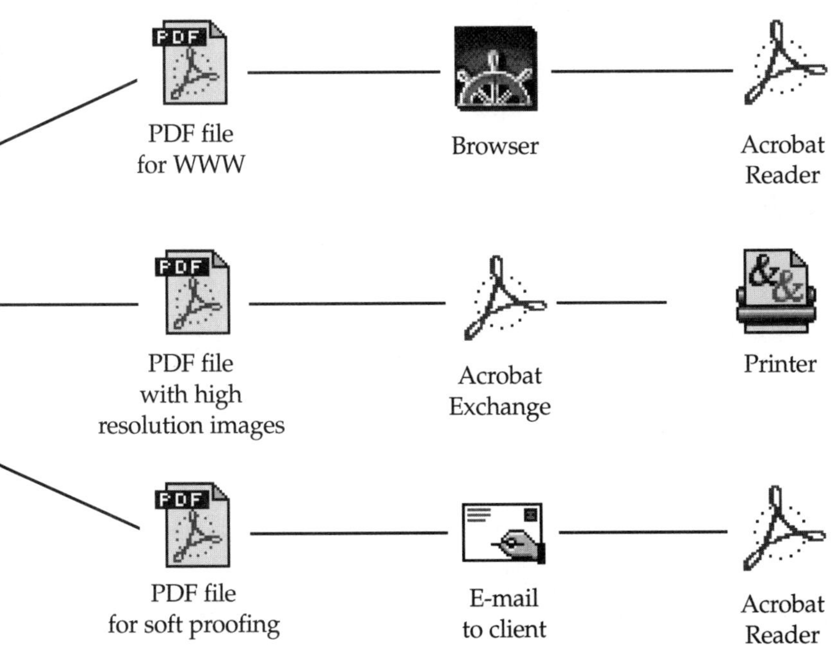

Sample Settings for High-End Print PDF

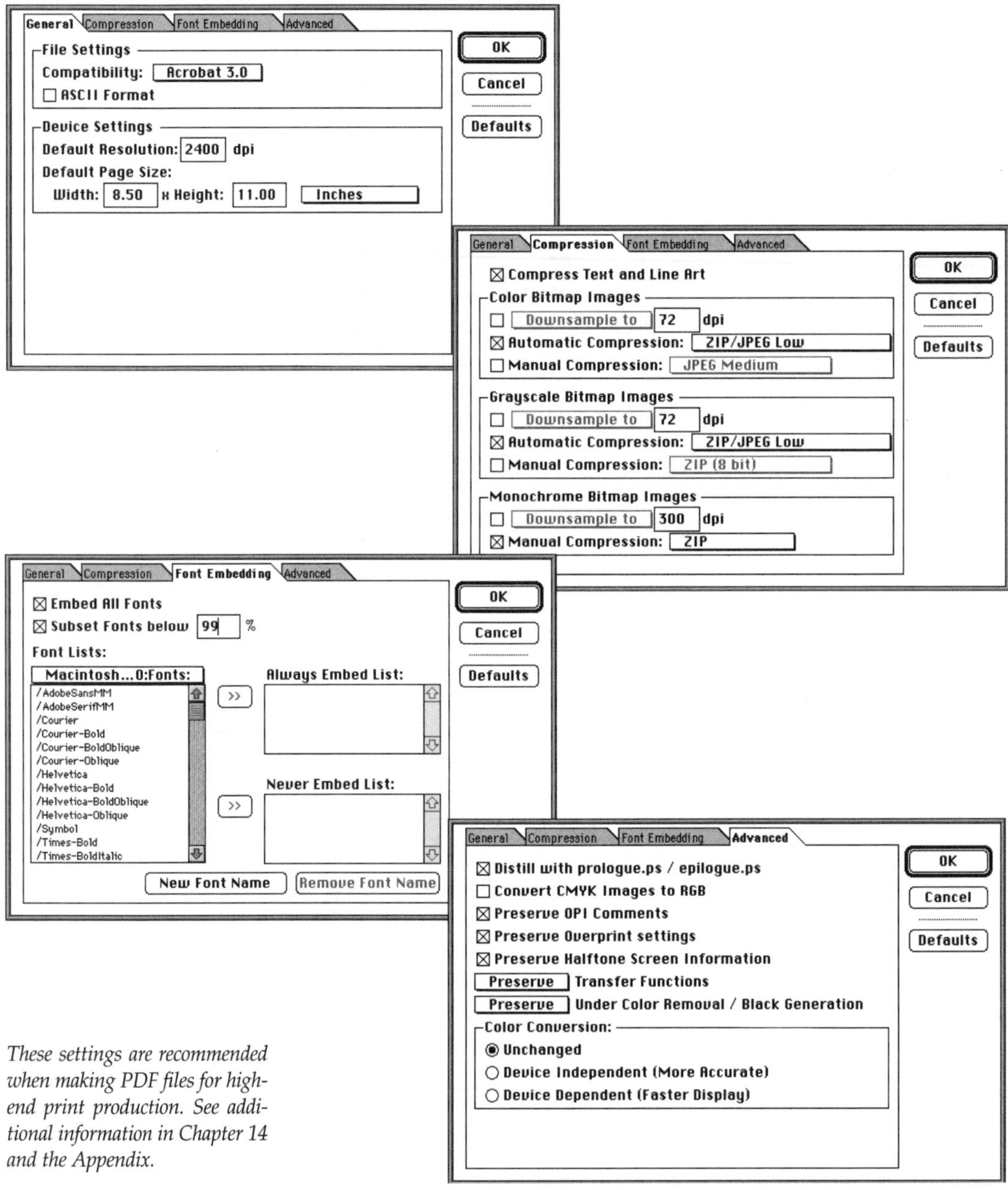

These settings are recommended when making PDF files for high-end print production. See additional information in Chapter 14 and the Appendix.

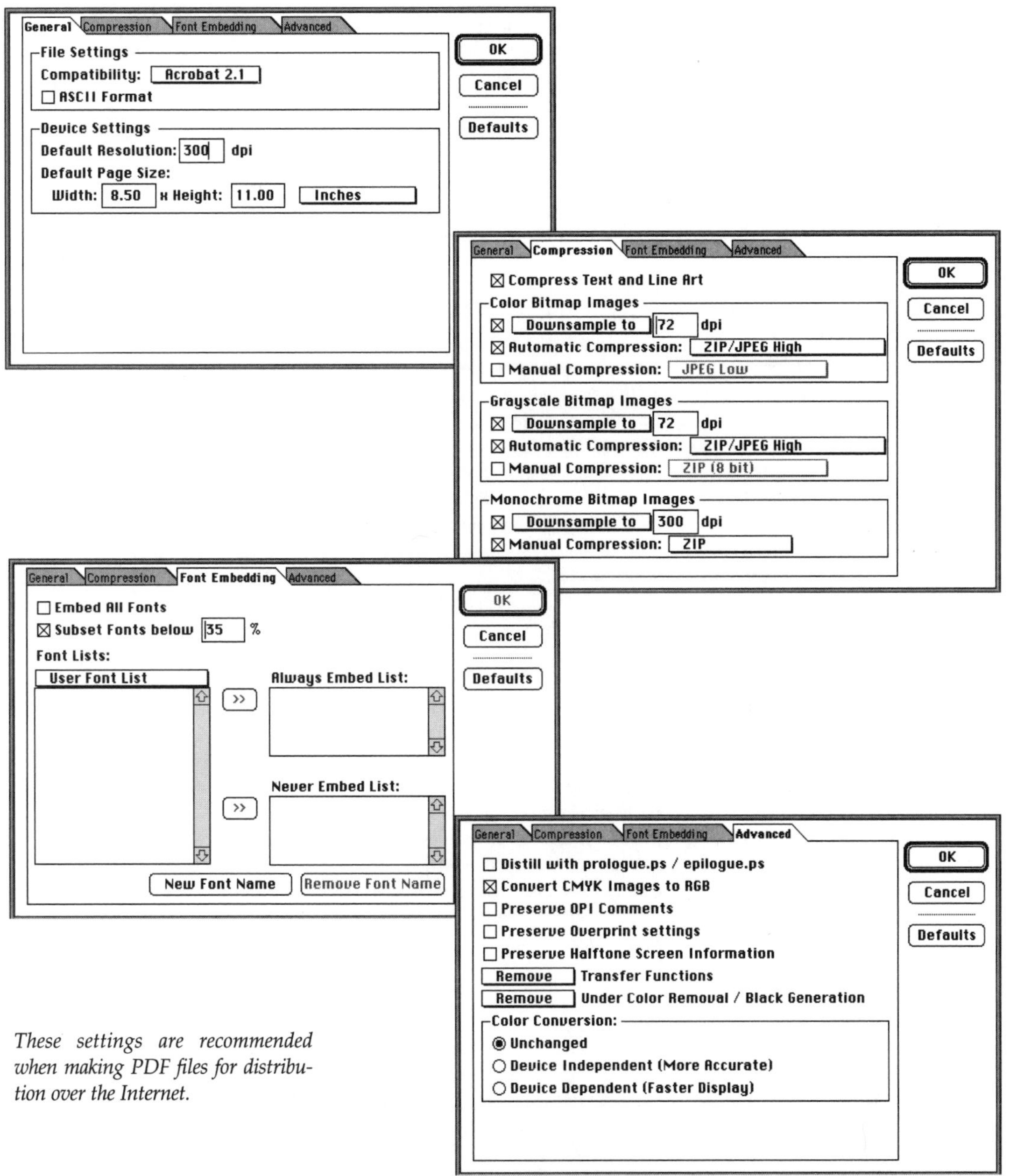
General
Compression
Font Embedding
Advanced
File Settings
Compatibility: Acrobat 2.1
ASCII Format
Device Settings
Default Resolution: 300 dpi
Default Page Size:
Width: 8.50 x Height: 11.00 Inches
OK
Cancel
Defaults
Compress Text and Line Art
Color Bitmap Images
Downsample to 72 dpi
Automatic Compression: ZIP/JPEG High
Manual Compression: JPEG Low
Grayscale Bitmap Images
Downsample to 72 dpi
Automatic Compression: ZIP/JPEG High
Manual Compression: ZIP (8 bit)
Monochrome Bitmap Images
Downsample to 300 dpi
Manual Compression: ZIP
Embed All Fonts
Subset Fonts below 35 %
Font Lists:
User Font List
Always Embed List:
Never Embed List:
New Font Name
Remove Font Name
Distill with prologue.ps / epilogue.ps
Convert CMYK Images to RGB
Preserve OPI Comments
Preserve Overprint settings
Preserve Halftone Screen Information
Remove Transfer Functions
Remove Under Color Removal / Black Generation
Color Conversion:
Unchanged
Device Independent (More Accurate)
Device Dependent (Faster Display)

These settings are recommended when making PDF files for distribution over the Internet.

Developers integrate PDF into workflow applications

Software developers are creating prepress solutions across a broad range of new applications that integrate PDF for graphic arts workflow. A complete PDF workflow ultimately means a "drag and drop" or automated process. For a service provider this offers benefits that allow savings up to 25 percent of sales revenue.

By leveraging the advantages of PDF, these new prepress applications allow:

- *Faster, streamlined, and more reliable printing, particularly since PostScript 3 and PostScript Extreme can accept PDF files directly. PDF page independence allows printing in any order from the single digital master file.*
- *Adobe Acrobat provides built-in preview and basic preflight capabilities for PDF files, which is important at the time of document creation so errors can be found before sending files to output. This can reduce the number of jobs returned to the creator with missing resources, or the time it takes to make the file print-ready at the print site.*
- *PDF's structured file format and extensibility allow applications more functionality for prepress workflows.*
- *PDF provides one file for viewing, distributing, archiving, editing, and printing.*
- *PDF's small file sizes streamline transmission.*

Imation (formerly Luminous) OPEN 1.1 automates workflows for PDF production such as the creation of PDF files from desktop publishing applications or Adobe PostScript files, separation of PDF files using Acrobat Exchange and PrePrint Pro, optimization of PDF files for Web viewing, and cataloging of PDF files into databases such as Canto Cumulus and Luminous Media Manager. In Media Manager, a PDF I-Piece adds the ability to catalog, preview, and navigate PDF files from within the database.

Cascade Systems Inc. offers MediaSphere, a content management system for storage and retrieval of digital objects including PDF files for integrated cataloging, management, preview, and repurposing of PDF content. Extensis' Portfolio 3.0, formerly Adobe Fetch, is a media management application with built-in file translators for the PDF format, allowing users to create thumbnails and previews of PDF files. Extensis plans to integrate PDF into an expanded family of prepress solutions. DigiServer from OneVision offers automatic processing of digital jobs in PDF or PostScript format.

Group Logic's Imagexpo v2.0 streamlines the creative review process with tools for remote soft proofing and annotation on PDF files, enhancing the many advantages of the PDF workflow.

QueuePic from Digital Image Bank Service (dibs) is a dedicated search and retrieval program that works across the Internet to connect to the dibs image database with more than 50,000 high quality consumer product images in PDF and JPEG formats. This enables the document creator to easily access low resolution design and proof images, while allowing the printing site to retrieve the high resolution version, via the Internet or the AP/Adsend network.

Once the PDF file is received at the prepress location, Markzware's FlightCheck can be used to detect possible problems with PDF files as they are sent to a final destination, whether that is to a printer for output, a computer screen for display, or the Web for viewing. FlightCheck can catch incorrect color and font usage, resolution, etc.

EnFocus Software Pitstop is an Exchange plug-in for visually editing PDF page contents, including text, graphics, and object attributes. DigiScript from OneVision offers an interactive suite of WYSIWYG tools for complete PDF file editing. Using DigiScript, users can open PDF or Adobe PostScript files and interactively edit any aspect of the files, including text, color, images, line art, and production parameters such as separation.

Imation PressWise will support PDF natively, enabling Adobe PostScript 3 printing systems to take advantage of prepress workflows that are based entirely on PDF. The new PressWise will have the ability to add PDF pages to any PressWise imposition process and produce job tickets for Extreme.

DK&A, Inc. has full PDF support in their imposition product INposition 2.0 through its Tempus integrated prepress plug-in technology. This will provide customers with comprehensive file support so they can impose native QuarkXPress and PageMaker files, and provide full support for PDF, Adobe PostScript, EPS, TIFF, and PICT files.

Control of screening, separations, and more can be defined using Crackerjack from Lantana. A plug-in to Exchange, it provides professional printing tools for PDF. Lantana's XLR8/C3—an accelerator card with Adobe's ColorBurst ASIC utilized by PostScript RIP vendors—accelerates rendering and enhances output of files made from PDF.

APPLYING PDF FILES

Adobe Acrobat Exchange and Reader are the two applications of the Acrobat suite which allow the user to view, navigate, search, print, modify, and enhance (Exchange only for the latter two) the PDF documents created with Distiller or PDFWriter. They are key programs.

While the ideal digital document would be wholly application-independent, the PDF format is reliant upon either Exchange or Reader to be viewed or printed. Reader, the simplest way to access PDF files, allows for the viewing, navigating, searching, and printing of PDF documents. Exchange goes one step further by including many editing features. Some new features available in Acrobat version 3.0 include enhanced security options, customizable forms, page-on-demand Web access, and plug-ins.

Adobe Acrobat Exchange
Exchange is the essence of accessing and working with PDF documents. Distiller creates PDF documents and Exchange customizes them. Exchange includes tools for enhancing PDF documents which build interactivity and security options into PDF documents, while allowing certain levels of editability such as the ordering of pages and text touch-ups.

Working with Exchange can be broken down into four logical areas: Viewing/Navigating, Editing, Interactivity Options, and Security Options.

Viewing PDF Documents
Becoming acquainted with Exchange is like a child taking its first steps or reading its first sentence. Learning incrementally adds up to understanding the whole. Learning how to effectively view and move through a PDF document is like taking that first step to understanding the whole application.

Page View Options
Exchange allows for the screen viewing of the page to be handled in many different fashions. Many of the viewing capabilities are similar to those of page layout programs and general platform software.

In addition to the display of the actual page contents, PDF documents can also carry information regarding the logical layout of the document. Enhancements such as bookmarks and thumbnails for the pages can be saved within the PDF document making navigating through the PDF a simple process.

Page Only, Bookmarks, Thumbnail Views
The tool bar offers some direct layout functions. The *Page Only* view does just what it says, it shows just the page on the screen. The *Bookmark* view splits the screen and brings up any previously created bookmarks in the left portion of the screen. The *Bookmark* view must be activated when creating new bookmarks as well. The *Thumbnail* view also splits the screen and shows any already created thumbnails in the left portion of the screen. By the way, 21″ monitors are almost mandatory.

Single, Continuous, and Continuous Facing Pages
Exchange enables the user to designate the document view when scrolling through the pages. *Single Page, Continuous Page,* and *Continuous Facing Pages* are options under the view window.

Single Page View displays only the current page in the window, while *Continuous Page View* will display documents in a scrolling fashion, allowing for the bottom of one page and the top of the next to be split on the screen. The *Continuous Facing Page* option displays pages in a spread type fashion which is useful for pages designed for magazine spread publication. A centerfold image would lose its pizazz if the two pages that make up the spread had to be viewed separately.

Continuous facing pages will not change the layout in the thumbnail view.

Actual Size, Fit Page, and Fit Width

Page view options control how the document is going to be displayed in the monitor—*Actual Size, Fit Page,* and *Fit Width. Actual Size* is a 100% view of the document, *Fit Page* fits the entire document into the window, and *Fit Width,* well, fits the width of the document in the window.

Actual size

Fit page

Fit width

Magnifying Glass

The magnifying glass found on the tool bar and accessed from the main menu bar allows for magnification at a number of predetermined percentages. The pop-up window accessed by the magnifying glass on the bottom page bar offers these predetermined percentages as well as a a user-defined percentage. This window also allows for *Fit Page, Fit Width,* and *Fit Visible* view options. Similar to most applications, the magnifying glass will become a reduction glass when the option key is held down.

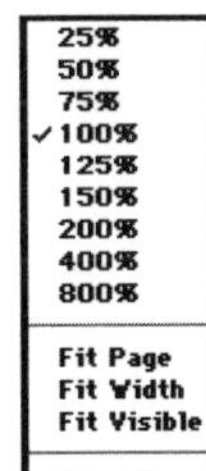

Magnifying glass

Bottom page bar

Create Thumbnails

Thumbnails are small display versions of the pages within a PDF document. The creation of thumbnails is a great viewing capability when the goal is page insertion/deletion or editing the page layout. Thumbnails are also very useful when viewing the contents of the pages. By scrolling through the thumbnails and clicking on the page you wish to view, that page appears in the page view portion of the screen.

By simply dragging down the Document window on the main menu bar and selecting *Create All Thumbnails,* the small page versions are automatically created and displayed. When thumbnails are created, a window opens to the left of the page view window, splitting the screen into two frames.

When initially creating thumbnails, they appear automatically, but they can be hidden by clicking on the *Page Only* icon on the

Document
Set Page Action...
Crop Pages...
Rotate Pages... ⌘⇧O
Insert Pages... ⌘⇧I
Extract Pages... ⌘⇧E
Replace Pages... ⌘⇧R
Delete Pages... ⌘⇧D
New Bookmark ⌘B
Reset Bookmark Destination ⌘R
Create All Thumbnails
Delete All Thumbnails

Create Thumbnails

tool bar or by selecting *Page Only* from the view window in the main menu bar. If you want to call up thumbnails you know have been created, or you want to check and see if they have been created, simply select the *Thumbnails* icon in the tool bar.

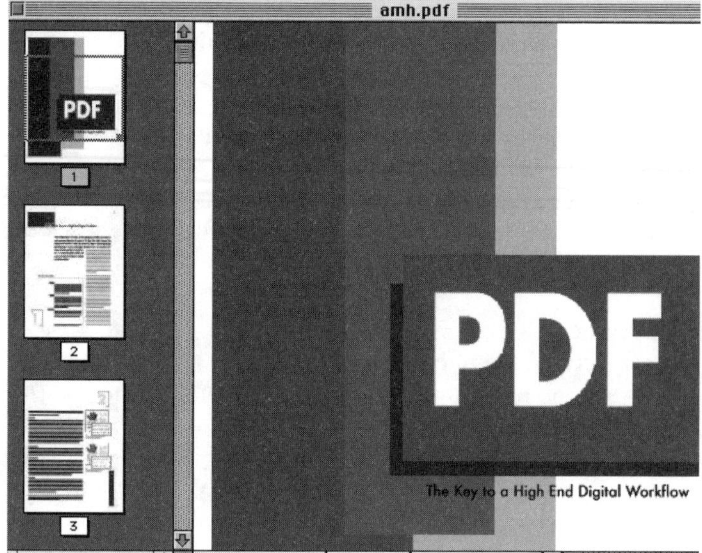

Thumbnail View

Exchange automatically numbers the thumbnail pages beginning with one and continuing consecutively in number order. The numbering is not related to any previous numbering in the document itself.

If you select the Thumbnails view option and thumbnails have not been previously created, blank thumbnails will appear.

Thumbnails are the most efficient way to move, copy, and delete pages within a single document, or insert pages from another document. These capabilities are editing issues and will be further discussed in the Editing section of this chapter. Once the thumbnail view is selected, thumbnails can be scrolled and clicked on to view the respective page.

Thumbnails are an all-or-nothing entity in Acrobat—either every page has a thumbnail or none of them does. The creation of thumbnails will increase the file size of the PDF document about 30 percent. So, if size is a crucial consideration, you might choose to skip thumbnails.

First Page *Next Page*

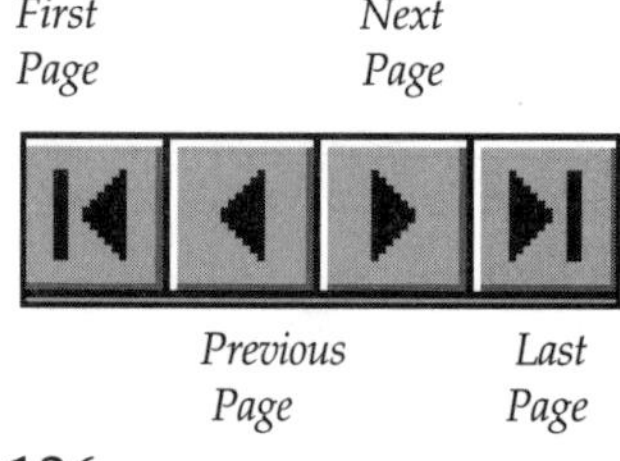

Previous Page *Last Page*

Navigating Through PDF Documents

As already discussed, one efficient way of navigating through pages is the use of thumbnails. The tool bar also offers simple page navigation tools. *First Page, Previous Page, Next Page,* and *Last Page* are all accessible with a simple click on the respective tool icon. Again, these destinations can be reached from the view window under the main menu bar or through shortcut commands.

Go Forward and *Go Backward* are other navigation tools found on the tool bar. Selecting *Go Backward* will bring you back to your previous page and viewing situation. If you had jumped from page 3 to page 64, *Go Backward* would return you to page 3 at the magnification you had been viewing the page. These commands can also be completed under the *View* window and shortcut commands. Exchange remembers 64 movements for this function.

Go Forward

Go Back

Do not confuse Go Backward *and* Go Forward *with* Undo *and* Redo. *These commands remember viewing conditions, not editing selections.*

Bookmarks

Bookmarks are another navigation tool, serving a purpose similar to that of an index or outline. The user can become oriented with the document page layout quickly and can easily navigate through an extensive file quite quickly. Bookmarks are strictly word-based as opposed to thumbnail's image-based capabilities. Bookmarks, however, account for less file size.

Once the *Bookmarks view* has been selected, the creation is rather simple:

1. Position the page on the screen exactly as the viewer should see it.
2. Select *New bookmark* from the document window on the main menu bar. (A page icon appears with the temporary name "Untitled.")
3. Type the name for the bookmark.

Bookmarks may be positioned as a sub-bookmark to create a true outline hierarchical structure. Once the bookmark is created (or when it is still untitled) it can be dragged down to the right to a subposition and can also be dragged out of a sub-position by dragging it to the left again. Basically, once marks are created, they can be repositioned to any position in the hierarchical structure. Bookmarks may be edited by:

1. Positioning the page on the screen exactly as the viewer should see it.
2. Clicking on the page icon to highlight the bookmark intended to be changed.

If the goal is to keep the PDF file size small, thumbnails can easily be deleted by selecting Delete All Thumbnails *under the* Document *window on the main menu bar. Just remember that if thumbnails are not created or are deleted in Exchange, they cannot be viewed in Reader.*

Document
Set Page Action...
Crop Pages...
Rotate Pages... ⌘⇧O
Insert Pages... ⌘⇧I
Extract Pages... ⌘⇧E
Replace Pages... ⌘⇧R
Delete Pages... ⌘⇧D
New Bookmark ⌘B
Reset Bookmark Destination ⌘R
Create All Thumbnails
Delete All Thumbnails

Create Bookmarks

3. Selecting *Reset Bookmark Destination* from the Document window on the main menu bar.
4. Clicking on *Yes* when asked if you really want to do this.

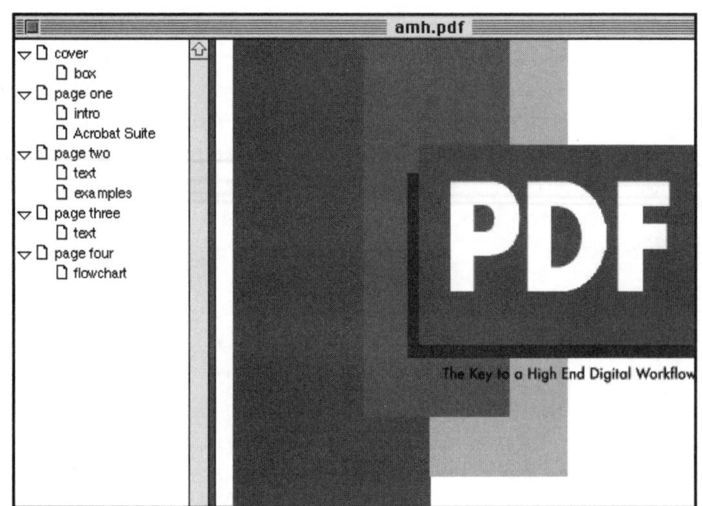

Bookmarks view

cover
box
page one
intro
Acrobat Suite
page two
text
examples
page three
text
page four
flowchart

Bookmarks

Bookmarks may be deleted by selecting the bookmark and pressing the *Delete* key.

Creating Articles

One of the worst aspects of on-screen digital publications is that they are not nearly as easy to read as the hardcopy publication. Trying to read a digital article requires enlarging to a readable level and then reducing it so navigating to the next article thread is possible. Acrobat Articles are a navigation tool that can be built into PDF documents to allow easy reading of selected text, or an entire article, throughout the PDF.

Acrobat's *Article* function solves much of the difficulty by enlarging the text to a readable level and following the article through the document. Much like a jump line in a newspaper, Article directs the reader where the article continues, the Article tool leads the PDF user throughout a document following the pre-defined path of text.

The *Article* tool of Acrobat is similar to a hypertext link (the text you click on in a Web page that jumps you to a different location). However, information regarding the article title, subject, author, and keywords can also be included. A list of articles for a PDF document can be viewed.

To set up an article within a PDF document, select *Article* under the *Tools* menu. The screen pointer becomes a set of crosshairs that are used to marquee text. Each successive area of text in the article is marqueed until the article is completely defined.

As users click on articles in a PDF, the predefined sections are enlarged to a readable level. As readers approach the bottom of the screen and click again, more of the article is displayed allowing for easier reading of on-screen text. Print applications for this feature are virtually none, but Articles provide an excellent tool for electronic publications.

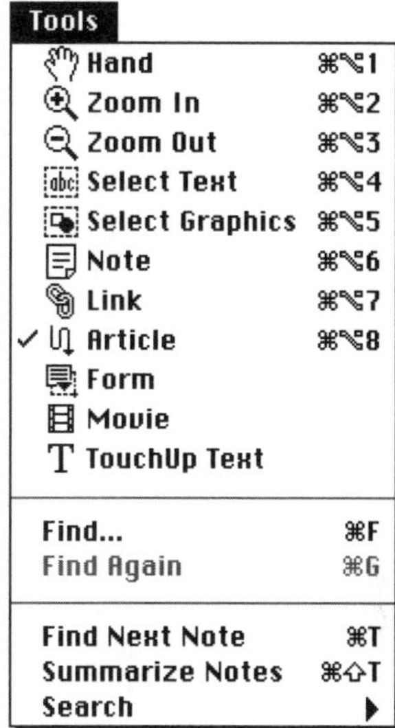

Creating Articles

Interactivity Options

PDF documents can have options like hypertext links, QuickTime movies, and forms added making them more interactive.

Creating Links

Links are useful tools that build interactivity between the user and the document by performing actions when clicked. Activated links can perform a number of operations including jumping to a referred Website, jumping to another section of the PDF document, or playing a QuickTime movie.

Link tool

Any portion of a PDF document can have a link associated with it. When the link tool is selected, users marquee the area that will be sensitive to the link—as small as a word or line or as large as the page.

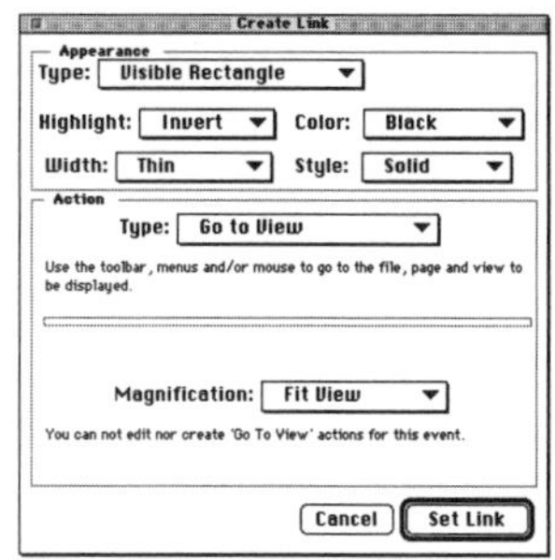

The Link tool allows Exchange users to specify actions for user-selected areas of the PDF document.

After the selection has been marqueed, the link attributes window is displayed. The top half of the dialog box deals with the appearance of the link—visible or invisible. If the link is selected to be visible, the characteristics of the link bounding box can be defined. For instance, the border of the link box can be set to either thin, medium, or thick settings, the color can be changed, and the effect when the link is clicked can be selected.

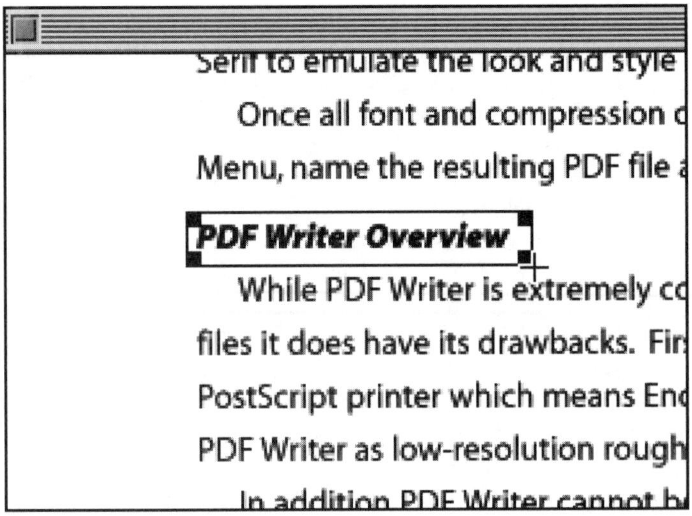

Setting Links within Exchange

Twelve actions can be specified by a link:

Care should be taken not to create links that can't be followed. For instance, an Execute Menu Item *command referring to a Menu Item available in Exchange, but not in Reader, will add to user confusion and unnecessarily clutter the file.*

Execute Menu Item—Any menu item (including the Apple Menu) can be selected using this action specifier. For instance, if a user wants to build a print button into the PDF document, the link could be set to select the *Print* option under the *File* menu.

Go To View—This action jumps the user to any particular page and magnification of the PDF document. For instance, if superscript numerals were used to reference endnotes, the link could be specified to jump to the endnote page at the appropriate location and magnification for viewing.

Import Form Data—This option would be used to import default form data from a Web server.

Movie data will not be saved with the PDF file. Only a reference to its location on the hard drive or network is saved in the file. The movie file must also be distributed, ultimately reducing the portability of the package.

Movie—Specifying this action will play a QuickTime movie that is placed in the PDF document. Specific QuickTime controls pertaining to looping and movie controls can be set from this menu.

Open File—This action will open another PDF document. This is useful for very long technical manuals. It may not be practical to have a very large PDF document, but rather break it down into chapters and then link the end of the chapters with the new documents.

Read Article—Specifying this action will bring up a window of readable articles within the document.

Reset Form—Clears all data previously entered into a form. This option is useful if a *Reset* button is designated in the form.

Show/Hide Field—Will show or hide any fields that may occur within the PDF document.

Sound—Lets the user designate a sound to be played upon link activation. As with movies, the sound is not embedded in the PDF file, only a location reference to the sound file is saved.

Submit Form—Any data that has been placed into a form will be submitted to the specified URL when this link is activated. *(See Forms for more detail.)*

World Wide Web Link—This link jumps the user to a specified Web page. For the jump to occur, the user must have Internet access and have a Web browser configured to work with Acrobat.

Creating Forms—Since Web publishing is the prevailing buzz, Acrobat provides a tool for interactive data submission over the Internet via the PDF format.

Forms creation in Acrobat 3.0 is something of a misnomer—it should more appropriately be titled "data field definition" because the look of the form is done in the original page-layout application or scanned directly to PDF format.

The concept behind forms is simple. Any document can be created containing boxes for certain types of data or end-user input. That document can then be converted into a PDF document and using the forms function of Exchange, those data fields can be described and defined.

Exchange lets users add functions like radio buttons, check boxes, text entry fields, list boxes, and other options which could be set to collect data over the Web via PDF.

The forms function would add great value for an employer who would want to post a PDF-version of its employment application on the Web. Like any paper document with check boxes for gender, text entry for address, and perhaps a list of job titles, the PDF application could have those functions built into it.

After the data had been entered on the user end, a button to submit the data could be added to the PDF, and a CGI-script on the Web server could collect and sort the submitted data. The forms function essentially allows the interactivity of HTML to be built into a PDF document.

Creating Notes

Notes icon

Closed note

Amie

This is what a note looks like when created in Acrobat Exchange.

The note can be sized, and the color can be changed by double clicking on the title bar.

The note can be closed by clicking on the box in the upper left corner. And it can be reopened by double clicking on the note icon.

Open note

Similar to those sticky notes you put all over your memos and office, Exchange allows you to apply notes directly on the page. Notes are a great way to add comments or bring attention to an area of interest on a specific page. To create a note:

1. Select the note icon from the tool bar.
2. A crosshair appears. Drag a box to the size you wish the note to be.
3. The note will appear, and the flashing cursor allows you to begin typing.
4. The name and color of the note can be changed by double clicking on the note's title bar. *When the title bar is double clicked, a Note Properties pop-up window will appear allowing these changes to be made. Note preferences can also be set in the Notes preferences pop-up window under* File, Preferences.
5. The note can be closed by clicking the box in the upper left corner.
6. Once the note is closed, it can be reopened and read or edited by double clicking on the closed note icon.

Editing

The editing of PDF documents is available on a document-level basis and a content-level basis. The document level includes features to:

- Move pages
- Copy pages
- Delete pages
- Replace pages
- Rotate pages
- Crop pages

Content level editing features include text touch-ups, provided the font has been embedded. Touch-Up options include:

- Character color
- Character size
- Character placement

Document-Level Editing

One of the chief advantages of the PDF format over its PostScript parent is page independence. The pages of a PostScript file cannot be separated within the file. PDF files are logically structured so that each page is individually defined and extractable.

Move, Copy, Delete, Replace Pages

Page independence functionality allows individual pages of the PDF document to be moved, copied, deleted, or replaced within a file. Pages can also be inserted from other PDF documents. This ability allows for the customization of PDF documents. For example, a PDF instruction manual could be customized for an individual product model, while still including all of the general information common to the entire product line. This type of customized service could be accomplished on a print or online, on-demand basis.

The best way to move pages around is in the *Thumbnails view*. Not only can you view the pages in succession, but they are easy to grab and move as one entity due to their size.

Move Pages

Moving pages is useful when restructuring the page order of a document.

1. *Thumbnails view* should be selected from the *View* menu.
2. Select the hand tool and click and hold on the thumbnail page number (a small page icon appears attached to the arrow cursor).
3. Drag the thumbnail to the destination of choice and a black line will appear between the already existing page order. *This line represents the placement of the page which is about to be made.*
4. Release the mouse and the thumbnail is placed in the new order as is the page itself.

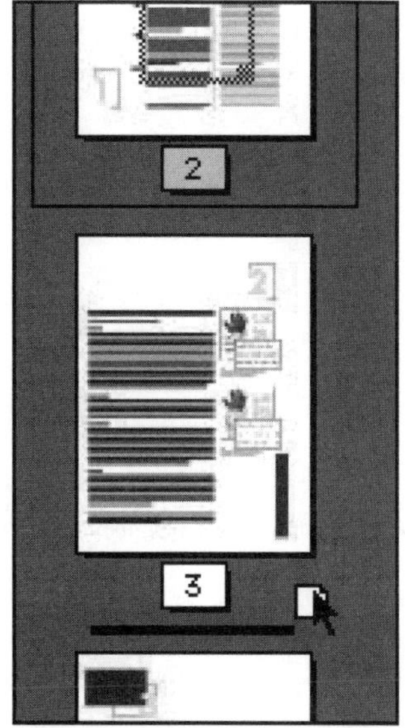

Moving Pages

The PDF thumbnails will reflow and will be renumbered if necessary.

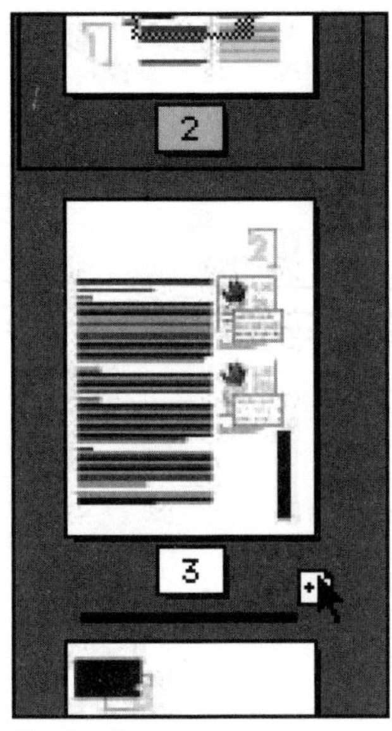

Copying Pages

Copy Pages

Pages may be copied within a document, or they may be copied from one document and inserted in another. To copy pages within a document:

1. *Thumbnails view* option should be selected.
2. Select the hand tool and click and hold on the thumbnail page number (a small page icon appears attached to the arrow cursor).
3. Hold down the *Option* key. A "+" appears on the small page icon.
4. Drag the thumbnail to the destination of choice and a black line will appear between the already existing page order. *This line represents the placement of the page which is about to be made.*
5. Release the mouse and the thumbnail is placed in the new order as is the page itself.

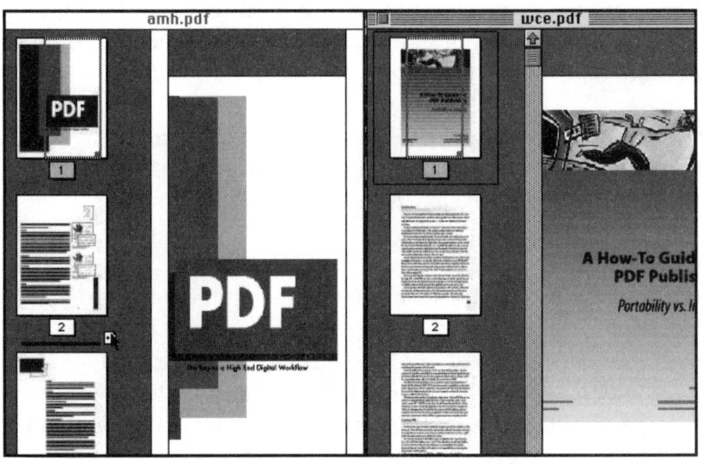

Copying Pages between doc uments

To copy pages from one document to another:

1. Open both documents with *Thumbnails view* selected.
2. Select *Tile Vertically* or *Tile Horizontally* from the *Window* menu.

3. Select the hand tool and click and hold on the thumbnail page number which is being copied (a small page icon appears attached to the arrow cursor).
3. Drag the thumbnail to the point of destination in the other document.
4. A black line will appear between the already existing page order. *This line represents the placement of the page which is about to be made.*
5. Release the mouse and the thumbnail is placed in the new order as is the page itself.

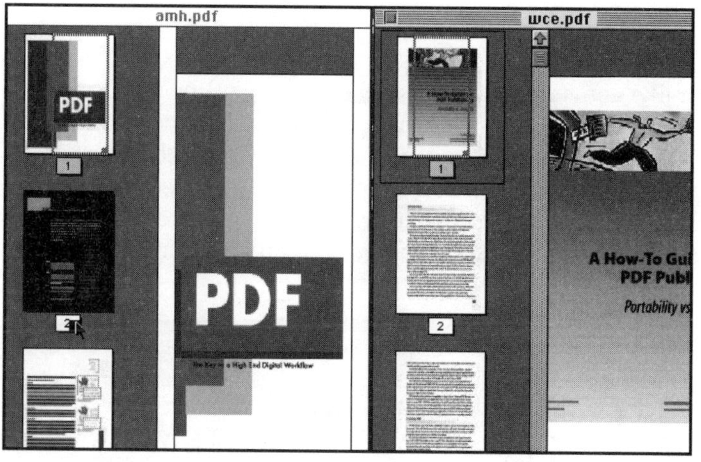

Replace Pages

Replace Pages

Pages may also be copied from one document and inserted into another document, replacing a page. This may be important for extensive document changes or additions such as the example of the PDF instruction manual. Instead of going back to the original application file, making changes or additions, and distilling again, just the changed or added pages can be distilled and added to the first PDF. To replace a page:

1. Open both documents with *Thumbnails view* selected.
2. Select *Tile Vertically* or *Tile Horizontally* from the *Window* menu.
3. Select the hand tool and click and hold on the thumbnail page number which is being copied (a small page icon appears attached to the arrow cursor).

4. Drag the thumbnail directly on top of the page number icon of the thumbnail which you intended to replace.
5. The page being replaced will be highlighted in black.
6. Release the mouse and the thumbnail is replaced.

The page will be deleted, but the memory allotment will still exist. In order to solve this problem, you must Save As *to remove the extraneous data.*

Delete Pages

Simply select *Delete Pages* from the Document window. A pop-up window will ask you which pages you wish to delete. Another pop-up window will follow asking if you are sure you want to delete these pages. If you're sure, click *Yes* and the page will be deleted.

Crop Pages

Unlike conventional cropping, either digital or analog, which removes and deletes the data, Exchange only removes the material from the visible page. Thus, all cropping changes can be undone. Even if a *Save As* is applied to a cropped page within the PDF, the original page information can be retrieved by going back into the *Crop* dialogue box and reducing the margins to 0 (zero) in all directions.

Crop pages allows the cropping of the page borders to any specified length. To crop a page:

1. Open the file you wish to crop.
2. Select *Crop Pages...* from the Document Window on the main menu bar.
3. A pop-up window appears. Make the necessary margin and page selections.
4. Press OK.

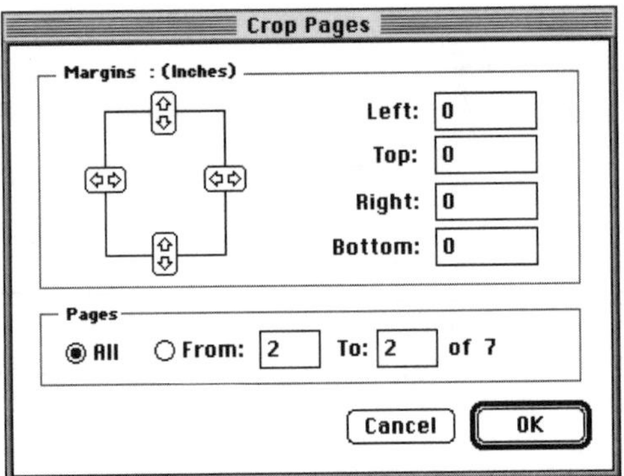

Crop Pages

Rotate Pages
Exchange allows you to rotate pages within a PDF document. All pages or individual pages can be rotated either clockwise or counterclockwise at 90 degree increments. It is not possible to rotate arbitrarily.

Content Level Editing
Another significant advantage of the Portable Document Format is the retention of vector-based information. This means that when fonts are embedded, the actual outlines are preserved, keeping them in a semi-editable state. This allows some degree of editability.

Text Touch-Ups
Probably the most common user misconception about the PDF format is in regard to its editability. Unlike other document formats (i.e., native QuarkXPress, Microsoft Word or Adobe PageMaker formats), the objects that make up the PDF document cannot be moved, deleted, or altered. (Except with a plug-in such as PitStop or OneVision DigiScript. *See Chapter 10.*) For the most part, PDF documents are locked, page-independent, data containers that can be viewed, searched, and printed. Pages as entire entities can be moved around, but the contents within usually cannot.

Keep in mind that changing characters with the Text touch-up tool cannot be done to fonts that have been subset. If you foresee the need for text revisions, then be safe and Embed All Fonts *when distilling the file.*

It is interesting that Acrobat PDF was attractive because the content could not be modified, as it could be in layout applications. Now, it appears that there is a demand for increasing levels of editability. The reason has to do with changes required at various stages of the workflow.

There is some editability available within Exchange, and this "some" may be all you need. However it's crucial to understand the limitations of that editability. Acrobat provides two tools for text selection.

Select Text Tool
The Select Text tool allows for text to be highlighted and copied to another application program as ASCII text. This function is very similar to the text copy functions of most other applications. To select text:

Select Text

The Select Text *tool allows text to be highlighted and copied to another application if allowed by the security features of Acrobat. See* Security *later in this chapter.*

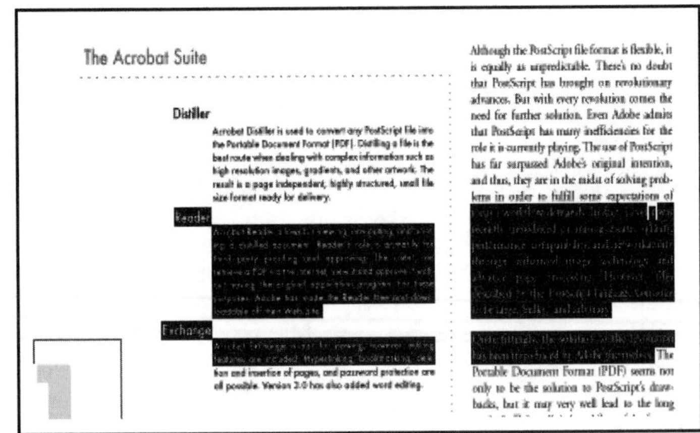

Selecting text

1. Click on the *Select Text* tool in the Menu Bar or under the *Tools* menu.
2. A cursor will appear. Highlight the text you wish to copy.
3. Select *Copy* from the *Edit* menu.
4. Paste in the text into any application.

The *Select Text* tool will select text on a line-by-line basis. If text was originally flowed into separate text boxes, then the *Select Text* tool, as shown above, may select text you do not wish to include. To select a specific portion such as a paragraph:

1. Click on the *Select Text* tool in the Menu Bar or under the *Tools* menu.
2. Hold down *Option* key, and a dotted box will appear over the cursor.
3. The cursor will allow you to drag a selection box over the text you wish to select.
4. The text within the box will become highlighted.
5. Select *Copy* from the *Edit* menu.
6. Paste the text into any application.

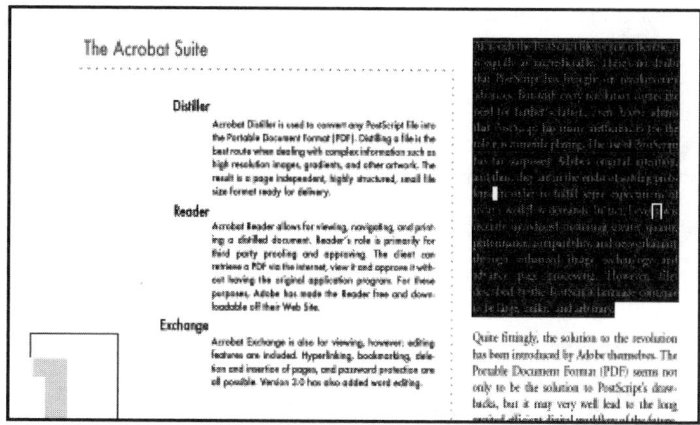

Selecting a portion of text

Text Touch-Up Tool

The *Text Touch-Up* tool offers limited text changes on a line-by-line basis given certain criteria. For instance,

- To change characters in a line, the font used for the text must either be available on your computer or the full font must be embedded within the PDF document. *(See font embedding in Chapter 5.)*
- If the font used on the text is an embedded subset, character changes will not be allowed.

The Text Touch-Up tool allows for small type changes to be made to PDF documents. The availability and functionality of this tool is limited by a number of factors.

To determine how a font is embedded in a PDF document, select *Document Info, Fonts* under the *File* menu. This dialog box will identify fonts used and how they were embedded.

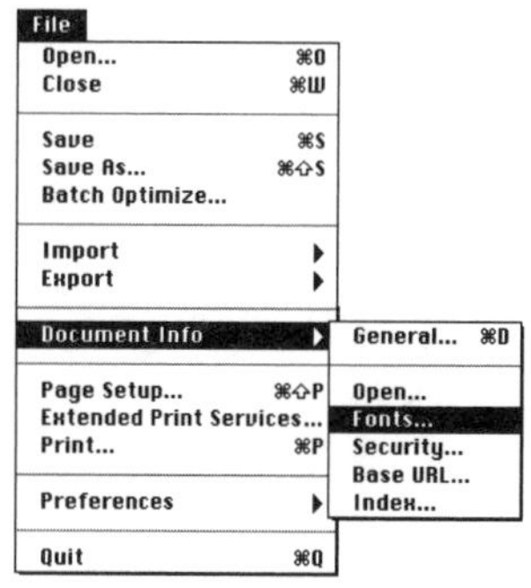

If the text can be edited, it can only be done on a line-by-line basis because Acrobat can't reflow text through a document. However, to fix a last-minute price change in a digital ad or a misspelled word in a lengthy document makes the Touch-up tool a valuable asset.

recently introduced promising greater quality, performance, compatibility, and networkability through enhanced image technology and advance page processing. However, files described by the PostScript language continue to be large, bulky, and arbitrary.

Quite fittingly, the solution to the revolution has been introduced by Adobe themselves. The Portable Document Format (PDF) seems not

In addition, *Text Touch-Up* provides other features such as applying color to text and scaling. To apply a *Text Touch-Up*:

1. Select the *Text Touch-Ups* icon on the tool bar.
2. Place the cursor where you want to edit the text.
3. A box appears outlining the line of text.
4. Highlight the text you plan to edit.
5. Select *Text Attributes* from the *Edit* menu.

At this point, a floating palette appears with choices for *Font, Character,* and *Line.*

Font

The text editing options of the Text Touch-Up Tool are broken down into three sections. The options are

- Font selection
- Size
- Fill color
- Outline color

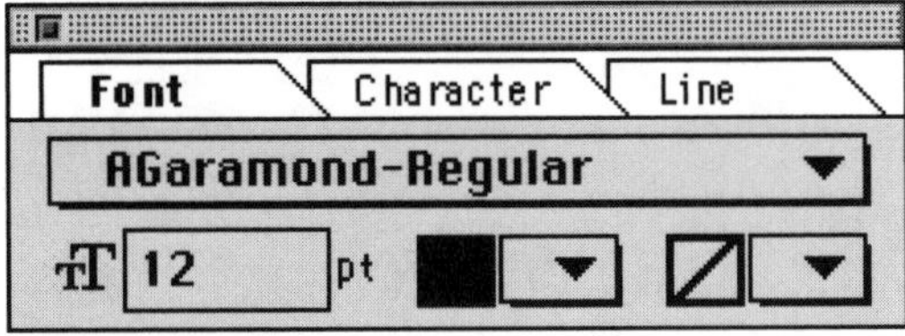

Text Touch-Up Font Options

If the font size is increased over the length of the line, the copy will flow off the page and will not be viewable, so be careful when enlarging font size.

The Font *option in Text Touch-Up is useful for adding color to links or highlights after the PDF file has been created.*

Character

The character options include the traditional PostScript controls for typographic manipulation and formatting—scaling, letterspacing, and word spacing.

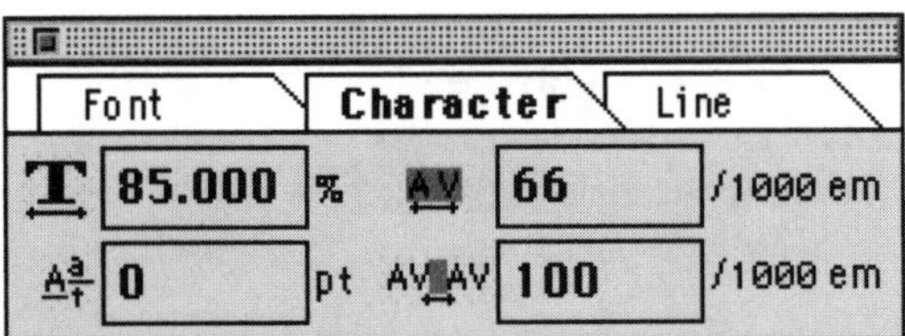

Text Touch-Up Character Options

Any changes that affect the line length and force the copy off the page will not be viewable. Please be careful using these functions since they can change the look of the type vis-a-vis the rest of the text.

Line

The line options handle the alignment of the line being edited. Flush left, center, flush right, and justify are the options available at this level. The two measurements at the bottom affect the placement of the text line from either the left or right page border. For instance, a value of zero entered in the left-side box will place the left edge of the line on the edge of the page.

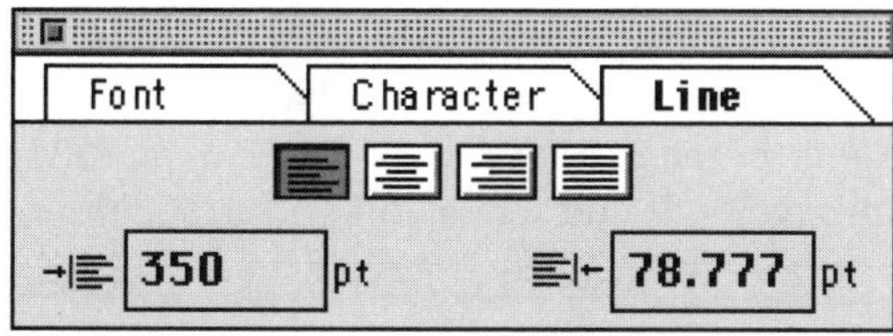

Text Touch-Up Line Options

Security

Acrobat Exchange also contains options for insuring PDF security. On the broadest level, a password can be set to open the PDF document. More specifically, printing, changing the document, selecting text and graphics, adding or changing notes, and form field entry can all be controlled with a password as well. Make sure you record the password so you can remember it.

To set security options, select *Save As* under the File Menu and click on the *Security…* button. A dialog box will appear and all of the functions can be set there.

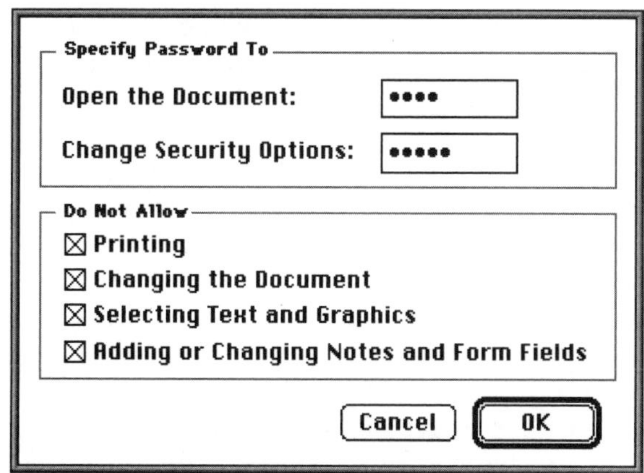

Will PDF re-H&J?
The PDF file format definition includes Marked Contents operators and Article Threads which may be used by applications to denote information needed to "re-H&J" (Hyphenate & Justify) a story, or even reconstruct features particular to a specific application such as layers and groups.

An example of this is Illustrator 7, which can save a PDF file and reopen it with article flows, layers, and groups preserved. Optional hyphens are also distinguished from "hard" hyphens.

These "Structures"—Marked Contents and Threads definitions —can even be defined in PostScript using PDFmark operators defined in Acrobat's pdfmark.pdf Help file. FrameMaker, PageMaker, and plug-ins to XPress like PageDesignXT and Quark's new PDFExport Xtension, all take advantage of some or all of these capabilities.

In future versions of both the PDF specification and application products, tagging and structure preservation will become more prominent. This will allow more powerful reuse and even reflow of text within PDF files and facilitate definition of prepress-specific structures within PDF files such as job tickets, trapping zones, and trap channels. Certain classes of "H&J information," such as algorithms used to determine when to break or not break a word, are native to an application and do not belong in a PDF file, but rather in the authoring application.

Acrobat's Extendibility
One of the most interesting functions with PDF is that third party developers have the ability to write plug-ins to extend Acrobat's capability. There are many commercially created plug-ins available for handling text in PDF files, but there are currently no plug-ins available which directly support high-end printing production like printing color separations of PDF files. Adobe is developing a beta plug-in that will allow both process and spot plates to be printed as well as custom settings for screen angles, halftone dot shapes, and color rendering. The intention for this plug-in is to show the possibilities that PDF can give high-end users and encourage third-party developers to supply further functions.

Extended Print Services, the plug-in for printing color separations was assigned to Lantana and released as Crackerjack (*see Chapter 11*). Acrobat outputs a composite file, which is fine for black and white or color laser printers but not for imagesetters or platesetters. Crackerjack is one of almost 100 plug-ins that add functionality and extend the PDF franchise.

Document
This part is basically the normal print dialogue box with the general settings of page range, number of copies, and PPD selection. It is also possible to save all the settings that are used and reload them later.

Pages
The Pages option includes the settings that are normally found in Page Setup like media size and orientation.

Output
Output controls let the user choose to reduce the size of the page (usually found in Page Setup), but the image can be scaled anamorphically which would be practical for flexographic printing. Also included in the Output options are Printers Marks, Mirror, and Negative options.

Color
Producing color separations is the heart of what PDF must do to be a viable part of the high-end publishing workflow. And

the Color options are where it's done. The first option is how the color output (screen angles, dot shapes, UCR levels) should be controlled. There are three main choices: either the printer's default setting, the document's setting, or both these can be overridden by the settings specified in the dialogue box. Next the file can be printed either as a composite page or as separations. Screening control allows the halftone frequency, dot shape, and screen angles to be set to the PPD-defined defaults or to custom levels. If the printer has Color Rendering Dictionaries installed, different rendering intents can also be specified from within the *Color Option* dialogue box.

Extended Print Services has a demonstration version that shows the functionality that can be added to Exchange and PDF. Other third-party developers will create plug-ins that will duplicate, and perhaps expand upon, the capabilities just described.

Reader

Reader is the baby brother or sister in the Acrobat family—definitely a part of the family but you don't want to let them play with your toys. This is to say that Reader can view, navigate, search, and print PDF documents. It can also enjoy any of the interactivity built-in to PDF documents through Exchange like Web links and QuickTime movies. However, that's about the limit of what Reader can do. It cannot touch-up text, add interactivity, or make page-level changes like cropping. Anything that might change the structure of the PDF file can't be accomplished in Reader.

And it's not designed to do those functions. Adobe markets Reader as "The free viewing companion to Acrobat..." It is designed to be a freely distributable way to share PDF documents across different platforms. It is available on all three major platforms—Macintosh, Windows, and UNIX.

Capabilities

Reader is a great way to soft proof, and it's the simplest way to view PDF files downloaded off the Web. Files can be viewed and printed, but they cannot be edited in any way. Reader does not have any saving capabilities. Text can be selected, copied, and pasted into another application but touch-ups cannot be applied. Basically, it's a "look, but don't change" application. Reader can view notes, but they can't be edited. This means that responses or further comments cannot be added to a preexisting note using Reader. Reader also supports searching through the *Find* command which further enhances the use of Reader as a viewing program.

An early version of this book is a good example of how this works. We never actually met with the cover designer. As the cover evolved he sent PDFs of it via e-mail. We affixed notes and sent it back. At each iteration we printed the cover out as a proof, first from a Canon color laser copier with an EFI RIP and later from an Imation Rainbow dye sublimation proofer.

Why Use Reader?

Acrobat Reader does have some advantages and is actually a good choice in some situations. If you are that designer sending a menu design to a restaurant for approval, Reader is efficient. Simply save the file as a PDF (*as explained in Chapter 5*) and send it to the restaurant client via e-mail. The client does not have to invest in Exchange just to view the menu. Reader is free and easy to download directly from Adobe's Website. The expense of printing proofs and the dependency on making that overnight mail pickup is no longer necessary either. The client can view the menu in full color on screen for virtually no cost on either end.

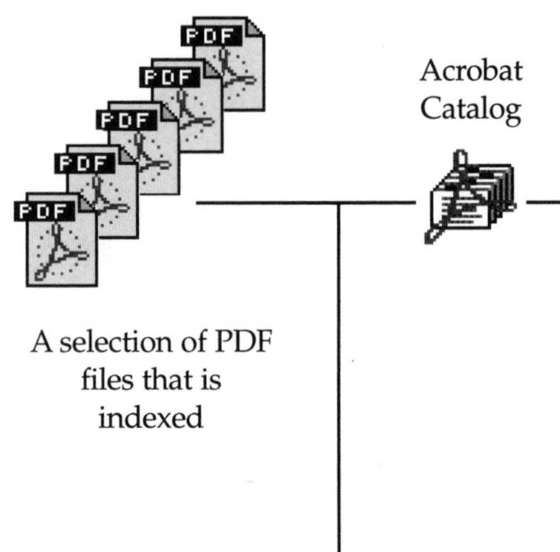

This is also a great example of an instance where you would want no editability in your digital document. You, the designer, would not be interested in your client moving images or changing fonts. Notes can be viewed, so if you wanted to include a few questions or concerns in need of consideration, Acrobat Reader will allow the client to access these notes. Comments cannot be directly added on the client end but, after all, the file is being e-mailed, so comments can attach as with regular mail.

Adobe Acrobat Catalog and Search
Files and the information contained within them are only as valuable as the ability to access that information. What good is information if it is buried deep within a file? Currently there is no direct and effective way to store and retrieve files created in any one of today's application programs. Acrobat's solution to the archival prospect lies within the Catalog and Search features in the Acrobat suite. Catalog is a stand-alone application, while Search is a plug-in packaged with Reader and Exchange. Both are important tools.

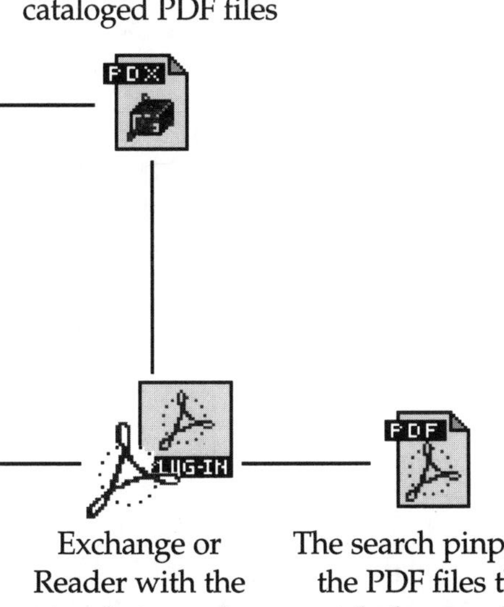

Catalog and Search Market

Anyone who needs to manage large volumes of PDF documents or wants to have instant access to specific portions of files will benefit from using Catalog and Search. Grouping all files and indexing them is an advantage which will lead to more streamlined workflows and will significantly decrease downtime in the location of files and images. The implementation of an index with searching capability for archiving is a necessary part of digital workflow. Since storage space is so expensive and digital workflows for printers are evolving and incorporating the usage of PDF files, direct archival storage in a structured manner is needed.

How Does it Work?

Similar to a filing cabinet, hundreds of individual documents can be grouped together in one location. This is called indexing and is possible through the use of Acrobat Catalog. But unlike the old file cabinet setup, documents can be found easily. Not only can they be found by name or author, they can also be accessed by one word or phrase buried deep within the document. This function is called searching and is possible when using Acrobat Search. So, if you want to rid the office of those stacks of paper documents and those bulky file cabinets, or you have trouble finding the one piece of paper you're looking for, Catalog and Search are worthwhile options.

The Planning Stage in Exchange

Prior to index building in Catalog and while the PDF is still in Exchange, there are several options which should be specified in order to ensure indexing efficiency. The most important areas of concern are:

- Document information box options
- Thumbnails/bookmarks
- Optimizing
- Notes

Document Information Box

Access to the dialogue box in Exchange is found in the File menu, Document Info, General menu. The dialogue box which appears is the key to all category searching. The box allows the user to specify document information such as title, subject, author, and keywords. Defining these fields allows Catalog to more efficiently indexed PDF files.

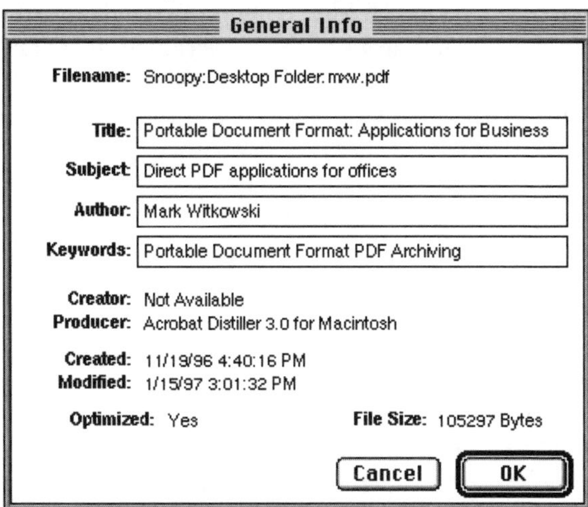
General Info

Filename: Snoopy:Desktop Folder:mxw.pdf

Title: Portable Document Format: Applications for Business

Subject: Direct PDF applications for offices

Author: Mark Witkowski

Keywords: Portable Document Format PDF Archiving

Creator: Not Available
Producer: Acrobat Distiller 3.0 for Macintosh

Created: 11/19/96 4:40:16 PM
Modified: 1/15/97 3:01:32 PM

Optimized: Yes   File Size: 105297 Bytes

Cancel   OK

PDF Document Info Window

The Document Information box is probably the most overlooked step in the process, and it is actually the most essential for archiving purposes. The choices should be completed in a similar manner for all files being indexed. This will help you later when you are trying to retrieve the PDF.

Thumbnails and Bookmarks

The prior creation of thumbnails and bookmarks in Exchange will help searchers navigate through the document after the "hits" are located. When a user is directed to a "hit" on the page, reading typically does not end there. Since you have full access to the entire document, thumbnails and bookmarks serve as an effective and necessary navigation tool, especially if the document being searched is lengthy. Bookmarks could get the reader to a particular page at a particular zoom to a particular area. This is how one packaging firm gets their proofers and checkers to the specific area they have to check.

Remember that if thumbnails and bookmarks are to be utilized in Catalog and Search, they must be created prior to indexing in Exchange.

Optimizing

Optimization of a file is an important operation to perform on all PDF documents which are going to be cataloged. An optimized file is more efficiently structured allowing Reader or Exchange better access to the objects in the file.

Byte-serving—*Aims at reducing file download times by only allowing single page transfers. Also produces quicker screen re-draw times by first displaying approximations of fonts, then replaces them later on.*

Notes are electronic annotations which are included on the screen view, but do not print out. Unfortunately, the notes contained within the files in the index are not searchable.

Storage Locations
Once the PDF files are properly prepared in Exchange, they should be saved to a dedicated folder in which all the files being indexed will go. Further subgrouping of these files at this point will allow separate, more specific indexes made for large volumes of PDF files. This will enable searchers to more accurately pinpoint queries later.

Presorting large amounts of related files and/or the breaking up of all extremely large singular files enables quicker, more directed searching. The creation of a structured organization and naming system will further streamline the searching function. You do want fast searching.

Using Acrobat Catalog
When Catalog is first opened the screen looks very similar to Distiller. The first step after opening Catalog is to immediately check and set the preferences. The preferences set at this point are kept every time subsequent indexes are built. If you are rebuilding an existing index, it will use the preferences set at the time of the re-build. These preferences may not necessarily be the ones used in the original build. It is necessary to determine the end use of the index when setting the preferences because these settings affect the later uses of the index.

The *Preferences* menu is found under the *Edit* menu. It consists of five sections:

- Index
- Index Defaults
- Logging
- Drop Folders
- Custom Fields

Purging is the deletion of the entire index and all of its contents. When an index is purged all of the files are irreversibly erased.

Index
The index box contains several settings regarding the index in general. The Purge time is a setting which delays the purge or deletion of an index. The default time setting is 15 minutes. This time span will allow users who may be using the index on a network to complete their searches before the index begins erasing.

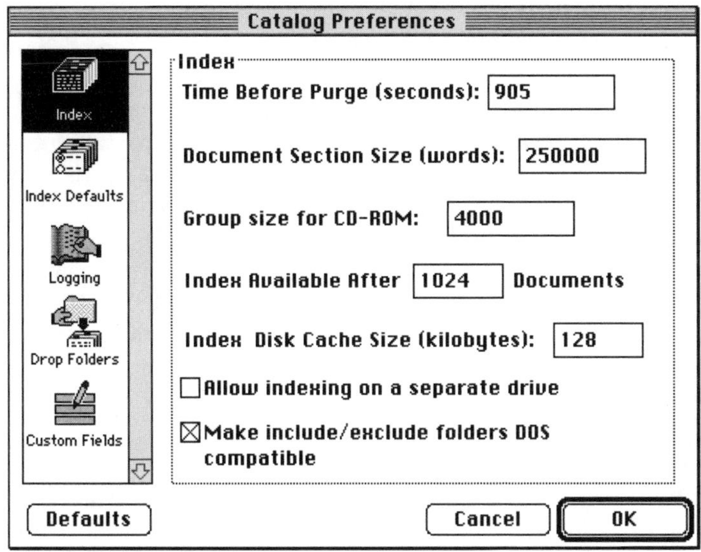

Catalog Preferences Window

The *Document Section Size* is the threshold at which Acrobat will cut off large documents and segment them into as many parts as specified. For instance, if the size is set to 250,000 words and a file containing 300,000 words is indexed, it will be cut off at 250,000 words and a second index file will be created including the remaining 50,000 words. The intention of this is to keep the catalog and search functions operating quickly.

Choosing the group size for CD-ROM allows Acrobat to cut off the size of the singular index to specified limitations for use on CD storage media. There is a limit and ideal format for CD-ROM storage. It is important for CD creation that particular attention be paid to this setting.

Making indexes available after partial completion is best used when indexing large amounts of information. The smaller the number in this field, the faster viewing and usage of the completed parts of the index. If large amounts of data are being cataloged, it is wise to set the value in this field to a low number so that users have access to at least some information.

Setting the *Index Cache Size* to larger values will allow faster index build times on a Macintosh.

On a Macintosh platform you have the ability to index files on different drives, but on a DOS platform all files must be in the same drive. It is recommended that all files regardless of platform be included within the same folder, and on the same drive.

Checking the box to allow indexing on a separate drive is not recommended if there is ever a possible future for cross-platform use of the index. The separate drive feature is only allowed on the Macintosh platform, not on the Windows platform.

The DOS-compatible folder names is also important for cross-platform functions. When this box is checked, the computer limits the naming of files to the least common denominator—which is MS-DOS names.

If you are working on a Macintosh platform and plan to transfer this index at any time to a MS-DOS platform, it is important to keep all file names in accordance to MS-DOS standards. Character names must be no longer than eight ASCII characters with a three character extension. Example: acrobat.pdf—"acrobat" is the file name and ".pdf" is the extension.

Index Defaults

The choices made in this section pertain to the limiting factors of the index. The choices also determine the functionality of the search. Selecting or deselecting each feature in this box can reduce the overall size of the index approximately 10 to 15 percent for each option. It is important to note that with these choices you are sacrificing storage space for functionality in the search process. It is the relationship between functionality and space that becomes a focal point for the selections made.

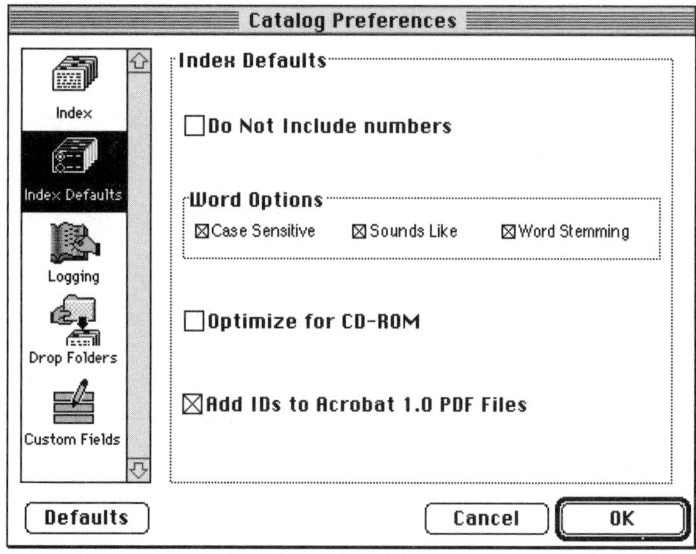

If CD-ROM or DVD-ROM storage is a possibility, now or in the future, it is important to check the *Optimize for CD-ROM* box. This option organizes the data in an order that is ideal for CD storage and retrieval, especially for older 2X and 4X CD-Readers.

The only absolutely necessary consideration that must always be checked is the *Add IDs to Acrobat 1.0 PDF files.* This will add a tag to PDF files created before PDF version 1.2. This tag will let Catalog recognize the older PDF 1.0 and 1.1 files and will include them in the field.

Depending on the desired user pool of the index, the choices in *Word options* should differ. If several users needing broad searching capabilities will be using the index, options for Case Sensitive, Sounds Like, and Word Stemming should all be enabled.

However, if a select group of users who know exactly what they are looking for is using the index, these options may not need to be included.

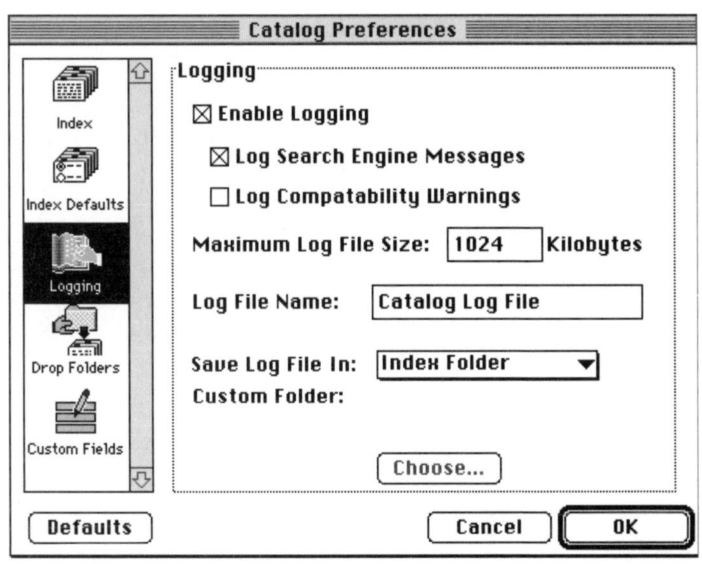

Log files are good feedback tools from the index. Information shedding light on the way in which the created index is working and how often the index is used can be provided.

Logging

Logging creates a report file which contains all information when indexes are built and records the status after building. Choices include having the log file updated every time there is an inquiry with the search engine. You can set the name and destination of the log file created at this stage. Even though the log file will be recognizable, it is a file name relative to the index which will insure correlation to that index.

The destination of the report file should be in the folder containing the index and related files. The information in the report file which is a SimpleText file includes time stamp and a message report. You can set the maximum size of the file so that it gets deleted and reset at a certain point.

Drop Folders

These settings determine the default index name and designate where the peripheral files will be created for the index. It is important to remember that all files for a particular index should be contained in one folder to eliminate confusion in the future. Taking these steps at the beginning will add to the longevity of the index.

Custom Fields

The creation of information fields for custom versions of Acrobat are created in this box. The declaration of integer, text, and string data fields can be specified at this point. This feature is supported by custom versions of Acrobat.

Building the Index

The actual building of the index is a relatively simple task now that all files are set up in a structured manner. It is at this stage that many of the important planning steps taken will help shape the index.

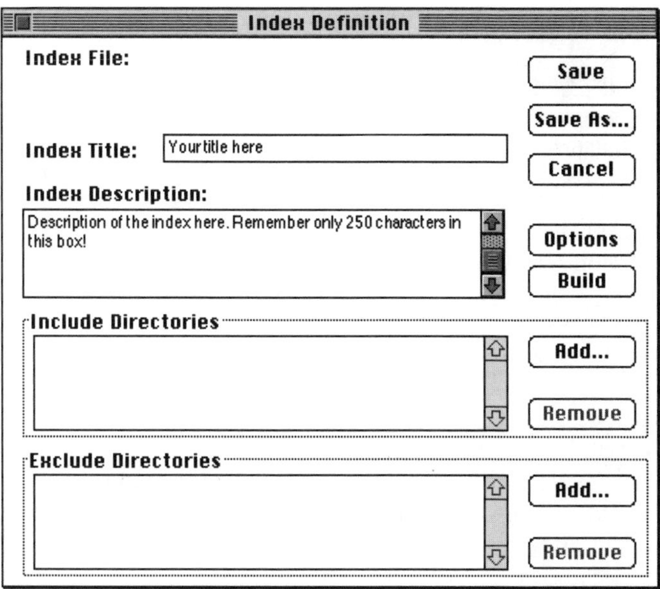

Where to Begin Indexing

With Acrobat Catalog running, select *New* from the *File* menu. The Index Definition dialogue box that appears controls everything that index will contain, as well as its file name and description.

1. Name the index.
2. Give a summary of the index. *There is a maximum of 250 characters in this box, so be concise, but descriptive.*
3. Choose the folders that will be included in the index.
4. Click on the *Add* button. A document selection box will appear. In order to select an entire folder, click on the bar at the bottom of the box which starts with select. This is where the careful planning of folders and subfolders becomes important.

Make sure you know where the folders are at this moment and where any new folders will be stored. We have all been known to lose folders.

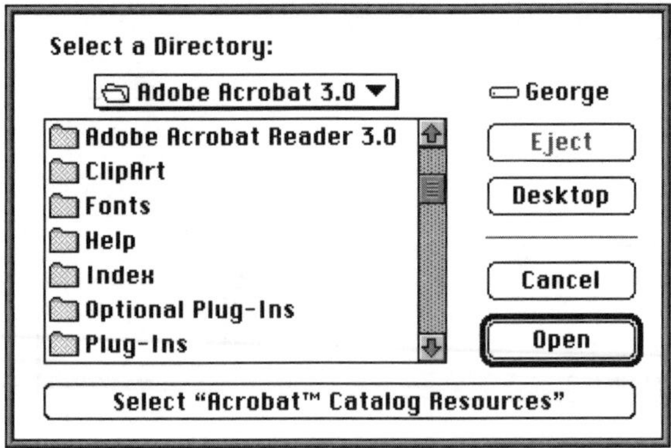

Now that the files are chosen,

5. Click on the *Options* button. The most important part of this box is the selection of stop words, or words that should be included in the index. Choosing words that will not appear in the index can have a significant impact on the index size. For instance, words such as: *and, the,* or *for* are not necessarily needed and can be cut out in order to reduce the index size. The choices made in this box are specific only to this particular index, and are used whenever that index is updated.

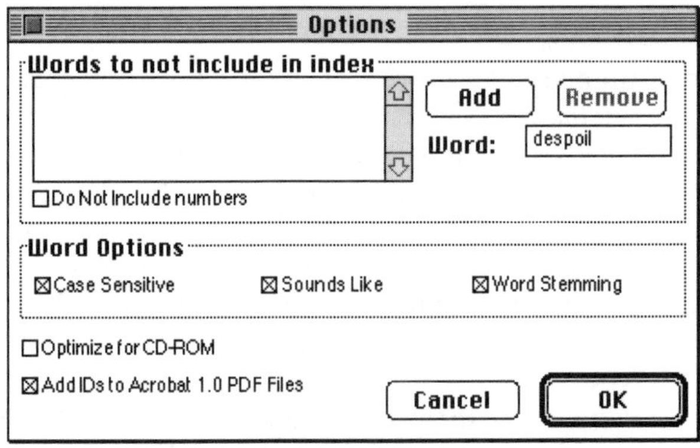

Use the Save *button in the index definition box for updating the information to an existing index definition.*

6. Click on *Save As*. Now that the overall index has been set in the Index Definition box, the *Save As* dialogue box

allows you to give the central index definition a file name. The index file should be saved in the master folder previously set up with the PDF files. Choosing the *Add to Index to Schedule* is the only choice left to make if you want to add the index to the automatic rebuild schedule. Once everything is set, click on the *Save* button. This will create a central index definition file with a .pdx extension.

7. Under the Index menu choose the *Build* option to do the actual building of the index. Once inside the build feature you will be at a file selection dialogue box. To build an index, highlight the index definition file (with a .pdx extension) you want, then on the open button, then let Catalog do its work. When the actual index is built, a series of nine folders is created to support the central index definition. Depending on the amount of text and graphics contained in the pages, cataloging times may vary. For more text, allow longer times for building the Acrobat index.

Maintenance

After the index is first built, your work is not done. It is important to keep the index and its contents up to date. Periodic rebuilding of the index and additions are necessary. This is very easily done.

1. The first step is placing the new PDF files into the desired index folders. In Catalog select *Build* from the index menu. Then select the index file with the .pdx extension.
2. If there are no changes to the overall setup to the index, just click *Build* and the index will be updated and include the new files.

Major Rebuilds

If there have been significant changes to files in the index or any new files have been added or options have been changed, then purging and rebuilding the index is necessary. Purging erases all information in the existing index so think twice—think three times—before you purge anything. The purge function is found in the *Build* menu, and should only be used when complete changes need to be made to the index. After the index has been purged, the previously outlined rebuild techniques can be followed.

Purge and rebuild indexes that have been rebuilt several times. This is because each time you rebuild an index it gets a little bit larger. Purging this index will reclaim disk space and make searching quicker.

Remember: you can add an index to a schedule menu when you are in the Save As *box of the index definition.*

Scheduling

In order for a streamlined service of the rebuilding process, the Schedule feature needs to be enabled. Scheduling will allow automatic updating of the index. This feature should be used if the catalog is being constantly updated and renovated.

1. The first step in the schedule build setup is to access the *Schedule Builds* dialog box. Go under the index menu to the schedule option.
2. Once inside the *Schedule Builds* box, select the indexes you want to add to the schedule. Use the same techniques outlined earlier for selecting indexes.
3. Decide how often you want the indexes to be built: *Continuously, once,* or *on a set time schedule.* Ideally, you want to rebuild the indexes when no one is using the index. You can set the time of rebuild to be overnight so it does not interfere with anyone's searching.

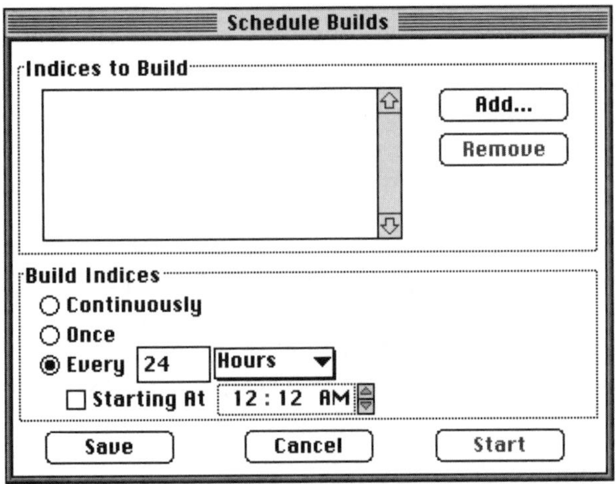

The drawback to the schedule tool is that the computer system must be running 24 hours a day, seven days a week. If there is any interruption either in electricity or manual switching, the schedule must be re-defined and re-started.

Acrobat Search

Acrobat Search is a plug-in supplied with Exchange and Reader. Search preferences must be set before you do your first search. It is a relatively easy task to change and redefine the preferences in this menu. Settings for queries, results, highlighting, and indexes can be set.

Setting Search Preferences

The Acrobat Search Preferences dialogue box can be found under the *File* menu, *Preferences, Search.* The check boxes found give the flexibility to customize the way the search reports hits. Results can be organized by a host of categories.

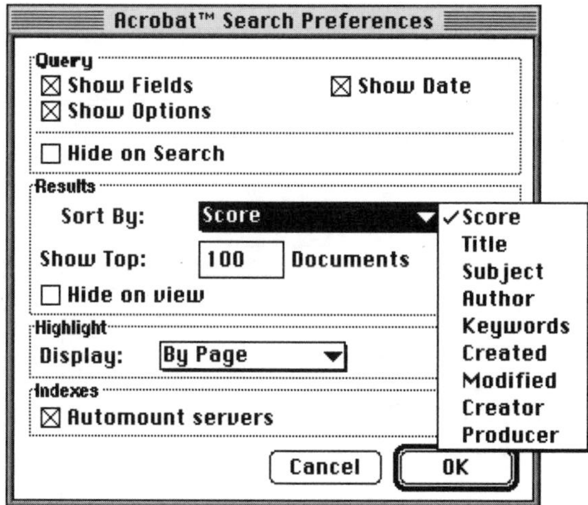

1. Go to the *Search Preferences* dialogue box.
2. Select how much of the query box you want users to see:
   - *Show Fields*: will choose whether or not to show document information fields.
   - *Show Date*: shows or hides *with date information* box.
   - *Show Options*: enables options set in Catalog such as sounds like, word stemming etc.
3. The *Hide on Search* check box refers to keeping the Acrobat Search window open or closed after the search is done. Checking this box will hide the window when the search reports back.

4. The order in which results of a search are displayed can be set in the results option field. Several options are available for sorting returned hits. *Choose the one that best suits your needs.* You can further limit the number of returned documents at this point. Also, you can click on the *Hide on View* box to hide the results box when you view a document.
5. Highlighting the hits on a page can be set in the highlight box. Highlighting by page, word, or no highlights at all can be chosen. Page highlighting is the default value.
6. Automounting servers in the indexes area will automatically mount all available indexes available when starting a search. This function is only available on a Macintosh platform.

Performing the Search

Now that all of the preferences have been set, it is finally time to perform the search. To get to the Search dialogue box, go to the Tools menu, *Search, Query.*

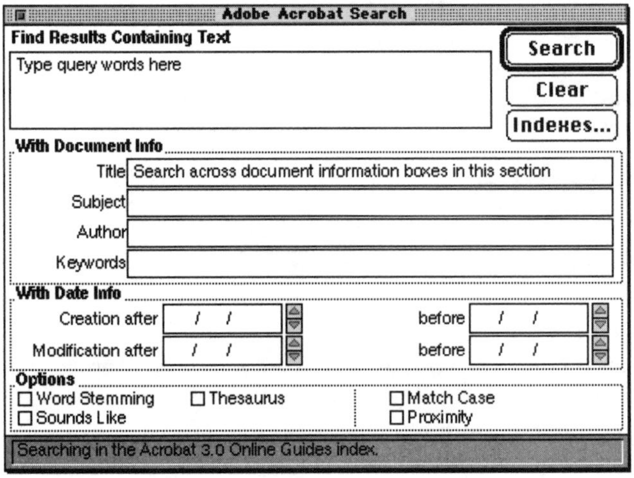

Adobe Acrobat Search
Find Results Containing Text
Type query words here
Search
Clear
Indexes...
With Document Info
Title Search across document information boxes in this section
Subject
Author
Keywords
With Date Info
Creation after / / before / /
Modification after / / before / /
Options
☐ Word Stemming ☐ Thesaurus ☐ Match Case
☐ Sounds Like ☐ Proximity
Searching in the Acrobat 3.0 Online Guides index.

Using the Search Box

Using the Search box is where you make the choices of where and what you want to search. The search engine does the rest of the work and reports back to you via a hit list dialogue box.

1. The first step is to decide where you want to search. Click on the *Indexes* button. You will be brought to a box where you can select or deselect indexes. The sensible division and subdivision of created indexes becomes important at this point. If an index you want to search does not appear in the box, de-select any index currently in the box and click on the *Add* button. This will bring you to a box which allows you to find your index. When you find it click on the *Open* button. After all indexes appear in the Index Selection box, click *OK*.
2. Now that you have decided where to search, you must decide what to search. There are several ways to drive the search engine. First, determine what options you want to include in the search, such as:
    - Word stemming
    - Sounds like
    - Thesaurus
    - Match case
    - Proximity
3. Searching for files created on, between, before, or after specific dates is the next set of options which must be determined. This is a useful feature because date information is automatically included with all documents, and is searchable.
4. Performing searches in the "With Document Info" area is where the document information box becomes vital. The fields in this area consist of the information provided in the planning stages of the index. Each of these fields can be used to perform a search within that particular field across the selected indexes. As you can see the proper and consistent information provided in these fields is invaluable at this point.
5. The final method for searching documents is the straight text calls made in the *Find Results Containing Text* field. Several methods and options exist for narrowing or expanding these specific searches. Wildcard, boolean, phrase, and comparison searching can be performed. This type of search uses typical protocols for the usage of these operators.

This icon can also be used to access the search query box.

If Automount Servers *is not selected in the preferences box, then either click on this button, or mount them by going into the tools search, index menu item.*

Explanation of Search restrictions and options.

Word Stemming: *returns words with the same stem or root as the query word.*

Sounds Like: *returns words that may be spelled differently (incorrect spelling) but are pronounced the same as the query word.*

Thesaurus: *returns words with the same meaning as the query word.*

Match Case: *returns words that match the letters of the query word in both majuscule and miniscule letters—upper and lowercase to non-type geeks.*

Proximity: *returns words with the boolean AND restriction of within three pages of each other.*

Boolean operators are typed in as all-capital letters:

AND: *both words*

OR: *either or both words*

NOT: *does not contain word*

Wildcard: *used when not sure of spelling of word, * stands for one or more characters, ? for one character.*

6. The last step in the search process is to click on the *Search* button. Acrobat Search will then access each index called for and search its text list. When it is done, it will return the list of "hits" in the order in which you set in the preferences menu.

Search Results

Each document on this list contains the information called for in the search box. To view a file from this list either double click on it or highlight it and click on view.

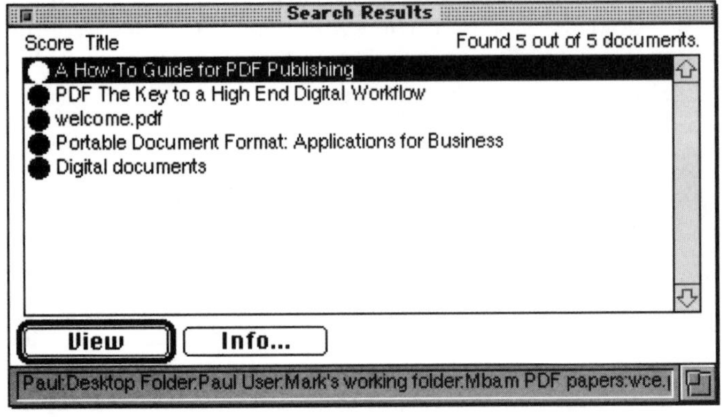

Clicking on the Info… *box will show the document information box of that file.*

Refining a Search

An option to refine a set of returned search files can be done by reopening the search dialogue box, keying in the restraining parameters, and holding down the *Option* key (Macintosh) or the *Control* key (Windows) which will change the *Search* button to *Refine*. Click on *Refine* and the new requirements will be applied only to the original search results.

Word Assist

This option can almost be thought of as a preflight for search with the stemming, sounds like, and thesaurus help functions. By using this function you can perform a mock search and see what words will be returned as *hits*.

To access this box go under *Tools, Search, Word Assist.*

Here is what the Word Assistant Dialogue box looks like:

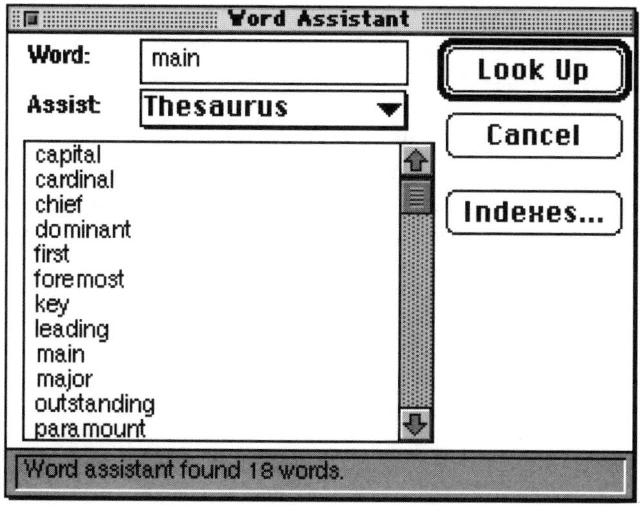

1. Select the indexes you want to search across by clicking on the indexes box. The process is now just the same as previously explained for search.
2. Choose what type of search you want to perform *Stemming, Sounds Like,* or *Thesaurus.*
3. Type in a word in the Word box.
4. Click on *Search.* A list will then appear in the lower box. This list consists of words that are in the indexes chosen to search. You can then use the information from this box as a guide in your searching.

Conclusion

The usage of Catalog and Search features in Acrobat seem to be relatively insignificant on the surface, but in reality they are the backbone of what could be a powerful archival system. These functions are the basis for a necessary structured system to store and retrieve data. You should plan ahead when preparing PDFs so as to facilitate search and retrieval.

Remember, it is not information until you find what you want.

Digital storage methods have consistently changed, as we have sought an ideal structure and format for archiving. The PDF file offers tremendous advantages and solutions over previous approaches. The efficiency and reliability that the Acrobat suite offers for archiving may very well be the answer to many concerns and problems.

It is important to realize that the construction of any storage system utilizing PDF files as the base needs to be extremely structured and well thought out. It is the planning aspects that will ultimately determine the success or failure of a system.

8

INSIDE THE ACROBAT PDF

This book is about high-end printing workflow, but it all starts in the creation of a PDF. In this chapter we summarize the more important aspects of creating responsible PDF files. Special thanks to Mike Jahn and Gary Cosimini.

Watched Folders Options

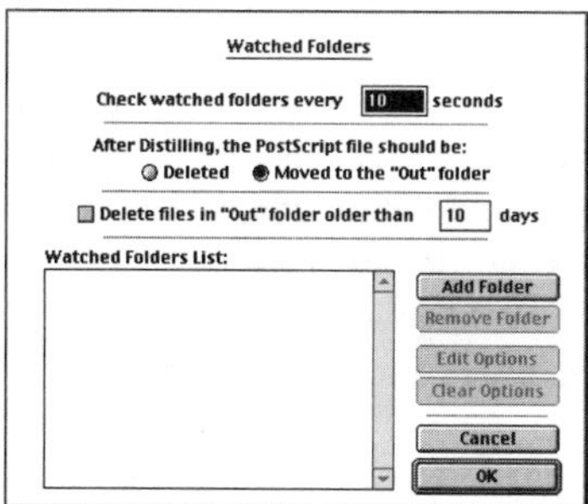

You can set up Distiller to watch certain folders on a network server by going under the *Distiller* menu and selecting *Watched Folders*. When Distiller watches a folder, it periodically checks the folders for PostScript files. When a PostScript file is saved or copied into a watched folder, Distiller automatically processes the file and moves it to an Out folder. Sharing Distiller on a network conserves resources, such as memory and disk space, and can help avoid having disparate Job Options settings. Acrobat Distiller can watch up to 100 folders. There is no way to create a new folder to watch, so you must select already existing folders or create new folders beforehand.

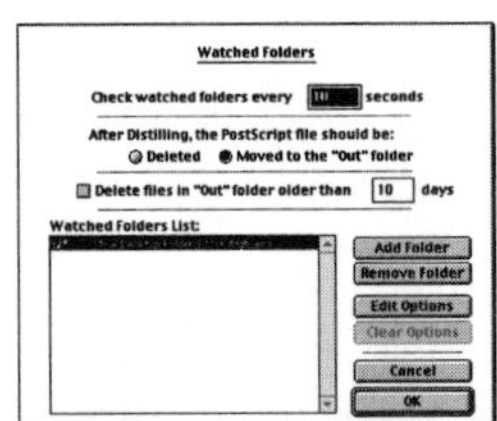

You can specify different options for each folder using the Edit Options tool. To add watched folders:

1. Choose *Distiller > Watched Folders;* then click *Add Folder*.

2. Select the folder location for the In and Out folders. Distiller creates an In folder and an Out folder in the selected folder. Distiller does not create new In and Out folders if folders so named already exist.

A PDF is a device-independent file format with good possibilities for compression. In addition, it does not "lose information" and retains the design richness. Depending on the complexity, you will most likely fit a menu in a compressed PDF file on a floppy disk (remember floppies?)

Our Suggestions on How to Set up PDF Files

In QuarkXPress, make sure any special spot color or Pantone color does not have "Separations" checked in the Edit/Colors dialog box. Either "Save as EPS," or use an Xtension that preserves this information or the PostScript you "print to disk" will convert the spot colors to CMYK.

Please note:

Turn off the "Smooth Graphics" option in the QuarkXPress print setup dialogue box before you use PDFWriter or before you make a PostScript file for Distiller.

Drag the files called "prologue.ps" and "epilogue.ps" into the same folder as the Distiller application from the folder called "High-end" (in the Xtras folder) which was created when you installed Acrobat Distiller.

PostScript files that conform to the PostScript Level 1 conventions for color separations use an operator called *setcustomcolor*, which gets defined by the application which receives/imports the file. The default definition is to convert custom colors into their process color equivalents using the *setcmykcolor* PostScript operator. This means that the separations information is lost, which may be preferable if the file is not to be separated later.

If you want separations, then a definition of *setcustomcolor* that uses separation color spaces in PostScript is needed. The Distiller will then preserve that information, and it can be printed from Exchange, either as PostScript Level 2 separation color spaces, or as a PostScript Level 1 file conforming to the conventions for color separations. To use this definition of *setcustom-color* which retains the custom color definitions, one must Distill files using the prologue.ps and epilogue.ps files.

Distiller's Job Options/General

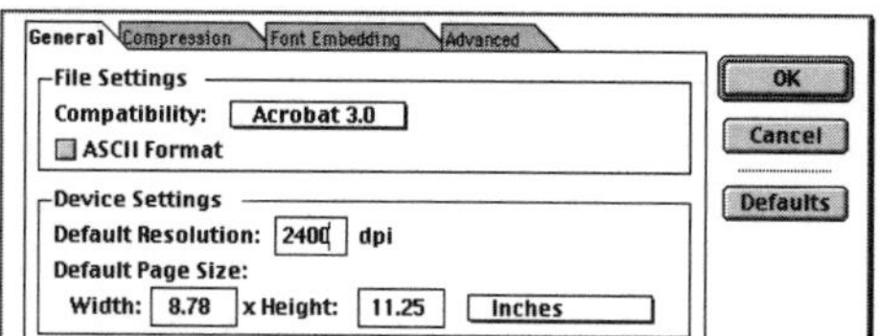

In Acrobat Distiller's Job Options *General* tab, select the Acrobat 3.0 option from the pop-up menu for Compatibility. This provides more advanced image compression settings. We see no reason to go backward to an older version.

Do not select "ASCII Format." This will create a larger file. Select ASCII to open and examine a PDF file in a text editor such as BBEdit.

In the Device Settings section, enter the resolution (dpi) of the file's final output device in the Default Resolution text box. The value you enter affects only object-oriented EPS files with device resolution-dependent elements, such as gradients or blends.

If the PostScript file you're distilling includes a paper size, not page size, which most high-end applications do include, you can ignore the Default Page Size option. Distiller only uses the values you enter in these text boxes when a PostScript file doesn't include a paper size. Distiller rounds to the nearest point.

Distiller's Job Options/Compression

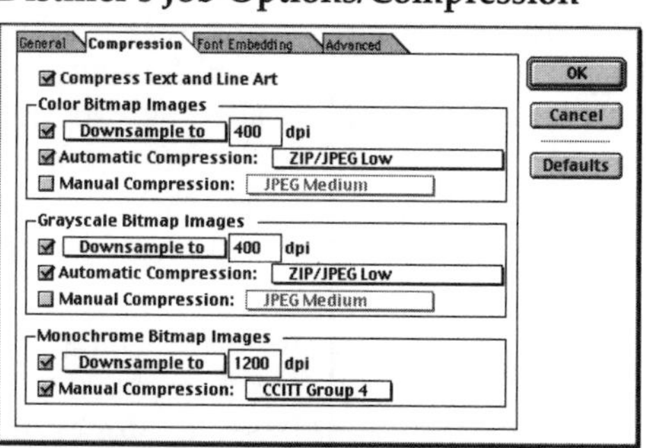

Distiller's *Compression* tab has controls which affect file size and image quality. Leave the Compress Text and Line Art option selected (vector EPS) since this compression is lossless and has no effect on the image quality of these items.

Distiller supports several methods of image compression, which can be controlled separately for monochrome, grayscale, and color images. For color and grayscale images, Zip and JPEG compression are supported. Zip compression is lossless, and will not affect image quality. JPEG compression is lossy, and may affect image quality.

Distiller supports five levels of JPEG compression: higher compression ratios result in greater lossiness, and have more effect on image quality. There may be some level of JPEG compression you find usable, depending on your requirements.

For monochrome images, Distiller supports Zip, run-length, and fax compression, all of which are lossless and will not affect image quality. Generally, fax4 (CCITT Group 4) compression works very well for monochrome images.

Some options offered in the Distiller interface combine both image depth and compression into one. LZW or Zip 4 bit is lossy, not because of the compression, but because it fiddles with other stuff as well. The 8-bit options are lossless (unless you have 12-bit data in the PostScript code).

The truth about "subsetting"
You have used the font "Hobo Extended Bold" for prices ("2 for $1") in an ad and when you print to disk *from QuarkXPress or PageMaker, the whole font is placed in the PostScript file, including the Yen symbol and all other option and option shift characters… even though you only used a "subset"—0 through 9, a $, and letters f, o, r.*

You can set Distiller to only place the characters you need in the PDF file, ignoring the unused characters by turning on "font subset." If you want all the fonts and all the characters to be embedded and don't mind the larger file, turn off "subset fonts." Subsets means just that—Distiller will place the specific group of characters from that font into the PDF file, so the file is smaller, and ATM (Adobe Type Manager) does not render a "this is close enough" substitute, it uses the original font metrics in that PDF file to render to screen and marking engine.

*Distiller 3.0 lets you set the Embed Threshold. Prepress PDFers should set it to **99 percent** to insure that **all** fonts are embedded. Embedded subset fonts also get a "machine-generated name" which precludes last-minute substitution of fonts at the RIP or the local printing system. Such involuntary substitutions might result in errors if old versions of a font or user-edited fonts exist with identical font names to those used in the PDF file.*

The *Downsample to 400 dpi* selection creates a baseline for the amount of image data included in the PDF file. If a bitmap image has been scanned at 300 ppi (scans are pixels per inch or dots per inch) then scaled by X percent, the actual image resolution is increased accordingly. The *Downsample* option allows you to catch these anomalies, create a smaller, more efficient PDF file that may image in less time. Do not use *Subsampling* unless you need to process extremely high resolution images down to proofing quality or for on-line distribution. Subsampling is faster than downsampling but image sharpness will be lost.

For Color and Grayscale Bitmap Images, select the Automatic Compression of ZIP/JPEG Low. Low compression means just that, a very "low" or small amount of compression is being applied. Low compression will provide high quality. JPEG Medium-Low and Medium compression will also produce pretty good results, and the files will be even smaller. Highly detailed images benefit from lower compression (and higher quality) but consult with your printing service for optimal settings.

Distiller also supports lossless ZIP compression for images, but this causes greatly enlarged file sizes. For Monochrome Bitmap Images, select the *Downsample* option and enter the resolution of the intended final output device. This will catch those scaled images that are oversampled. All compression choices for Monochrome images are lossless—select CCITT Group 4.

Distiller's Job Options/Font Embedding

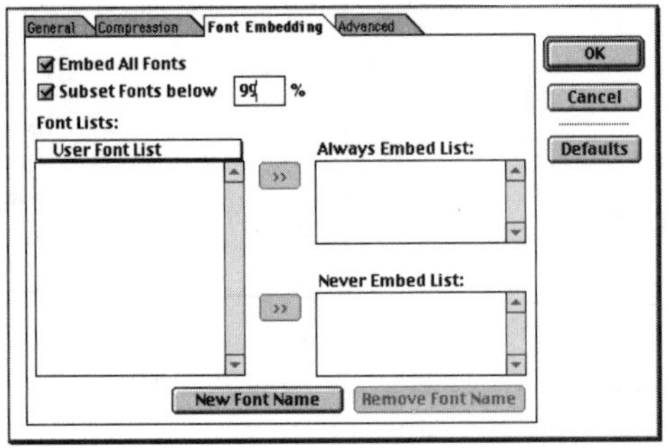

Under the F*ont Embedding* tab, specify which fonts you want included in the PDF file to prevent font substitution. Distiller never embeds the Base 13 fonts of Helvetica, Times

Roman, Courier, and Symbol because these fonts are included in all PostScript devices. Select the *Embed All Fonts* so that Distiller includes all fonts used in the document in the PDF file. Select the *Subset Fonts Below* option and specify 99 percent. When you select this option, Distiller includes only the characters used in the document for each typeface, and it renames the subset fonts in the PDF file to prevent fonts with the same name from being used at print time. This makes the file extremely reliable. Including subset fonts in a PDF file decreases file size and print times, but prevents late-stage editing with text touch-up.

If you have the original font that was subsetted, you could use Acrobat Exchange, and go under the *Tools* menu and select the *Select Type* tool, select the type that you want to edit, and under the *Edit* menu select *Text Attributes*, and change the font from the embedded font to the font you have loaded on your system, make the change and then *Save*. This will solve your problem, but if you are sending this file to another machine or location, the PDF file requires the other machine or site to have that particular font installed.

Distiller's Job Options/Advanced

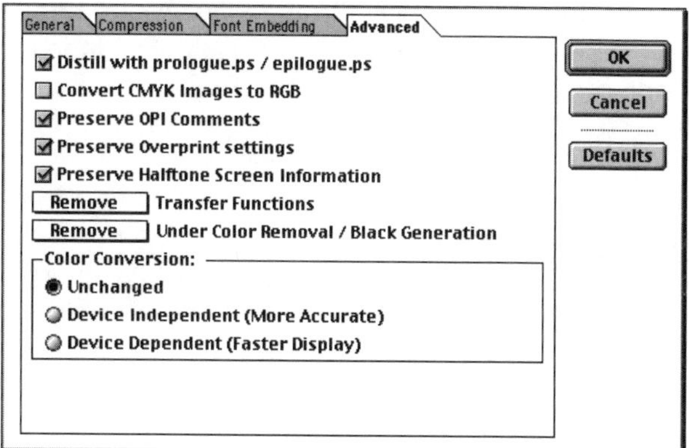

The default options in the *Advanced* tab are for online documents. These options affect the images in your document, regardless of whether you're distilling an online or a print document. If your document includes spot colors, select the *Distill with prologue.ps/epilogue.ps* Spot Colors option. (In UNIX, use the

If you want the smallest size file and don't mind font substitution, turn off Embed All Fonts *and turn on* Subset Fonts *and set it to "99 percent."*

With Embed All *turned off, Distiller will not embed any font, just their metrics to allow substitution, with one exception: if a font appears to Distiller like a non-ISO Latin font (Carta, for example), one which will be misrepresented by substitution, then Distiller will embed it, and subsetting will reduce file size because only the characters used will be saved. If you open this on a computer with the supposedly correct font, or print it to a RIP with same, the correct font will be used.*

Prepress User Note: Don't forget to remove the ***SuperATM.db*** *file from your Distiller's Fonts folder or else Distiller will fail to embed Adobe Library fonts even though you are set to* Embed All. *It will perform "silent substitution"—substituting fonts but not alerting you.*

Example: Job with 18 fonts: Bodoni, BodoniItal, BodoniUltra, etc.
Scenario 1:
Embed All Fonts—Subset Off: Resulting PDF file has 18 embedded fonts, about 300 Kb. Fonts are named Bodoni. BodoniItal, etc.
Printing Possibility 1: the local Mac has Bodoni that you've modified with Fontographer: ATM will use local Bodoni when printing even though Bodoni is embedded. Bad! Possibility 2: the RIP has Bodoni, an old version with different glyphs. The RIP will use its local version over the embedded one.
Bad! But, see next sidebar.

Scenario 2:

Embed All Fonts—Subset On, 99%: Resulting PDF file has 18 embedded subset fonts, about 100–150 Kb. Fonts are named ABCDEFG+ Bodoni, BCDEFG+ BodoniItal, etc.

Printing: Subsetted fonts have unique names and always download. Since no local or RIP font has the same name as subset font, embedded font is always used.

99 percent threshold assures that all fonts are subsetted unless 100% of the characters are used, a practical impossibility, and thus each one gets a unique name. Bulletproof printing, regardless of local state.

When Distiller is set to Embed All, *it should always embed but when* ***SuperATM.db*** *is present it may not. Exchange will always download embedded fonts (which it does when you Export PS/EPS).*

-includebookends parameter to use prologue and epilogue files.) Move the prologue.ps and epilogue.ps files from the high-end folder (in the Xtras folder) to the Acrobat Distiller folder (Macintosh), or move them from the Distiller/Xtras/High_end folder to the Distiller folder (Windows). Distiller needs these files to include spot colors in the PDF file instead of converting them to process colors.

Deselect the *Convert CMYK Images to RGB* option to prevent Distiller from converting CMYK images to RGB images. If your document includes placeholder images for Open PrePress Interface (OPI) replacement images, select the *Preserve OPI Comments* option. If you want Distiller to include the overprint settings included in the PostScript file in the PDF file it creates, select the *Preserve Overprint Settings*; if you want it to include the halftone screen information included in the PostScript file, select *Preserve Halftone Screen Information.*

You can apply, remove, or preserve Transfer functions and Under Color Removal as well as Black Generation information from your original PostScript file in the resulting PDF file. We recommend *Remove* in both cases. By choosing the *Apply* option, the options are applied to the PDF file and viewable on-screen. Once these options have been applied, they are not included in the PostScript print stream from Acrobat Exchange. If these options are needed for final print production, select *Preserve.*

In the *Color Conversion* section, select *Unchanged* to ensure no color conversion takes place. However, device-independent colors that do not map directly to calibrated RGB or LAB are converted to CIE Lab. Consult with your imaging service regarding these options.

9

THE DIGITAL WORLD

Now that you can create, view, and edit PDF files, we're going to bring it all together and discuss PDF in the job workflow environment. There's no doubt that changing customer demands are driving markets toward completely digital workflows. Every technology involved in the production and reproduction of information on paper is now electronic.

Short Run Market

Digital press technology is driving short-run, on-demand jobs, which are the ticket to the future. Printing trends are leading toward full color printing which is faster and cheaper. Entire markets have sprung up seemingly overnight. Digital color presses like the Xerox Docucolor, Agfa Chromapress, and Indigo E-Print 1000 are making inroads where traditional lithography once reigned. Making money in printing requires keeping the presses running. This is even more so for digital color presses. In order to keep them running, data must come in a reliable self-contained package that is easy to process. Because the runs are smaller, the profit margins are very tight. To make money on 300 copies of a color brochure, the workflow must be easy-in, easy out. The workflows must be virtually snag-less. PDF files have the most to offer this market. No other file format can accurately render a page in such a compact and efficient manner—font

Dynamics of Market demand

- *right person: generalized, customized, personalized*
- *right content: text, graphics, images, sound, video*
- *right time: fixed vs. continuous delivery*
- *right place: centralized, regionalized, localized*
- *right form: print, multimedia, Web-based*

Sending PDF for On-demand
You've received approval for the menu from the client and want to send a PDF file to the print shop for reproduction. Instead of e-mail though, you are going to send the file on some type of media.

Q: Should PDFWriter or Distiller be used to create the PDF?
A: Distiller is the best choice.

Q: What compression options apply?
A: Since the PDF is going to be sent via removable media, file size is no longer critical. Image quality is the deciding factor. The designer wants to ensure that all of the illustrations and images in the menu reproduce at the highest possible resolution. Downsampling is probably not a good idea. JPEG-Medium compression won't degrade image quality to unacceptable levels.

Q: Should the fonts be embedded?
A: Since this is the final output for the PDF, the designer wants to make certain of all of his/her typeface choices. Embedding the fonts is the only option.

The work is ready to be proofed. But instead of sending the QuarkXPress files with the illustrations, you send the "okayed" PDF file to the reproduction company contact person. The reproduction company now receives the single PDF file and does not need to load the typefaces or to have your version of the creating application. Instead Acrobat Exchange is used. From here the proof is output through the OPI system, where the low-resolution images are exchanged with the high-resolution versions.

formatted text, vector objects, and contone images all packaged into one neat, viewable file. United Lithograph, a commercial printer in the Boston area, uses PDF files this way to keep its Xerox Docucolor and computer-to-plate system running three shifts a day.

Designer/Printer Relationship
In order to create a seamless production environment and to best use the benefits of new reproduction technologies, there must be an efficient exchange of files throughout the entire life of the document. Partial digital workflows have dominated the exchange of files from designer to printer for quite some time, but the results are often far from seamless.

Whether you are the designer or the printer, you have most likely witnessed some very, let's just say, less than perfect situations. For instance, how many times have you opened a file, and that horrible window appeared saying, *Fonts Missing*? How many times have you begun to preflight when you realized pictures were missing? How many times did these problems occur when the job needed to be output no later than yesterday? PDF provides the solution to these nightmares.

Currently, the majority of jobs are layed out and paginated in an application such as QuarkXPress or PageMaker. The scans are either done in-house or are sent out and placed in as FPOs. Once the designer has completed the job, the client must then approve the job. From there, the job is sent to a printer where it is trapped, imposed, proofed, approved, and printed. Since the file changes hands so many times, it is essential that the file be all-inclusive and consistent. PDF may not decrease the change in hands, but it becomes the common denominator making the process easier, quicker, and more trustworthy.

Let's create a specific scenario. Imagine that you are a designer producing a menu for a restaurant chain. You have received the photographs via FedEx, have sent them to the printer to be scanned, who in turn has supplied you with the low-res images to work with for your page layout. The menu has been designed in QuarkXPress and is ready to go to your client for approval.

How do you send the job to your client? At this stage in the game, we are past the usage of faxes. Fax requires retyping, fax quality is yukky, fax is yesterday. Since this job is four colors, the client needs a more accurate representation of the design richness. Traditionally, you would send the file together with any digital artwork and illustrations back to the printer who then opens the file, and makes sure that images are correctly linked in the OPI system. Fonts, which are (hopefully) from the same supplier and have the same set of kerning information, are loaded into the system. The prepress operator then sends the file to film, makes a proof and charges you $100 for labor and material. Even if the proof is mailed directly to your client, the entire process still takes 2–3 days.

The proof is then sent back to you and for you to show the client. Of course the client will be eager to make even more corrections, but the initial soft proofs are managed with PDFs.

Not only is this a tremendous hassle, but you have already added a decent chunk of money to your client's bill. After the job gets revised, and even more proofs, it becomes obvious that there must be a faster, cheaper solution. How about PDF as a soft proof? As a designer, your job will be easier, and more importantly, you can provide a better price for your client. So, instead of sending the original application file together with pictures and illustrations to the printer for hard proofs, make a PDF file and send it to your client, who can then view the job with detail and accuracy on screen.

Creating PDF Soft Proofs
Q: PDFWriter or Distiller?
A: Distiller! Because the document uses EPS files and PDFWriter does not work with EPS files very well.

Q: Compression options?
A: Because the PDF needs to be compact to send via e-mail and is going to be viewed on screen, the images in the document should be downsampled to 72–96 dpi. JPEG medium compression could also be used to help reduce the file size.

Q: Should the fonts be embedded?
A: Chances are the client doesn't have the fonts on the receiving computer. And since the typeface choice of the menu will carry much of the "design richness" of the document, the fonts should be embedded.

Generating the Soft Proof

The generation of a soft proof (an on-screen proof, not hard copy) is not difficult, but very crucial. PDF will be your best friend if, and only if, you distill your file correctly. For a soft proof there are several things you should play close attention to:

- Preferences in Distiller
- Font Embedding
- Compression

After the PDF file is generated, you can open it in Exchange and add notes for further description or to ask about different problems or ideas you may share with the client.

Client Approval

When the client receives the PDF file it can be opened in Acrobat Reader. Acrobat uses anti-aliasing to represent the text on screen so the overall appearance will be more realistic than just looking at a faxed copy. Images on screen are not high resolution. After the client reviews and approves the design, it's time to send the file to the printer.

The Repurposing Market

Repurposing is emerging as an integral part of digital workflows. Web publishing and CD-ROM publishing become another step in addition to print media. Rather than being an alternative to print, they are complementary formats. PDF files customized for the Web or CD-ROM can be created using the same PostScript that generated a print version PDF. Through the use of customized drop folders discussed in Chapter 5, PDF files can be customized for their intended delivery—print, Web, CD-ROM, or e-mail. If your job is Web bound you want to make sure that download times are as short as possible. Some suggestions for setting specific compression job options in Distiller:

- ***Print***—*print and distribute—an old model slowly changing*
- ***Digital media***—*replicate and distribute—like print, only send a disk*
- ***Networked print***—*distribute and print—lots of potential with new digital printers*
- ***Networked digital media***—*display and transact—the Web-based model*

File
- Acrobat 2.1 compatible

Images
- High JPEG compression for gray and color images
- Downsampling to 72 dpi for gray and color images
- CCITT Group 4 compression for monochrome line art
- Downsample monochrome line art illustrations to 300 dpi
- Convert separated CMYK images to RGB

Fonts
- Choose not to embed fonts unless important to the design
- If a big headline is used, include a subset for that font

The Advertising Market

After looking at the issues for PDF and its application to the designer/printer relationship, a focus shift to yet another market segment—advertisement distribution—is in order. The distribution of advertisements is filled with different scenarios, but an overriding paranoia on document integrity has always been present in advertising. It is this need for integrity that led the newspaper industry to reproduce ads on films or veloxes, then physically ship them to each individual newspaper. If you are distributing to hundreds of newspapers, this can be both time-consuming and expensive.

Newspaper Advertising

Even with the onslaught of other media, newspapers still remain a potent advertising market for retailers to sell their goods and services. According to a Newspaper Association of America (NAA) report, $36 billion dollars were spent on newspaper advertising in 1995. That figure accounts for about 22 percent of all money spent on advertising in 1995. Required delivery time poses a problem for advertiser lead time. To guarantee delivery by press time, advertisers must have completed ads ready to be reproduced at least three days prior to insertion. That cuts a lot of flexibility out of their advertising message... especially in today's "just-in-time" business world. And on top of that, shipping ads overnight to 100 newspapers could cost over $1,000. Also, not a practical solution.

World Digitization

As the world began digitizing in the 1990s, advertisers and newspapers looked for a way to integrate the ad delivery process into a digital workflow. Retailers realized that they could save thousands of dollars in reproduction costs by delivering digital ads to newspapers. Initially, advertisers began sending original application files to newspapers via disk media. However, this brought up the problem of reliability. Films and veloxes were reliable. The digital realm at this time was not.

Digital Growing Pains

While the entire graphic arts industry experienced these digital growing pains, the effects were especially hard on newspapers. If a printer had a problem with a digital file, he/she could reschedule the job. If a newspaper couldn't print a digital file, that revenue was lost for that edition. If the ad was about a "One-Day-Only" sale, the revenue was irrevocably lost. So, both the newspaper and the advertiser lost. Why not send PostScript files? This is also impractical because PostScript files are generally written for a specific output device. If an advertiser has to generate customized PostScript streams for each newspaper, they might as well send films. Sending films would be more productive and certainly more reliable than sending huge customized files to newspapers. On top of file format problems, delivering the ads was still a problem, when sending veloxes or removable media. The ad still had to be shipped through expensive ground or air delivery. The newspaper industry needed a file format that was self-contained, cross-platform, reliable, and

PDF for Ad Delivery?
Is PDF a standard for digital ad delivery? The answer is no, but it has the potential to become one. Currently the only ANSI & ISO standard is the TIFF/IT P1 format. TIFF/IT is also endorsed by the Digital Distribution of Advertising for Publications Association (DDAP).

Some publishers, like Time, Inc., have embraced the TIFF/IT standard. Time will accept ads in PostScript but recommends TIFF/IT. Time will not accept ads as application files. The problem with TIFF/IT is that it is raster only (in other words a bunch of pointless pixels). Last minute changes are impractical and difficult. While some consider the uneditability a good thing, it can have drawbacks.

For instance, a TIFF/IT ad is sent via modem to 100 hundred newspapers with a wrong phone number in it. How do you solve the problem?

1. *Edit the TIFF/IT LW file in a raster editor like Photoshop. (Sounds easy, but did you ever try it?)*
2. *Print films from the TIFF/IT file and have the newspapers strip in the correction.*
3. *Correct the mistake at the originator site and resend to all 100 newspapers.*

None of the solutions is practical especially in a deadline situation. What if the same situation happened with a PDF file? Solution:

Open the PDF ad in Exchange and use the Text Touch-Up tool to

compact enough to be transmitted quickly. (Can you see where this is headed?)

The PDF format provided the newspaper advertising community a reliable way to economically and quickly reproduce digital newspaper ads. With reliability, fast turnaround, and cheap reproduction out of the way, inexpensive distribution became the focus. The Associated Press was the first to really tackle this issue.

AdSend
Beginning in 1993, the Associated Press began offering a digital ad delivery system to newspapers. Since most newspapers were already receiving some type of AP data, either photo or copy, why not send ads using the same distribution system? AP chose to use PDF as the file format.

The Associated Press is now sending 70,000 ads a month to newspapers in PDF form. The 955 member newspapers either print the pages directly or use the "Export to EPS" to place their ads in their pages. At peak, 2,000 ads a day are handled. Included in the AdSend workflow is a job ticket which gives the newspaper information regarding the size, placement, and run dates for the ad.

While being used mostly for black-and-white ads, some retailers have used color. Boscov's, a retail-store chain centered in Reading, PA, began sending pre-separated color ads in early 1996 using Distiller 2.1. This is even more effective now because Distiller 3.0 can embed halftone screen information.

The workflow is identical to traditional workflows until output. At output, the advertiser or agency generates a PDF file instead of film. This PDF file is sent along with a job ticket and a list of selected newspapers to the AdSend site. Once received, the PDF is distributed to the desired newspapers.

Delivery Criteria
To be successful, a digital ad delivery system must be able to meet four criteria—low material costs, low transportation costs,

fast turnaround time, and reliability. PDF meets all of these criteria:

- Low Material Costs: Films or veloxes are generated at the printing site instead of the distribution site.
- Low Transportation Costs: Sending data via telecommunications, be it ISDN, modem, or satellite, is much cheaper than sending hundreds of overnight packages.
- Fast Turnaround: Ads can sent at the last minute and still be relatively on time.
- Reliability: Because fonts and images can be embedded, all necessary components are available for output.

The Archiving Market

How many times have you wished you hadn't trashed a file or a document? Archiving is critical for a printer. It serves as a history of completed work. After a job has been printed, it is not just thrown away. What if the client needs a reprint? In traditional workflows, archiving is storing the physical consumables such as the films or plates.

Stacks of films and plates pile high and soon you have rooms fully consumed by this archival method. Space is real estate and real estate is money. Since markets are driven by making money, printers are looking to digital archiving.

Digital archiving is the way to go for archiving documents that are electronically composed, as most are today. As magazines and newspapers migrate to complete electronic pagination on systems that support PostScript, they have the opportunity to create an archive of pages for printing, faxing, reprinting, or viewing on the screen. The real question is what format should be stored?

Some may choose the original application file, such as Quark or PageMaker. This raises longevity concerns since application versions are constantly being upgraded. The other choice is to store the PostScript file. This can also be messy due to the huge file size and the near impossibility of editability. The goal of archiving is to save the file that can be repurposed or reprinted.

correct the wrong phone number. Done!

Currently, the ANSI-sponsored Committee for Graphic Arts Technology Standards (CGATS) Subcommittee 6 is working on a standard which would utilize PDF as the delivery vehicle for digital print jobs.

As Acrobat 3.0 continues to improve, full color ads could be sent as composites and then be separated by the newspaper or exported as EPS and placed on the composite news page. In addition, Acrobat 3.0's forms capability could be used as an interface to the newspaper's ad scheduling system. Ads could be delivered to a newspaper, be automatically scheduled, exported as EPS files, and pulled into QuarkXPress or PageMaker page templates.

If there are fonts that are crucial to the look and feel of your document, or are of a large enough size that the simulated fonts will be very noticeable, make sure they are embedded. Since the file may be sent via e-mail, the size should remain as small as possible, but you do want your client to get a clear representation of the design.

Compression, especially of continuous tone images, will play a large role in the file. A 30-megabyte picture transmitted on an Internet connection of 10K per second will take fifty minutes to send. If a medium JPEG compression is applied, time will be reduced, to an average ten minute transfer.

TIFF/IT stands for Tag Image File Format for Image Technology. TIFF/IT files come in four flavors: LW for linework and type, CT for continuous tone images, HC for high-resolution contone information, and FP for merging the previous three into a single page. Because the files offer low editability and high reliability, TIFF/IT is oftentimes referred to as "digital film."

PDF Archiving

Using PDF as the storage medium for archiving print jobs allows the customer, the printer sales rep, or the printer to see a history of past jobs. Some commercial printers have been archiving PDF versions for use by print sales reps. The files are kept on a central server which allows the reps to view a history of jobs printed for a given client. So instead of having a huge file cabinet of printed jobs in a storeroom, the rep can access a copy of the job from his/her desk.

Other Archiving

PDF is a natural file format for archiving digital documents. They are not only predictable, but they are considerably smaller in file size than other digital options. Books in PDF form could be connected to a text retrieval system and used for research purposes. With an Acrobat-based approach, users could retrieve whole pages, with graphics in place, not just text. Reference publishers who need to keep an archive of revisable text might also want an Acrobat archive for reprints, but they would probably maintain that archive alongside an editorial database.

As commercial (and even corporate) printing and publishing worlds migrate towards increasing reliance on digital methods, what are and where are the markets going to be? In a landmark study of digital workflow, visionary industry analyst Mills Davis predicted a new world order where automated information factories churn out new products and deliver them in new ways.

Core markets for printing and publishing will remain substantially intact into the 21st century. While the quantity of commercial printing and publishing may gradually level over the next decade, the quality of demand will change rapidly. Networked interactive media and information will grow rapidly over the next five years, but measured by advertising revenues, digital media will still be less than 10 percent of print media. Most categories of printing and publishing now have print, digital media, networked printing, and networked interactive product alternatives.

The most important change is not the displacement of print to nonprint media, but the evolution of printing and publishing processes from craft-based manufacturing to computer, and communications-based services. New categories of demand are emerging as key attributes of printing and publishing products are redefined. The dynamic of market demand is about new ways to reach the right person, with the right content, at the right time, in the right place, in the right form for intended uses.

According to a 1994 study by the Sterling Resource Group, film costs for advertisers ran up to $11 for a single-color film. At that rate, sending a single, full-color ad to 100 newspapers would cost $4,400 in reproduction costs alone.

Changing Business Conditions

The printing and publishing business environment is changing. An emerging digital economy is restructuring the industry as well as transforming relationships both within and between customers, service providers, and suppliers. The need for rapid innovation and rapid response to changing markets are facts of business life. The emerging digital infrastructure will propel interbusiness communication, workflow, and content management to new levels of performance, flexibility, and service. The business of printing and publishing wants to be real-time, with zero lag time between identification and fulfillment of need. Advantage will go to companies that, together with their customers, providers, and suppliers, move information better and respond more quickly to changing market needs than their competition.

Metaphors for printing and publishing workflows include "the market of one," "just in time printing and publishing," "mass-customization of media," "on-demand," and "1-to-1 communications." To address emerging market requirements, printing and publishing workflows will need a higher metabolism in order to be more responsive to customers, with failsafe quality, faster, more flexible and just-in-time delivery, with the capability of handling an increasing volume of smaller transactions profitably. Printing and publishing processes must and will be reengineered to provide the level of performance required by new categories of demand as measured by cost, quality, service, speed, and flexibility.

The need for more rapid response to changing markets, better service, higher quality, lower costs, and greater flexibility are driving businesses in the printing and publishing industry to restructure and to reinvent the way they do business. To drive out costs and reduce processing latency, industries and businesses must take steps to compress their value chain.

Networked Digital Workflows

The focus is on process reengineering to achieve rapid response, short cycle time, quality fail-safeing, online customer service, low transaction costs, low materials usage, minimum inventory costs, and minimum distribution costs. Networked digital workflows introduce new forms of printing and publishing, conducting all business over the Internet and intranets, establishing print networks for distributed printing, publishing, and document management services, and supporting both "push" and "pull" demand models.

Content can be either "pushed" or "pulled" through the network from databases. High performance networked systems with links to databases make variable page, personalized, and custom content an option. Through printing networks, the distribute-and-print model emerges as an alternative to print-and-distribute. Internetworking business enables lean, flexible printing and publishing with just-in-time, on-demand delivery. As customer, provider, and suppliers internetwork and make information and systems interoperable, they can molecularize to achieve minimum inventories and processing costs, as well as more rapid response to changing market conditions.

Specific networked workflows will vary depending on the type of business, its markets, technology base, and the roles it chooses to play in the networked digital process. Networked digital workflows support a richer and more coordination-intensive information logistics in which content, workflow, and business information streams are fully integrated. Digitization begins sooner in the process, ends later, and encompasses more of the total communication and information flow between businesses than has ever been possible with analog or digital analog workflows. All business-to-business communication and as much work-in-process as possible is handled across networks.

Customers can inquire through the Net, learn how to prepare jobs, obtain estimates, submit work, determine status, and conduct business transactions. Workflow quality fail-safeing begins by aligning processes across the value flow to head off problems, and by communicating preliminary specifications to all affected parties before ever producing the job. Prepress services, printers, binderies, and fulfillment services, for example, could simulate the job; suggest alternatives to customers; estimate and quote production; and provide job-specific instructions, plug-ins, color profiles, business forms, and applets to handle preflight at the customer site. Before transmitting a job (such as a digital advertisement) the source files could be prechecked to ensure not only that the PDF would process correctly, but also that content elements had been made to the correct specifications for the application, medium, and reproduction process.

Networked digital content creation adds digital photography to the repertoire of digital-analog techniques. All input capture devices will evolve into color-managed network appliances. As the price performance of desktop tools to manipulate image and graphic content and master pages continues to improve, new levels of capability emerge for feature-based content editing, cross-media authoring and meta-design, and variable and custom data merge, to name a few. Many applications will be re-engineered to function as software objects across Internet and intranet front-ends.

Prepress, printing, and post-press functions will become increasingly automated processes across networks. Incoming work will be digitally logged into content, workflow, and business transaction databases, triggering credit checks, content file preflighting, scheduling, and resource allocation. Digital job specifications will provide the information needed to program individual prepress, press, and post-press operations. Networked digital process steps will be threaded, multitasked, or concurrently executed as needed, with status updates posted to a common database visible to everyone concerned. Even offline functions will be coordinated digitally.

One of the hallmarks of networked digital workflows will be color-managed digital printing, proofing, and remote proofing. The defining application will be digital advertising in newspapers, magazines, and catalogs. Pigment-based ink-jet printing may provide a near-term breakthrough towards direct proofing on actual stock with colorants that behave like inks on press. Prep will move from files, imagesetters, and imposetters toward databases, variable and custom data merge, and computer-to-film, computer-to-plate, and computer-to-press. The benefits of moving to an integrated content, workflow and business database are major, impacting operations upstream as well as downstream. The benefits of computer-to… are basically incremental and depend on successful front-end integration of the digital workflow that feeds the prep step.

Changing Workflows

The series of charts on the following pages show how the integration of PDF into current prepress workflows will streamline those workflows.

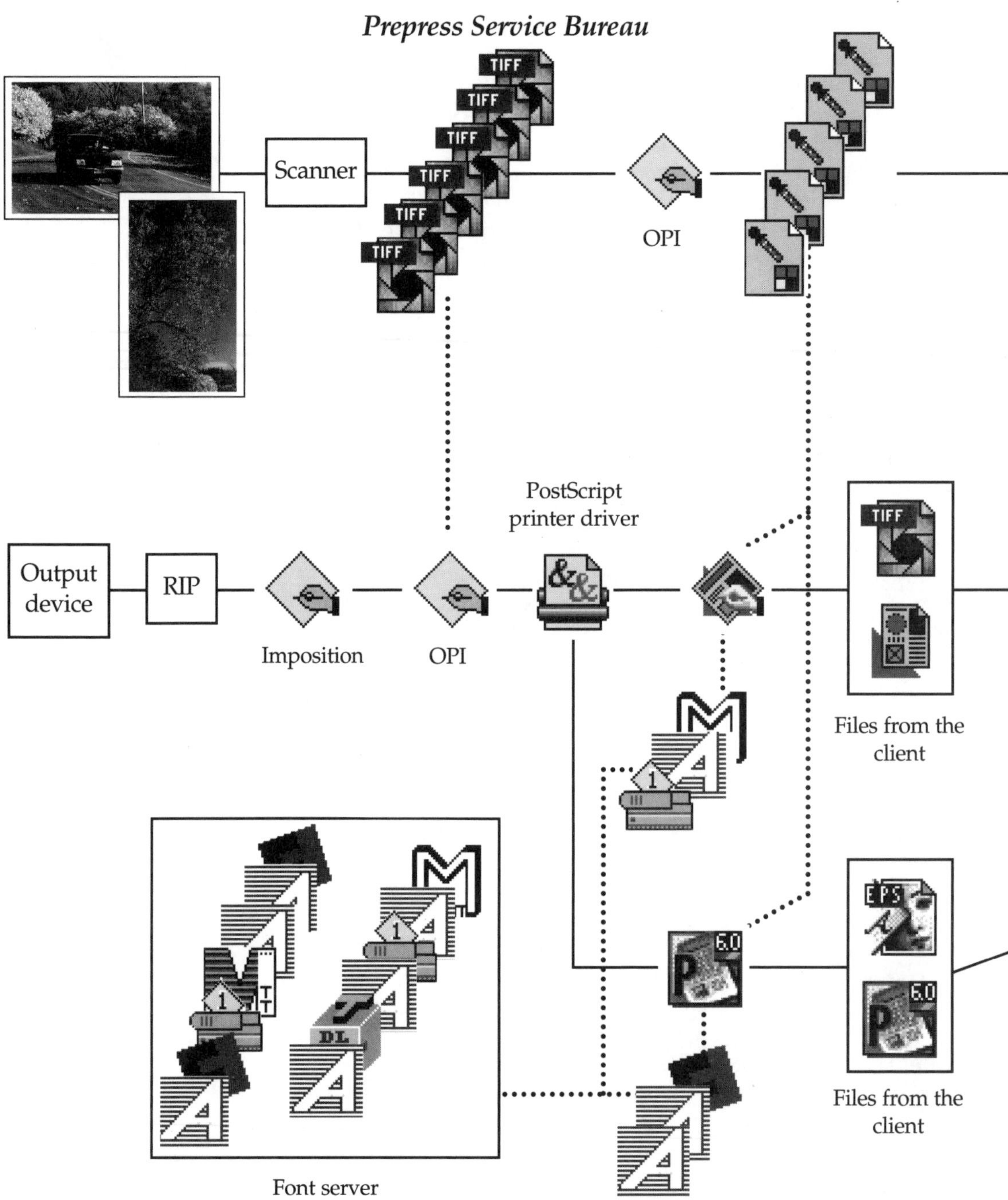
Prepress Service Bureau
Scanner
TIFF
OPI
PostScript
printer driver
Output
device
RIP
Imposition
OPI
Files from the
client
6.0
EPS
Files from the
client
DL
Font server

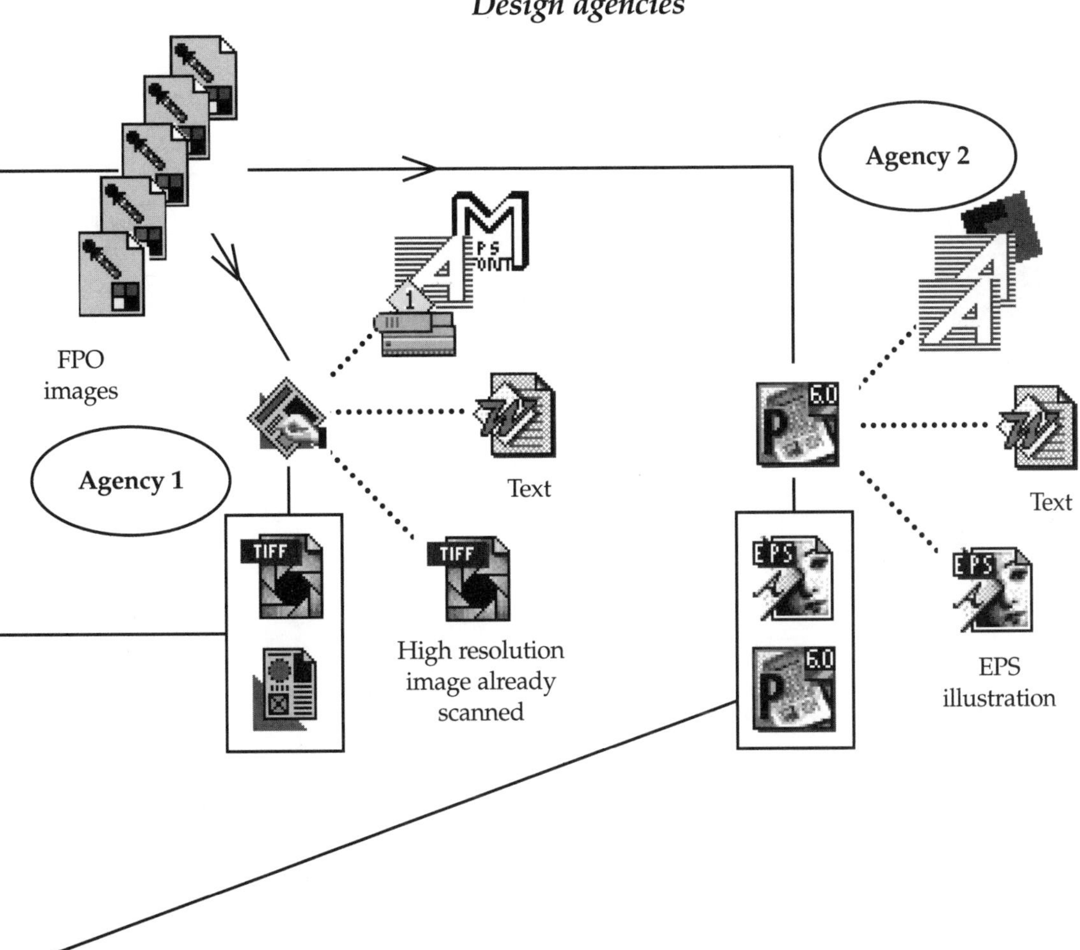

Traditional digital prepress workflow between prepress service bureaus and their clients

Pictures are sent from clients to the reproduction company where they are scanned and placed in the OPI server. FPO images are sent back to the clients, via disk e-mail, or FTP site, where they are placed into a layout program. The client may also include pictures that they have had previously scanned in high resolution (for instance, images from a previous job.) These non-FPO images together with the layout file are sent back to the reproduction company. Because of legal ramifications, fonts cannot be included. This forces the service bureau to purchase a large font library to ensure that it can meet client typographic needs.

When the service bureau receives the files from the client, the file is opened in the application where the font is used and which the reproduction or service bureau company owns, and is loaded into the system. The job is printed through the OPI server and then sent to the RIP and imaged. PDF solves most font problems.

Prepress Service Bureau

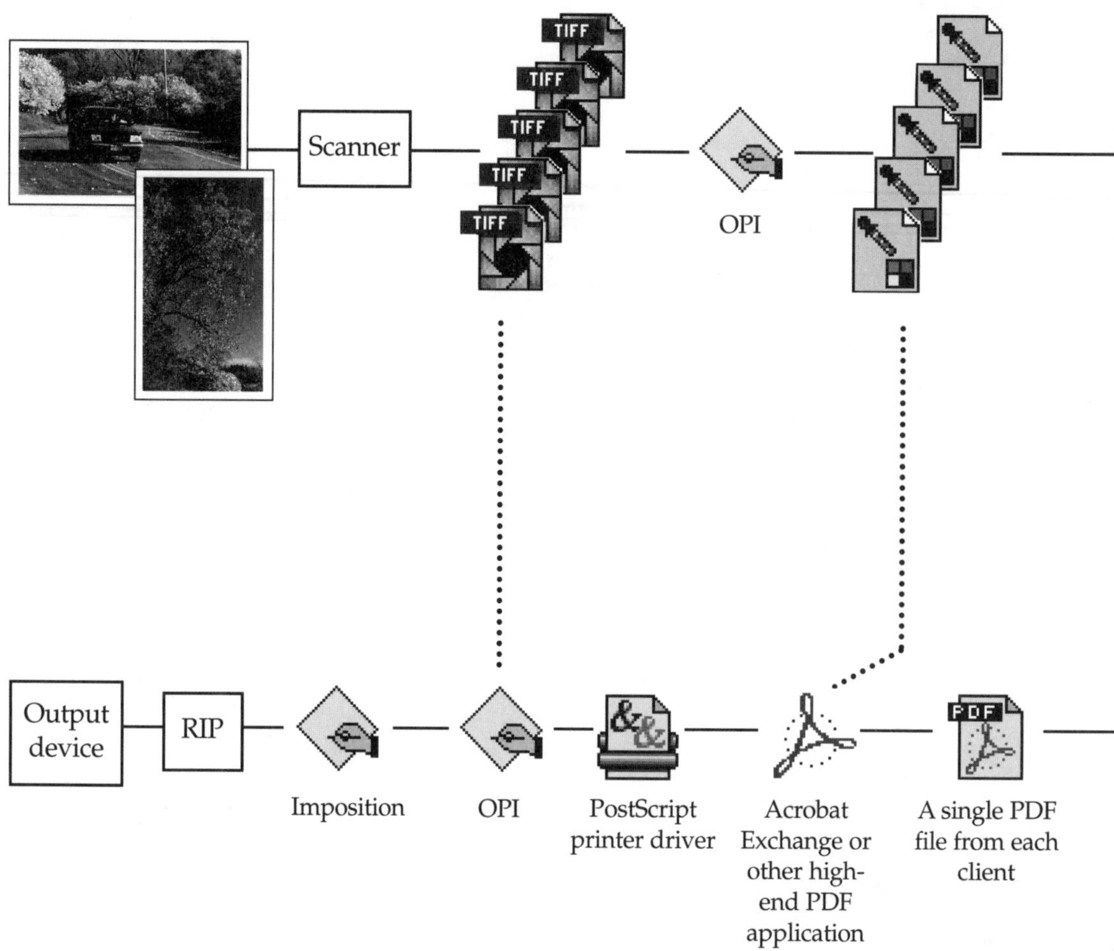

Design agencies

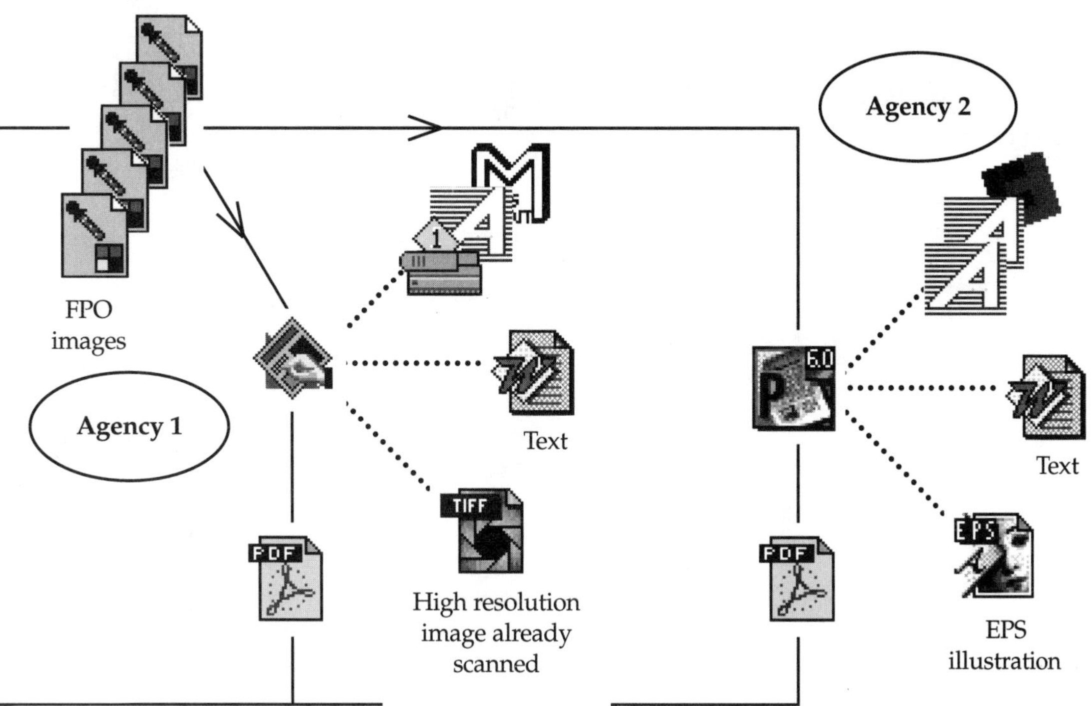

Digital prepress workflow when using PDF files

As in the traditional workflow, the reproduction or service bureau company sends FPO images to the client. The client uses the layout application of their choice. When it is time to send the work back to the services company a PDF file is generated. Because the PDF file includes all fonts and images, only one application-independent file is sent. This means creative people need to learn to make good PDFs.

At the services company a PDF compatible print application is used, for example Acrobat Exchange, with the plug-in Extended Print Services. From here separations can be output with registration marks to the OPI server where the FPO images are replaced with high-resolution images. Further, the service bureau may use an imposition system before the data is sent to the RIP and imaged.

Prepress Service Bureau

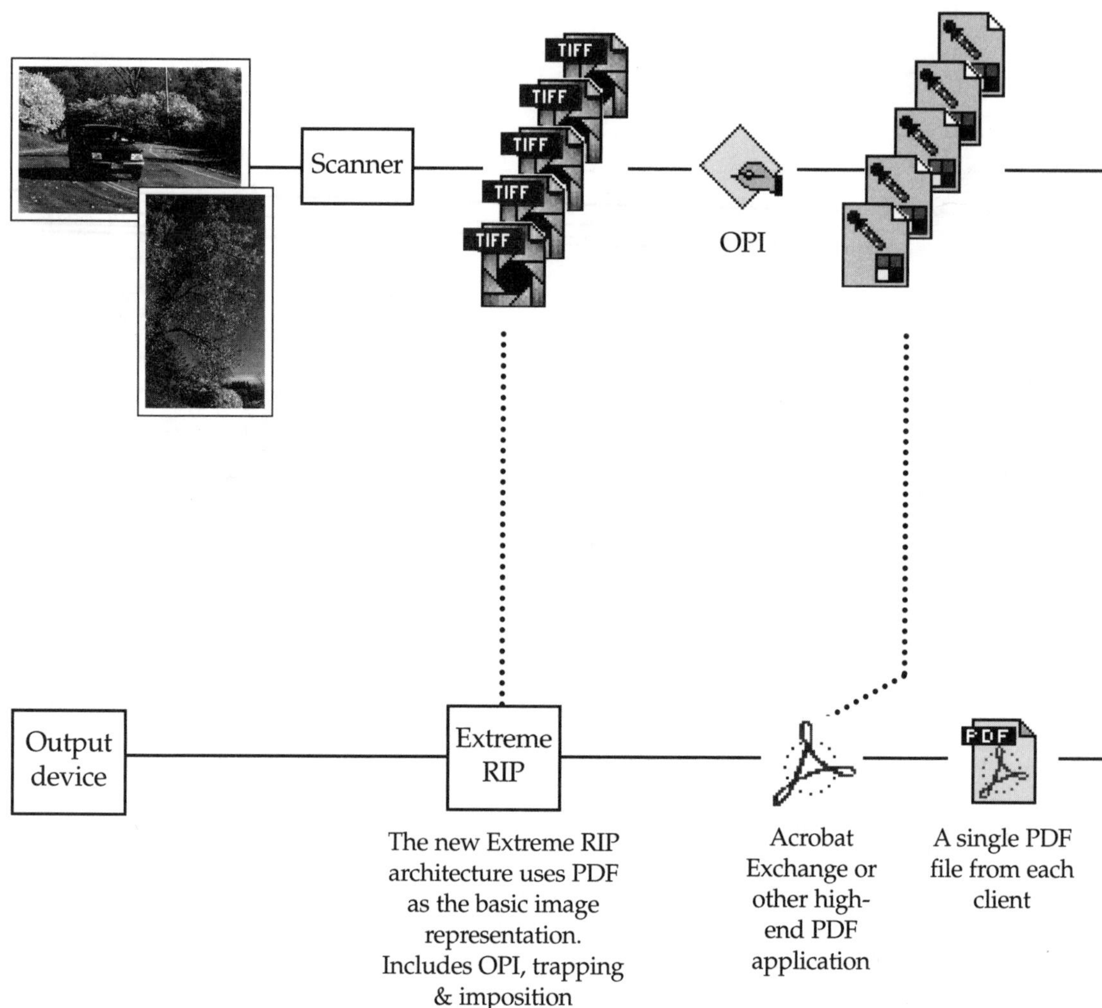

The new Extreme RIP architecture uses PDF as the basic image representation. Includes OPI, trapping & imposition

Acrobat Exchange or other high-end PDF application

A single PDF file from each client

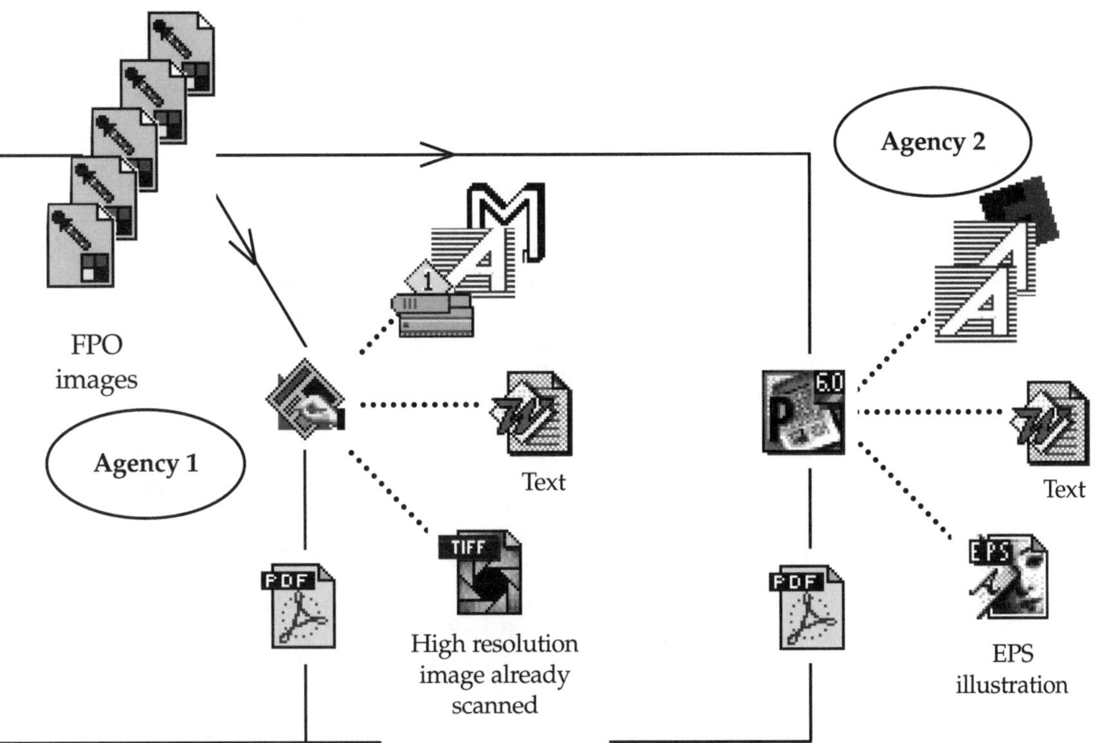

Digital prepress workflow when using PDF files and Extreme

As a continuation of the PDF workflow, Adobe announced a new RIP systems architecture, called PostScript Extreme. The major difference is that Extreme can handle both PostScript and PDF information it "normalizes" PostScript to PDF. The new RIP architecture is also *multitasking,* which means that several pages can be RIPped simultaneously. The pages can then be "coordinated" for imaging on a high-end output devices. Best of all, high-speed printers can operate at full speed.

Network digital workflow leverage all kinds of printing output—analog sheet-fed or web-fed, offset, gravure, and flexo presses, and hybrid presses as well as digital ones. Specifications have been developed for digitally-driven press rooms and digitally-coordinated binderies. These workflows enable multiple distribute-and-print and on-demand printing models as well as print-and-distribute. Networked digital workflow management is based on new control structures.

Integration across multiple businesses is achieved through open network infrastructure standards, shared process semantics, application-level content specifications, standard file and database formats, and industry standards for electronic data interchange. Distributive workflows are coordinated through network communications to common (synchronized) databases containing evolving content and product information, workflow schedule and current job status, business relationship and financial data, and management information.

Networked digital content management involves file formats, standard page description languages, and digital archives with dedicated librarian applications to index, search, and retrieve data. Multipurposing requires maintaining multiple versions of source content. Networked digital business systems are fully integrated with work-in-process and content management. Electronic data interchange and, in some instances, electronic commerce are standard operating procedure.

Quantum improvements in printing and publishing workflow are possible by combining principles of business process reengineering with architectures for distributive workflow, integrated business systems, and media-independent content management. The PDF is unique in that it is both the product and the enabler of this new world order. As a product it is the view file delivered on disk or over the Web. The information consumer receives their content in a format-rich form where type and image are preserved. As an enabler, the PDF is the raw material of new workflows that re-engineer the way we print or present. In the history of human communication there has never been a method that could be so totally repurposed, reused, replayed, and even regurgitated on demand.

10

THE DIGITAL DOCUMENT

It all comes down to how you want to distribute information. This is our opinion chapter. It's not as far out as blue sky and not as close as down-to-earth. Let's start by saying that TIFF-IT and other bitmap files are just a dumb buckets of bits. They cannot help you repurpose information into other media. They cannot help you drive different output devices from the same data. They cannot get you on the Web. They can be archived but there isn't much you can do with them when they come out of hibernation—especially if you have changed output devices in the meantime. They cannot be read on different platforms—or even any platform. They are just a dumb buckets of bits. It is WYGIWYD—what you get is what you deserve.

According to the Sterling study, common problems in digital distribution included:
- *Missing fonts*
- *Corrupt files*
- *Missing graphic elements*
- *Lack of accuracy*
- *Variation in application software*
- *Use of software extensions not available at the newspaper*

Some commercial printers like bitmap files because they see them as the digital equivalent of film—unchanging, unchangeable. But they will soon find that the world of information dissemination is fickle. It wants what it wants when it wants it. That means print today and electronic publishing tomorrow. Proof on one device now and a remote proofer later. Print on an ink jet machine today and an offset press next week. Bitmap workflows were a reaction to the eccentricities of PostScript. They were a good idea at the time but now there is PDF.

Who owns TIFF?
TIFF was developed by Aldus and Microsoft, and the specification was owned by Aldus, which merged with Adobe, which may hold the copyright for the TIFF specification. TIFF is a trademark, formerly registered to Aldus, which is now probably claimed by Adobe but is not listed on their Web trademark page.

The TIFF format permits both MSB ("Motorola") and LSB ("Intel") byte order data to be stored, with a header item indicating which order is used. There are old, poorly written TIFF programs on the PC that assume that all TIFF files are Intel byte order. It is easy to write a TIFF-writer, but very difficult to write a fully TIFF-compliant reader.

TIFF uses 4-byte integer file offsets to store image data, but a TIFF file cannot have more than 4 gigabytes of raster data (and some files have begun to approach this boundary). This is 4Gb of compressed data, and so if the compression ratio is high enough, theoretically a TIFF image could be much larger.

There are problems with TIFF/IT-P1 that need to be addressed, such as support for spot colors (including names of color channels and CMYK simulation values), a palette that should be increased from 256 to 65,535 colors, and compression supported in CT (Packbits, LZW, Flate). There is also a need to convert from PS/PDF to TIFF and back to PS/EPSF. Also proofing and format verification tools are needed.

PDFs are smart files. They carry each element—text, images—as both a separate and an integrated unit. You can keep the file intact or break it apart. You can set and then reset color management information. You can read it and print it anywhere at almost any time. Only PDFs meet the demands for CD-ROM (and DVD-ROM), Web and print publishing. PDFs and PDF workflows are the future of printing and publishing.

PostScript—The Almost Standard

The world of digital prepress and digital printing exists because of PostScript. Although it is the "standard" for driving almost every high-end printing device, it has never been a standard standard. It is a de facto standard, which means that everyone uses it as a standard but no one want to admit it is a standard.

The PDF takes PostScript to a higher level. It removes the variability. It virtually pre-RIPs the document to speed its progress through the workflow. PostScript Extreme is an architecture with a lot of little RIPs distributed throughout the system. It divides and conquers. Think of Extreme and such systems as Hydra, the mythological creature with seven heads. By the way, it had one main head as well.

Now, add in the functionality of trapping and imposition and OPI and hot folders and more—the PDF-based workflow that Agfa is assembling as an example—and you have one of the most efficient methods for moving jobs around an electronic system.

The Present

This book was our attempt to centralize much of our research about the Acrobat PDF in one place at one time. We have provided tips and tricks on how it works and how you can apply it for high-end printing. A smattering of information on RIPs and systems and workflows has been included because the PDF does not stand alone. It is a part of a system, a piece of the whole.

There is still a lot to come. Plug-ins will proliferate. New systems will evolve. Functionality will improve. Hopefully this book will provide the foundation for your use of the PDF and an understanding of its place in the digital printing world of today and tomorrow.

The Future
There are lots of ideas in the printing and publishing industries about how work will flow through automated systems.

- CIP3 stands for Consortium International Prepress, Press, and Postpress and it is being developed by the Fraunhofer Institute for Computer Graphics in Darmstadt, Germany with a number of industry suppliers involved. The effort was initiated by Heidelberg. The goal is to link the prepress, press, and postpress parts of the process into one cohesive system. Where does PDF fit in? Plug in! We think you will see plug-ins for many special purposes and the links between all print-related functions makes sense.
- Magazines and newspapers will finally get digital ads. Some might be bitmaps until the comfort level with PDF grows. DDAP will go PDF as ad agencies discover its power and prepress services discover the many new value-added services they can provide. Like converting the print version of an ad to a Web version. OK, the format and size might be a problem. But new conversion programs might convert the ad into something more appropriate for the Web.

PDF is cross-platform compatible—MS-DOS, MacOS, Windows, and UNIX. Outline font information is embedded within the document, potentially resolving font problems. Postscript files can be distilled to PDF and PDF files can be previewed on a monitor for verification prior to printing. However, until the 3.0 version of Acrobat was announced on June 3, 1996 there were several major limitations to Adobe Acrobat:
- It was incapable of handling CMYK data.
- Incompatibility with OPI precluded workflows employing high resolution images.
- Printing attributes, color management data, and resolution were not be included in the file.
- Embedded EPS files created unworkable situations.

Now digital ads are a reality.

Consortium International Prepress, Press, and Postpress
The CIP3 group has released version 2.0 of its Print Production Format (PPF) description for the standardization of communicating digital data between prepress, press, and postpress (finishing) equipment. Version 2.0 includes several additions and improvements, a result of continued dialogue between the CIP3 members and the information obtained from beta sites of CIP3 users. The main differences between version 1.0 and 2.0 are in the areas of compression techniques available for images, used to generate ink setting information, and more detailed descriptions on how PostScript is used. For the postpress or finishing data generation the folding information has been positioned in a separate structure providing more direct access.

Version 2.0 specifications of the CIP3 PPF are available from Fraunhofer-IGD at http://www.igd.fhg.de/www/igda1/cip3.

Currently the members of CIP3 are: Adobe, Agfa, Barco, Creo, Crosfield, Ekotrading-Inkflow, Eltromat Polygraph, Ewert Ahrensburg Electronic, Goebel, Harlequin, Heidelberg, Koenig & Bauer-Albert, Kolbus, Komori, Linotype-Hell, MAN-Roland, Mitsubishi Heavy Industries, Müller Martini, Polar Mohr, Scitex, Screen, Ultimate, and Wohlenberg.

We predict that CIP3 will be incorporated into PDF encoding.

Problems with Digital Files

Inadequate instructions	51%
No proof	44%
Unspecified fonts	38%
Nonprintable fonts	19%
Unspecified file types or software version	37%
Missing images	36%
Proof not latest version	31%
Improper bleeds	35%
Improper page size	32%
Unspecified embedded graphics	31%
Incorrect trapping	19%
Proof not a verifiable color proof	18%
Unspecified color	16%

These limitations are addressed in Acrobat 3.0 and 3.0x. Magazines could be in a position to accept PDF files for ads and send PDFs for computer-to-plate. With such a file format standard in place the next step will be to build a series of recommendations/specifications for the submission of ads, including instructions, media, resolution, fonts, colors, page sizes, etc.

Future Speculations

- Color management will become a no-brainer. Color management is like the weather; everyone talks about it but no one has really done anything about it. There are partial solutions out there but they are just 10-foot logs trying to ford a 12-foot stream.
- Acrobat will not be the only PDF kid on the block anymore. Third party vendors will create PDF writers, readers, editors, and printers. Remember, Acrobat is only the interface, not the format. So, from now on say a PDF file, not an Acrobat file.
- CGATS will continue to push TIFF-IT as a standard and perhaps it will play some role in the future. A walk-on.
- Within a few years there may not be PostScript as we know it—only PDF.
- Where functions are performed in future workflows may not be an issue. OPI, trapping, imposition, and other functions can be done before the RIP, in the RIP, or beyond the RIP. The RIP will be just another function in an automated workflow. The RIP-centric world will change to a PDF-centric world.

- "Computer-to" approaches will continue to accelerate, mandating new workflows that automate individual processes. In the printing plant of the past people spent a lot of time carrying things around—disks, films, plates, proofs, job folders, and more. In the printing plant of the future the only carrying-on will be over a cable. Or maybe in the lunch room.
- PDF editing applications will abound. Because of PDF's object-oriented structure, you will be able to move objects (text, images, line art) around the page like a page layout application. You will be able to open a PDF file and move the objects on the page. So, when the client says, "Can you move that up a smidge?," you can.
- Standards will continue to evolve. There may always be a disparity between what the standards groups create and what the industry actually uses. Our problem has not been that we do not have standards; our problem is that we have too many of them.
- The operative word may be "remote." Creative professionals will send view files to clients; clients will send annotated files back. Final documents will be sent to graphic services; remote proofing data will be sent back. The graphic arts firm of the future will be a wired wonder.
- It's the PDF, stupid. By now you are getting tired of the term. And our comments about it. But keep in mind that it only takes one technology to make an industry. The lowly PDF will revitalize print by making it easier for people to get to print. And beyond.

And look for the following areas to be improved in upcoming iterations of Acrobat:

- Better handling of TrueType fonts.
- Handling of trapping (QuarkXPress, for instance, only includes trapping with separations, but omits the Overprint operator in composite output).
- Improvement in handling some word processing files.
- Increase in maximum page size from 45 inches square to four times that to support large format printing.
- Better handling of color monochrome images (which we now convert to EPS in Photoshop).
- Incorporation of CIP3 data in the PDF.

Traps from Quark or Illustrator not showing up on my output.
These programs output the overprint commands for traps only when "separations" are chosen at print time. These separations are "split" into separate pages by Acrobat Distiller, thereby removing many of the benefits of a PDF workflow. Overprint commands from these creation applications are not included for composite color output. Composite color files take maximum advantage of Acrobat's benefits. To trap these PDF files, output them from Crackerjack as composite color PostScript files and use downstream prepress applications.

Where are my spot colors?
Spot colors only show up on the Crackerjack Color tab when they exist in the PDF document. If you expect spot colors and still don't see them, the problem is likely in the way the PDF file was created. When Distilling color PostScript files, ensure that the "Distill with prologue.ps/epilogue.ps" option is turned on in the Distiller Job Options, Advanced *dialog. In order for this to work you need to first move the prologue.ps and epilogue.ps files from the "XTras:High-end" folder into the same folder as the Distiller application. Depending on whether you are using the Windows or Macintosh versions of Distiller, the "High-end" folder is located at different places within the Acrobat 3 folder.*

Merging several sources of information to a single PDF file

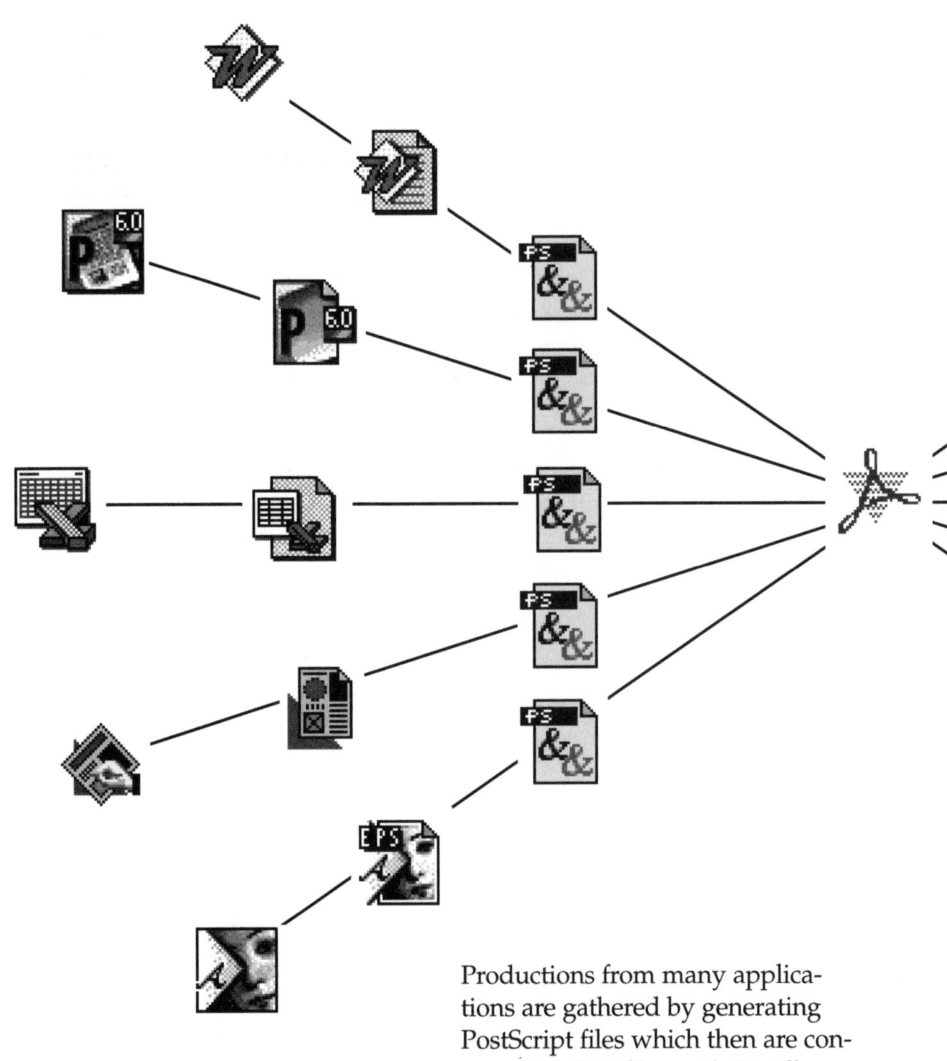

Productions from many applications are gathered by generating PostScript files which then are converted to PDF files with Distiller. These can then be merged into one big PDF.

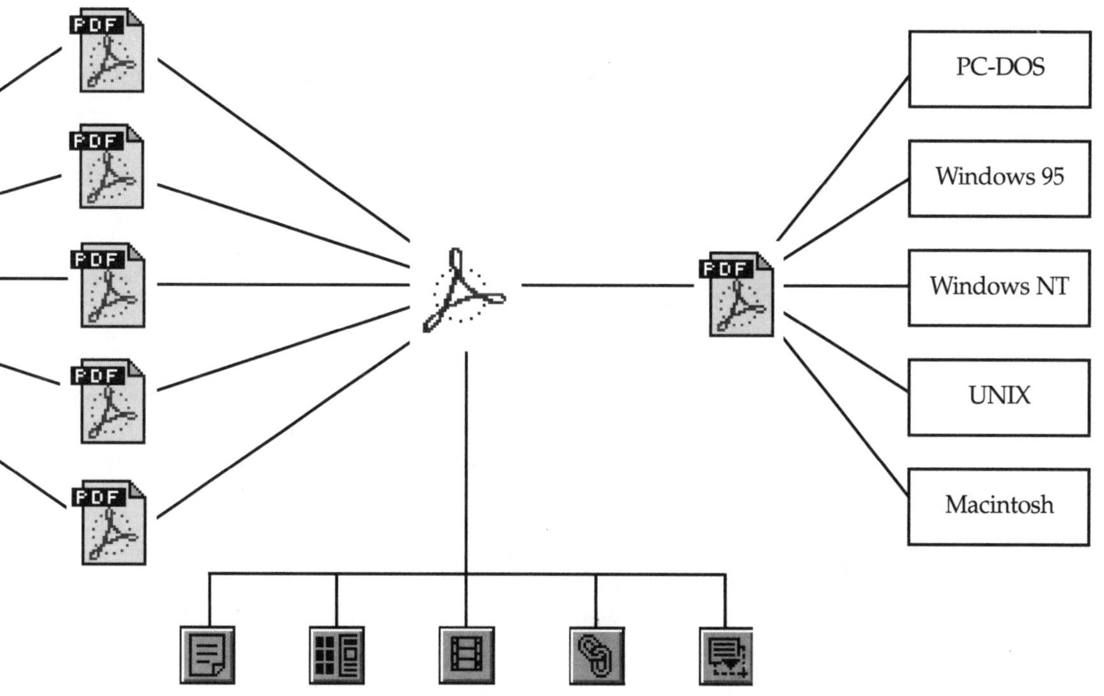

The individual PDF files are opened in Acrobat Exchange or via a plug-in or a PDF editing application. Here the files can be merged into a single file. QuickTime movies, sound, forms, and interactive linking is done to produce a single device-independent file that includes all information.

The Benefits of PDF

Device independence

The need for printing drivers or printer description files has made printing more device-dependent than users would have liked. But now the Acrobat 3.0/3.01 PDF provides the best method yet for storing and defining a document for print. The same file can be used for digital proofing, imposed film imagesetting, computer-to-plate, black and white document printer, color printer/color press, Web viewable and printable documents, and archived formats.

Media independence

Use the medium that best suits your message: page or imposed film, imposed plate—polyester or aluminum, digital color proof, demand printing from digital printers and presses, Web files, CD-ROM files, or digital image archives. Publishing has never had more opportunity for extending its franchise and reinventing itself.

PDF publishing

Publish in print or nonprint form. For instance, convert a year's worth of your publication to PDFs and record them on a CD-ROM. Sell this reference archive at a value-added price. Why? It's not just the publication, you can also search through all issues to find the keywords and information you want. Users will pay a premium for search and retrieval. You can also put the PDFs on the Web with a password and give it only to paid subscribers. Create an archive of issues from past years. PDFs retain the look and feel of your publication. Users can read them onscreen or print them out on almost any PostScript printer.

Distributed printing and remote proofing

Send PDFs with the efficacy of electronic communication to additional print sites to bring reproduction closer to the point of distribution... with the assurance that each site will print a uniform and predictable document. Send PDFs back to the client to proof on a digital proofer with proper color transforms. PDFs speed the production process... and also speed the delivery process.

11

PLUG-INS EXTEND ACROBAT PDF

Plug-ins are a significant development in the use of application software. A plug-in is an accessory computer program which extends out the functionality of a "host" program. On its own, a plug-in can do nothing since it needs the host program to operate.

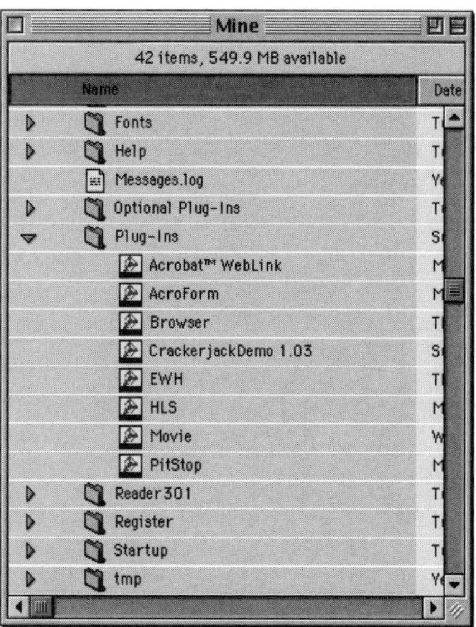

Plug-ins can be programmed to perform exceptionally simple or complicated tasks. They can be configured to appear when certain conditions are met, such as a particular file being open. They can even cause the Acrobat interface to be completely modified.

Creating plug-ins is a job for software development professionals. The Acrobat Software Developers Kit is a set of C-language routines which can be called by other programs. Plug-in developers have used these tools to create dozens of useful Acrobat extensions. If you are thinking of integrating Acrobat into your business, you'll need a plug-in or two.

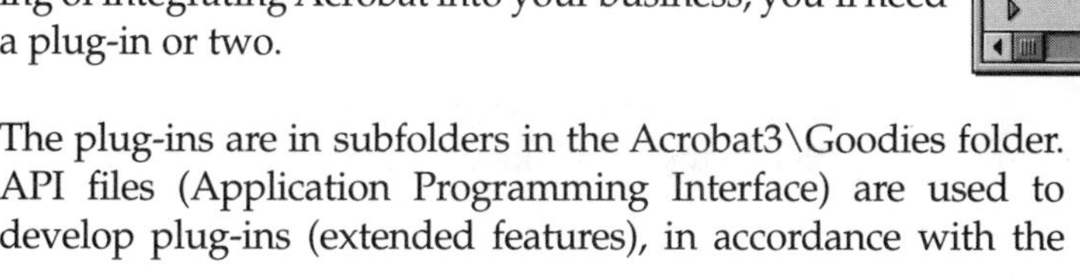

The plug-ins are in subfolders in the Acrobat3\Goodies folder. API files (Application Programming Interface) are used to develop plug-ins (extended features), in accordance with the

The Acrobat Software Developer's Kit (SDK) provides information to developers who want to write Acrobat plug-ins using C or C++, and for those who want to utilize Acrobat from within another application. The Acro_sdk folder on the Acrobat 3.01 CD is specific to the platform of Acrobat you purchased, whereas the full Acrobat 3.01 Plug-ins SDK supports development for Mac OS, Windows, and UNIX.

The following API files are included with the Acrobat SDK on the Acrobat CD: - Addps.api - Balloon.api - Ddeclnt.api - Debugwin.api - Extrnwin.api - Formdemo.api - Hftquery.api - Modpdf.api - Notify.api - Progbar.api - Rfs.api - Rot13.api - Rplcdemo.api - Setsec.api - Snapzoom.api - Stamper.api - Template.api - Weblhft.api - Wordfind.api - Imagesel.api - Templtex.api - Wrdfndex.api

There are now about 100 developers developing PDF plug-ins, with about 35 or 40 products actually out in the market.

information in the Acrobat Software Developer's Kit (SDK), and provide automatic access to features of an Acrobat application. The following plug-ins, developed by Adobe Systems, are in the Acrobat3\Goodies\Acro_pi folder on the Acrobat 3.01 CD.

- The AutoClose plug-in automatically closes the oldest of the currently open documents (the one that's been open the longest since last visited). By default, Acrobat allows up to nine open PDF documents at a time. When you open a tenth document, AutoClose closes the oldest document. You can retrieve closed documents by clicking Acrobat's GoBack button. Autoclos.txt, Autoclos.ini, and Autoclos.api are used.

- The SuperCrop plug-in adds the SuperCrop tool to the button bar in Acrobat Exchange. It is similar to Photoshop's crop tool. SuperCrop uses the files Supcrop.txt and Supcrop.api and works with Acrobat Exchange 3.0x.

- The SuperPrefs plug-in creates new preferences for Acrobat Exchange in Mac OS or Windows. You can access these preferences via Edit > *Preferences > Super Preferences.* The plug-in adds a Hot List menu to the main menu bar to access the preferences. SuperPrefs adds new preferences: File Open Behavior, Hot List, Auto Tiling, Acrobat Always On Top (Windows only), AutoSave Currently Open Docs, Replace Rotate Dialog, and more. SuperPrefs uses the files Supprefs.txt and Supprefs.api.

The Acrobat 3.01 CD also contains API files, which Acrobat Reader + Search uses to search PDF documents. The regular version of Acrobat Reader can't search PDF documents.

The following plug-ins, developed by third-party (non-Adobe) manufacturers, are in the Acrobat3\Goodies\Plug-Ins folder on the Acrobat 3.01 CD. Adobe Systems does not provide technical support or warranties for third-party plug-ins.

The Alliant folder contains the InfoLinker plug-in, which lets you specify parameters for automatically creating multiple hyperlinks. Refer to the Infolink.pdf file for information about this plug-in. InfoLinker uses the files Infolink.api, Infoln32.api, Rule32.api, Infolink.pdf, Sec7.pdf, Kill32.api, Killlink.api, Rule 32.api, and Rules.api.

The Ambia folder contains the Aerial, Compose, and Re:Mark plug-ins. Aerial lets you navigate PDF files more easily, Compose lets you specify parameters to automatically create bookmarks and hyperlinks, and Re:Mark lets you add editorial comments to a PDF file.

Crackerjack

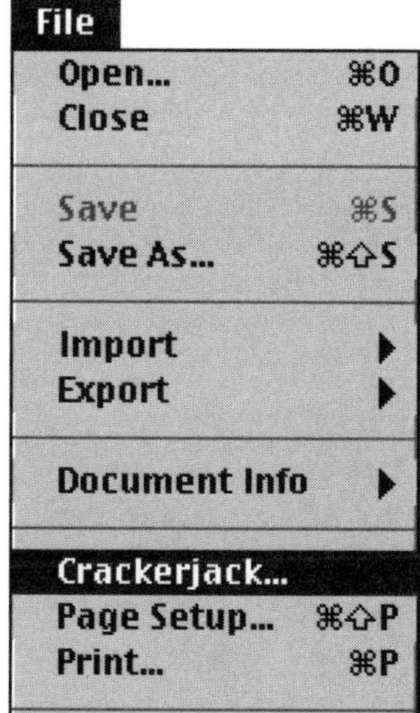

Adobe Acrobat outputs composite files. That means that all four colors are contained in one file. This kind of file will drive a color laser printer or digital color press but it will not drive an imagesetter or platesetter—any device that requires preseparated files. There was a need for a mechanism to do this from within Acrobat.

Extended Print Services was the first major plug-in and it has been refined and introduced as Crackerjack by Lantana. Because of its importance in printing, we have more detail on it. This plug-in adds print related features to Acrobat Exchange. With this plug-in the user is able to print separations to an imagesetter or platesetter. The dialog box has four tabs: *Pages*, *Output*, *Page*, and *Color*. Print-related information is edited and sent to the RIP in four monochrome separations, or if spot colors are used, either separated into CMYK or printed as the spot colors.

Crackerjack Functions

The settings that relate to how the document will be printed on the page are interactively shown in a second window, *Current Page Fit*, that is brought up as soon as Crackerjack is chosen. In this window paper size (as specified in the PPD), page size of the document, crop marks etc. are shown as they are changed.

The benefits of Crackerjack

Crackerjack is installed in the Plug-in folder in the Acrobat folder. When Acrobat Exchange is opened, Crackerjack will be found in the File *menu. Even though the normal* Page Setup *and* Print *options are still available, all the control, and more, is found in Crackerjack. The main functions that can be set and or modified with Crackerjack are:*

- *The range of pages in the document to be printed.*
- *The PostScript Printer Description file to use.*
- *Resolutions supported.*
- *Print or save the file as PostScript or EPS.*
- *The page format.*
- *Offset of page on media.*
- *Offset of image on page.*
- *Crop marks, color names.*
- *Mirrored output.*
- *Negative output.*
- *Composite CMYK or separations.*
- *Screen ruling, screen angle, and halftone pattern.*
- *Screening as specified in document or EPS images.*
- *Control over the rendering if separations will be made in the RIP.*
- *Convert spot color to CMYK process colors.*
- *Specify GCR and UCR.*

Crackerjack and PostScript Level 1 RIP

Crackerjack was designed to work with PostScript Level 2 (or above) applications and devices. This allows a broader array of screening solutions and enables composite color workflows so that the same data can be used for printing, CD-ROM creation, and online distribution.

Document

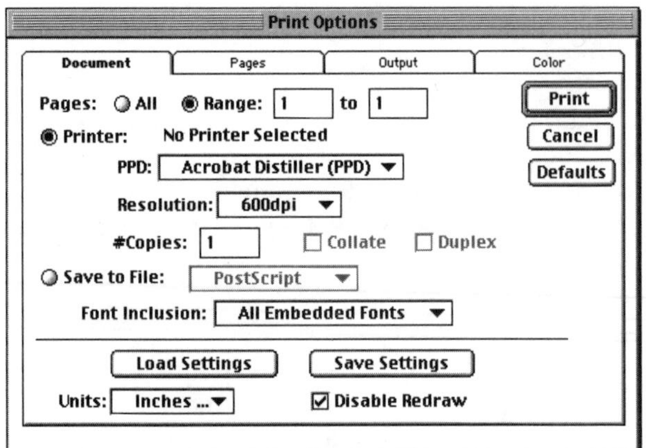

Crackerjack makes it possible to set the PPD file directly from the print dialog box This function makes it easier to have control over the setting even though there is no difference than if it was specified in the *Chooser*. The *Current Page Fit* window changes the printable output size as the PPD is changed. Instead of printing the document to a printer it can be saved as a PostScript or EPS file, with or without font inclusion. The other document functions are very similar to other printer dialog boxes. Either all of the pages or range is printed.

Separations from Word or Excel

It is possible to print separations from a document created in Microsoft Word, even if it has embedded graphics, and even if the graphics were created in Microsoft Excel. First, use Type 1 fonts—avoid TrueType. The next step is to create "good" PostScript output from Word by using a high-end PostScript Printer Description (PPD) file. By high-end, we mean a PPD for a device like an imagesetter. When printing from Word you must choose the high-end device and specify "print to file." The resultant PostScript file is then fed into Distiller to create a PDF file. On most PCs, the PostScript file will have a .prn file suffix. You can either edit the file name to give it a .ps suffix, or simply let Distiller open the .prn file. Once you have distilled the PostScript file into a PDF document you can now use Crackerjack to create separated output on your PostScript Level 2 RIP.

Pages

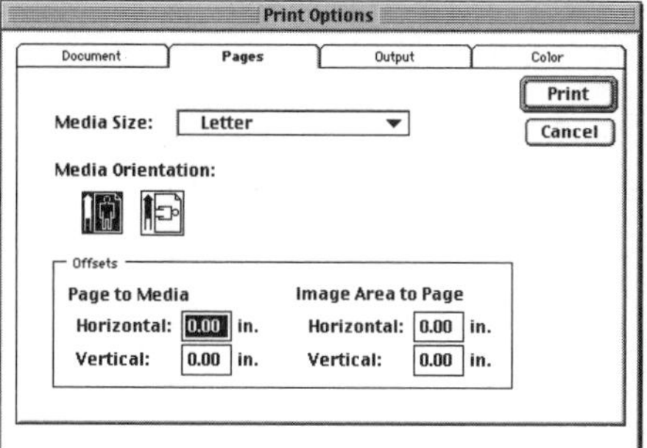

For each PPD there is a set of predefined output sizes. These are found in the *Media Size* pop up menu. If none of them is suitable for the document that will be printed it can be customized in a dialog box that appears if the last option in the pop up menu, *Custom Page Size*, is picked. All the *Page Size* choices are shown on the *Current Page Fit* window. The user can determine from this window if the document will fit on the available page size. If the page needs to be offset on the output media the *Page to Media* option is used in x-y direction.

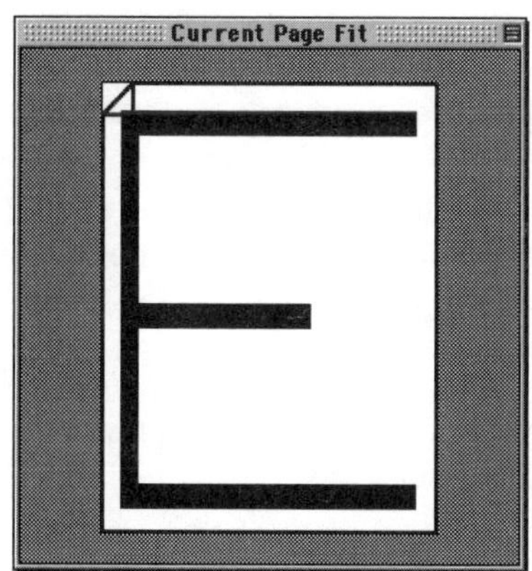

A similar function is the *Image Area to Page* setting, but here the document information is offset relative to the page. However, this function will change the entity of the page as the margins are changed. If the customer has made a mistake and specified a larger size than available on the output device, there are two options on how this can be solved without making new PDF files. The document may have enough margins to cut some of these so that the page does not need to be reduced to fit the paper size.

Here the capital E in the *Current Page Fit* window becomes important. The big E occupies the same amount of space as the objects on the page do. The margins can easily be seen and no guesses have to be made as to whether the information might fit on a smaller page size, for instance. For further control of the reproduction of the document use the options in the *Output* tab.

No screen angle or frequency saved in a PDF file

Grayscale TIFF images in an Adobe Acrobat PDF (Portable Document Format) file do not have the same screen angle and frequency as they do in the original file.

- *Download the free AddPS Plug-in module (AdDiskR2.sit.hqx "Acrobat Ad Sample Disk") which is available on the Adobe BBS (206-623-6984) and Adobe's FTP site: ftp://ftp.adobe.com/pub/adobe/acrobatdistiller/mac/addiskr2.sit.hqx The AddPS Plug-in lets you set screens and angles as well as lighten and darken images.*
- *Print the PDF file to disk as an EPS graphic, then place that EPS into an application in which you can change screen parameters (e.g., PageMaker) and print it from there.*
- *Create a custom printer file and change the default screen settings for the printer.*

Because screen angle and screen frequency information are considered device characteristics, Acrobat does not include that information within a PDF file. Doing so reduces the intended portability of PDF files. When Acrobat Exchange or Reader prints PDF files, it adheres to the default screening of your printer. If your printer driver uses a PPD, you can modify it to include the screen settings from the original file.

Printer not printing separations.

Desktop laser printers are not enabled to do in-RIP separations. Therefore, they are unable to process Crackerjack's commands to create separated output.

Adobe Acrobat now includes a "job ticket" with your print job—this feature will be expanded in a future version of Adobe PostScript Extreme as more PostScript 3 features are incorporated into the architecture. These "job tickets" let the print job carry a set of instructions for its handling at various stations along the way. They can also convey device-specific information so the same job can be delivered to two different output devices. Eventually, job tickets may provide a method for tying jobs into job-management databases and perhaps tracking jobs through the work sequence, or even attaching postpress instructions for devices like automated binderies. Companies like Imation and Agfa, among others, are implementing this technology.

Output

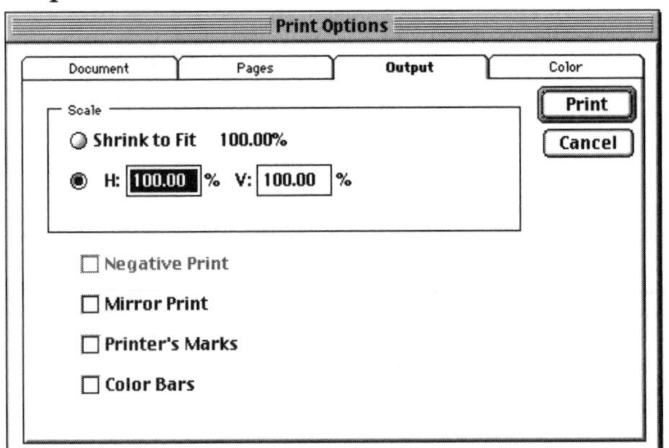

There may be times when the document has a page size that is larger than the possible output size on the imaging device. If the client accepts the page to be scaled in size to fit the maximum page size available this is easily done by choosing the *Shrink to Fit Page* option. The user then has a combination of offsetting the document on the printed page and a reduction x and y percent which can be entered.

The results that can be created with the scaling function in the *Output* folder tab and the *Image Area to Page* setting, in the *Pages* folder tab are quite special and give the printer and customer more options when the deadline is close and there is no time for re-creating the design and PDF files. Usually the *Current Page Fit* window will only serve as an informative guide on how the document will be imaged.

Further options in the *Output* folder tab are to choose if the output is to be printed mirrored and/or negative depending on the printing requirements. Printers' marks will image crop marks, registration marks, and color names.

Color

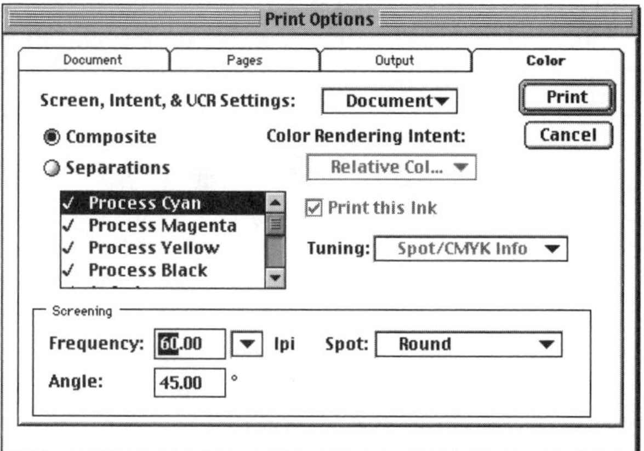

This is the part of Crackerjack where the most benefits are enabled—separations. Without Crackerjack, color separations cannot be output from Exchange. In the *Color* tab this is an easy procedure: choose *Separations* and you can also choose if any spot colors used should be printed as spot color or if they could be converted to process colors. When it comes to screening there are some further decisions. Depending on the creator of the document there may be a demand for multiple screen rulings on the same page. This may have previously been defined in a image application like Photoshop. If these customized screen rulings should be saved one have to change to *Use document* in the top of the *Color* tab dialog box in Crackerjack.

If the page will be reused for a different printing process that can not reproduce the same screen ruling it is a good idea to override the document setting by choosing *Dialog* instead of *Document*. In the bottom part of the *Color* tab dialog box the screening and screen angle can thus be specified.

When dealing with halftone screens it must be remembered that not all screen rulings and certainly not all screen angles can be used. Screen angles in almost all cases are restricted to 15, 75, 45, and 0 degrees. The screen rulings available depend on the RIP. The same thing is true for the raster shape. The RIP has to be set up to use certain shapes, and there is not much visual result to change the shape on the screen.

Crackerjack Pilot

Lantana Research Corporation's Crackerjack Pilot is an automation option to Crackerjack. PDF print production can be streamlined to a drag and drop operation as a plug-in to Adobe Acrobat Exchange and is available in Macintosh and Windows versions. Crackerjack Pilot allows the user to set up "hot folders" which are associated with a different output device and/or application-specific output parameters. Folders can be established for an imagesetter, plotter, brochures, data sheets, for client Jones, Lee, or combinations of these. Once folders are set up, all the user needs to do is drop PDF documents into the appropriate folder(s). The Pilot plug-in scans folders and ensures that each document is processed using Crackerjack which includes professional control over positioning, scaling, separation, screening, and more.

Plug-ins from EnFocus

EnFocus Software, a Belgian developer, has products that fit a new class of tools needed for handling PostScript files and PDF files for document editing, correction, and checking.

Tailor

Tailor is not really a plug-in. It allows PostScript or EPS files to be read, displayed, and edited, before being output in a cleaned-up, DCS-compliant PostScript format. In the process, files are "normalized" and stripped of all unnecessary overhead. Tailor can also convert PostScript to a number of export formats and is Imation OPEN-aware. Tailor enables the operator to open a PostScript file, inspect its objects, and check the attributes. It supports software to edit any type of object.

It also has an inspector that identifies errors in the PostScript file and cleans up many of them. Tailor includes support for PostScript fonts with embedded TrueType fonts by converting the TrueType to outlines. It also handles characters that are not present in the Mac encoding vector. This is significant for processing PostScript from Windows systems and it supports OPI comments. The graphics inspector allows relinking of an OPI path and modification of the crop rectangle.

Check-Up

A plug-in from EnFocus called Check-Up will enable users to check a PDF document using an editable report for "preflighting" PDF files. The report is comprised of five sections and lists all the qualities of each section. The first two areas are the most general: Errors, Warnings, and File Information. These areas include general information about the PDF document and any problems within the PDF. Check-Up provides a register of all the fonts used in the document.

The register specifies the PostScript name and font type; it also identifies whether fonts are embedded or subsetted, and encoding. The Color and Image Info section lists all the color spaces used in the document. Any additional data available about the color space is also listed. A record of all images in the document is included in the Image information. The image inventory also includes the physical and effective resolution, the positioning of the image, and any custom knowledge (halftone, transfer curves, etc.) This also allows bimodal viewing of the original document on the front of the screen while the reported object is shown in the corner of the screen.

PitStop

PitStop 1.5 is a new version of the PDF editing plug-in for Adobe Acrobat. Since the first release in July, 1997, PitStop has enabled the visual editing of any PDF page opened in Acrobat Exchange 3.0. For the first time, editing, moving, coloring, rotating, and resizing objects such as text, line art, and images were done right inside Exchange. This is a unique way to edit PDF documents in the native PDF format. Copy-and-paste of objects such as line art, pixel images, and text is possible. Copy-and-paste can be done between pages within the same PDF document as well as between pages from different PDF documents. Users can copy graphics, text, or images such as ads or logos from one PDF document into another.

All resources used in the copied object such as fonts or color spaces are automatically brought over into the new document. To replace an image on a PDF page, one saves the new image as a PDF in Adobe Photoshop, opens it in Acrobat, and copies-and-pastes it into the appropriate PDF page. Users can also apply fonts installed on their computer, or fonts embedded in any other open PDF document when editing text in PitStop 1.5.

Adding text in any font from your system and embedding it is a true timesaver when updating PDF documents. This function also supports embedding any of the base 13 PostScript fonts, which Acrobat does not do.

Third-Party Plug-ins

The next few pages list almost 40 plug-ins (or products that work very closely with Acrobat). With a list this extensive, we cannot guarantee 100 percent accuracy. We have tried to get as much contact information as possible.

Niknet
5D Solutions Ltd.
Guardian House, Borough Road, Godalming, Surrey, GU7 2AE, UK
Tel: 44 1483 426 421 Fax:44 1483 419 541
www.five-d.com
Niknak's sole purpose is to offer efficient and low-cost creation of PDF 1.2 files compatible with Adobe Acrobat products, or third-party PDF tools. Installs as a printer in the Windows Printing System allowing users to "print" to a PDF file directly from any application. Niknak combines the simplicity of Adobe PDF Writer with Distiller's ability to interpret arbitrary PostScript and EPS files. Appears as an icon on the desktop allowing drag-and-drop conversion of any PostScript or EPS file directly to PDF.

ODDJOB
5D Solutions Ltd.
Guardian House, Borough Road, Godalming, Surrey, GU7 2AE, UK
Tel: 44 1483 423 421 Fax:(44) 1483 419 541
www.five-d.com
ODDJOB is a PostScript and PDF workflow product offering viewing of PS, PDF, or EPS files with optional anti-aliasing translation between any combination of PDF v. 1.0, 1.1, 1.2, PS level 1, 2, 3, or EPS. Includes options to output low-resolution GIF/JPEG/TIFF file splitting and merging, page reordering; watermarking; mailmerge using Acrobat Forms plus simple imposition (2- and 4-up, step and repeat); color separation; batch-scripted processing; and "watched folder" processing where appropriate.

Self-Service Literature
Adobe Enterprise Publishing Services
2040 Raybrook SE, Grand Rapids, MI 49546
Tel: (616) 954-9500 Fax: (616) 954-9402
www.digidox.com
Deliver customized, up-to-date business data without incurring the usual costs and response delays that accompany paper-based dissemination methods. Self-Service Literature solutions combine electronic form technology with Adobe products and integration strategies to allow viewers to compile personal literature packets complete with the most relevant content. Self-Service Literature Fulfillment is perfect for companies looking to automate the efforts of field sales personnel or streamline marketing avenues by conducting paperless tradeshows. Self-Service Literature fulfillment solutions include:
- Source document conversion/preparation
- Custom form interface design
- Multiple interface security configurations
- Instant distribution with e-mail notification
- Hosting on an Adobe Web server
- Database integration and exports for input tabulation

Alliant Techsystems
13133 34th Street, North Clearwater, FL 33762
Tel: (813) 572-2200 or (800) HELP-102
Fax: (813) 572-2658
http://ais.atk.com
InfoLinker is an Acrobat Exchange plug-in that adds navigational capabilities to PDF documents through the generation of automated hyperlinks and bookmarks. Hyperlinks can be created based on a set of user-defined rules or through the use of an automatic rule generator called the Maestro. InfoLinker provides the ability to link from one document to another

or to incorporate multimedia or other software applications into your PDF document. It also supports URL links.

Library Manager
Alliant Techsystems
13133 34th Street, North Clearwater, FL 33762
Tel: (813) 572-2200 or (800) HELP-102
Fax: (813) 572-2658
http://ais.atk.com
Library Manager is a front-end user interface tool that organizes PDF files by a descriptive title. The descriptive name can include up to 60 characters. A search on a portion of the title will yield a list of matching documents. Alias path names and volume labels are used for variable pathing to repositories, such as CD jukeboxes, disk arrays, and networks for easy document retrieval.

Link Manager
Alliant Techsystems
13133 34th Street, North Clearwater, FL 33762
Tel: (813) 572-2200 or (800) HELP-10 2
Fax: (813) 572-2658
http://ais.atk.com
Link Manager is used for easily modifying links in PDF files. It allows users to selectively modify manual or automated links by changing attributes, or delete specific links, notes, and threads. Link Manager also can refresh hyperlinks in documents that have had minor revisions and can change the color of hyperlinks.

PrintShop Mail
Atlas Software BV
Buys Ballotstraat 17-193846 BG Harderwijk
The Netherlands
Tel: 31 341 426700 Fax: 31 341 424608
www.atlassoftware.nl
PrintShop Mail is a production tool for Variable Data and personalized printing. PrintShop Mail lets you create all kind of personalized documents varying from simple labels and newsletters to complex (variable images) color mailings. Sophisticated PDF and PostScript technology is used to realize a short process (SPOOL + RIP) time.

Redwing
BCL Computers
600 W. Cummings Park, Suite 1500, Woburn, MA 01801
Tel: (781) 937-5930 Fax: (781) 937-5940
www.bcl-computers.com
Redwing lets you easily extract text or tables from even the most complex PDF files with great accuracy. Extracted information can be sent to a spreadsheet, database, word processor, or other desktop application. Redwing's zoning tool allows you to pick out just the text and tables you want. You also can sequence text, tables, footnotes, and titles, so they all go in the right place and order.

pdfToolbox
callas software
Pappelallee 9D-10437, Berlin, Germany
Tel: 49 30 443 90310 Fax: 49 30 441 6402
www.callas.de
pdfToolbox:

- pdfBatchMeister applies predefined Distiller settings for prepress/CD-ROM/Internet to EPS/PostScript in batch mode
- pdfOutput is for cross-platform EPS file-generation with preview and embedded fonts
- pdfInspektor is for preflighting PDF files for output: resolutions, colors, embedded and subsetted fonts, etc.

- pdfCrop&Measure is for cropping and measuring areas and distances of PDF files
- Batch preflight and convert PDF files into RIP-friendly EPS from a single dialog box.
- pdfCropMarks add crop marks to your PDF file.
- Preflight OPI & compression information with pdfInspektor
- Full separation output for Level 1/2 RIPS.

MadeToPrint
callas software
Pappelallee 9D-10437, Berlin, Germany
Tel: 49 30 443 90310 Fax: 49 30 441 6402
www.callas.de
MadeToPrint XT 3.1: Batch-printing workflow tool now creates PDF files from QuarkXPress.

- MadeToPrint's preconfigured PDF settings mean you don't need to touch the Distiller settings.
- integrates Distiller settings and destination folders into MadeToPrint jobs.
- MadeToPrint can now launch PDFDesign XT (TechnoDesign) for user-defined placement of automatically generated bookmarks within QuarkXPress.
- Flexible options to create one PDF document per page/document and hot folder locations.
- Creates PostScript/perfectly cropped EPS files, calls up Distiller and PDF Design XT directly for PDF files for prepress/Internet/CD-ROM use in ONE print job.
- Updates modified picture without printing
- Prints to single or multiple devices simultaneously with different print settings.
- Fully automated when used with AutoPilot XT.

Computerised Document Control Ltd.
PO Box 5, Chepstow, Monmouthshire
NP6 6YU, UK
Tel: 44 (0) 1291 641 715 (direct)
USA: (888) 240-1752 Fax: 44 (0) 1291 641 817
www.docctrl.com
Document publishing software to enable the assembly, dissemination, and distribution of critical business documents. Forging the link between document systems and Adobe Acrobat, CDC's products offer solutions for:

- Dossier compilation and publishing.
- Database publishing for customized documents on demand.
- Controlled printing for regulated document environments.
- "Intelligent" PDF creation

Our products are available as either integrated solutions for document management systems or System Integrator tools for Web-based publishing solutions.

Publisher
Data Technology Group, Inc.
221 E. Main St.Milford, MA 01757
Tel: (508) 634-1099 Fax: (508) 634-0898
www.dtgsw.com
Publisher is the first software package created specifically for the generation of FDA-compliant electronic submission of Case Report Forms (CRFs) in Adobe's Portable Document Format (PDF). The software performs on-the-fly PDF generation including TIFF conversion, bookmarking, and Table of Contents generation without the use of Adobe Capture, Distiller, Plug-Ins, or print drivers. The comprehensive functionality provided by CRF Publisher virtually eliminates the problems that can be introduced with the manual steps

required by other solutions. The software is designed for unattended operation.

Reax
Digital Applications, Inc.
215 E. Providence Rd., Aldan, PA 19018-4129
Tel: (610) 284-4006 Fax: (610) 284-4233
www.digapp.com
Redax for Text and Redax for Text and Images are plug-ins that allow the user to edit PDF documents in compliance with Freedom of Information Act and Privacy Act requirements.

DateD
Digital Applications, Inc.
215 E. Providence Rd., Aldan, PA 19018-4129
Tel: (610) 284-4006 Fax: (610) 284-4233
www.digapp.com
DateD is a set of plug-ins that adds dynamic date/time information as well as a static message to documents when opened and printed.

TimedOut
Digital Applications, Inc.
215 E. Providence Rd., Aldan, PA 19018-4129
Tel: (610) 284-4006 Fax: (610) 284-4233
www.digapp.com
TimedOut adds additional security features and expiration dates to documents. Expired documents can only be accessed with the proper passcode established by the System or Document Administrator.

SecurSign
Digital Applications, Inc.
215 E. Providence Rd., Aldan, PA 19018-4129
Tel: (610) 284-4006 Fax: (610) 284-4233
www.digapp.com
SecurSign adds digital signatures to PDF documents using public/private key pairs.

AppendPDF
Digital Applications, Inc.
215 E. Providence Rd., Aldan, PA 19018-4129
Tel: (610) 284-4006F ax: (610) 284-4233
www.digapp.com
AppendPDF is a server application that appends PDF files or page ranges within files.

StampPDF
Digital Applications, Inc.
215 E. Providence Rd., Aldan, PA 19018-4129
Tel: (610) 284-4006 Fax: (610) 284-4233
www.digapp.com
StampPDF is a server application that adds text messages, page numbers, or other static information to numbers of PDFs in an automated process.

Ari's Ruler
Dionis
167 Milk Street, # 478, Boston, MA 02109-4315
Tel: (617) 227-0903 Fax: (617) 227-5274
www.dionis.com
Ari's Ruler gives the ability for quick, precise measurements of PDF files on screen.

Ari's Print Helper
Dionis
167 Milk Street, #478, Boston, MA 02109-4315
Tel: (617) 227-0903 Fax: (617) 227-5274
www.dionis.com
Ari's Print Helper gives you an expanded print dialog box to print multiple page ranges. Page ranges can include even or odd numbered pages or pages in reverse numerical order.

D Soft
(ADA 823)Sparrestraat 24B-9920,
Lovendegem, Belgium
Tel: 32 9 372 70 41 Fax: 32 9 372 41 66
www.dsoft.be
The company develops plug-ins for clients (mostly publishers). These plug-ins provide a unique navigation interface for the user giving direct access to the requested information. They wrote an alternative to the Acrobat Search engine. By using this plug-in a user can for example limit their search to certain chapters within a PDF file rather than the file itself. You can browse through a complete table of contents that is extracted from the PDF files. These are plug-ins for special CD-ROM purposes.

DynaDoc/PDF
Dynalab Inc.
41900 Christy St., Fremont, CA 94538
Tel: (408) 735-0774 Fax: (408) 735-9070
www.dynalab.com.t or www.dynalab.com.hk or www.dynalab.co.jp
DynaDoc/PDF plays back documents with Chinese or Japanese characters through the reader into the English Windows environment. Allows users to view and print Asian character documents across a varying range of platforms. DynaDoc utilizes the convenient print driver option to generate the formatted document. Offers two ways of generating PDF formatted documents—through the Adobe PDF printer driver or through a PostScript file to a PDF converter. Generates and reads PDF documents across platform, application, and software version. Handles 2-byte data and embedding CJK fonts.

Fiery DocBuilder Pro
Electronics for Imaging, Inc.
2855 Campus Drive, San Mateo, CA 94403
Tel: (650) 286-8556 Fax: (650) 286-8686
www.efi.com
Fiery DocBuilder Pro is an optional upgrade to the standard Fiery Command WorkStation application. It features the industry's first server-based imposition by way of Adobe's PDF architecture. In addition to imposition, Docbuilder Pro also includes all of the classic DocBuilder capabilities, now at a pre-RIP stage. This includes the ability to view thumbnails and full screen previews, full page editing by way of third-party plug-in support, as well as deleting, duplicating, and combining of pages between multiple-source PDF documents. All changes are retained in the original PDF file, so they may be archived or re-RIPped.

PitStop
Enfocus Software
234 Columbine Street, Suite 3008, P.O. Box 6410, Denver, CO 80206
Tel: (303) 393-7282 or (888) 363-6287
Fax: (303) 393-7290
Technologiepark-Zwijnaarde 3B-9052 Gent, BELGIUM
Tel: +32 9 241 57 05 Fax: +32 9 245 03 04
www.enfocus.com
Enfocus PitStop is a plug-in for Adobe Acrobat to visually edit PDF documents inside Acrobat Exchange. You can edit any PDF document in Acrobat Exchange no matter where it was originally created. Open any PDF document in Acrobat Exchange and click on the Enfocus PitStop button in the toolbar. A PitStop window pops up with the page ready

for editing. Simply click-and-drag text or graphics to select, edit, move, scale, rotate, and/or change color. A tool for PDF editing.

CheckUp
Enfocus Software
234 Columbine Street, Suite 3008, P.O. Box 6410, Denver, CO 80206
Tel: (303) 393-7282 or (888) 3636287
Fax: (303) 393-7290
Technologiepark-Zwijnaarde 3B-9052 Gent, BELGIUM
Tel: 32 9 241 57 05 Fax: 32 9 245 03 04
www.enfocus.com
CheckUp lets you preflight and check any PDF document in Acrobat. Verify whether the document is properly created to suit the intended use. Does it contain embedded fonts? Are the images in the desired resolution and color space? Compression? The rules on how and what to check in a PDF document are defined and saved in preflight profiles. Just select the preflight profile of your choice and click on the Check button. Enfocus CheckUp generates a comprehensive preflight report divided into four main areas: fonts, images, color, and general information. The report lists warnings and errors, and hyperlinks point you to the flagged objects in the checked PDF document.

Ferrari
Enfocus Software
234 Columbine Street, Suite 3008 P.O. Box 6410, Denver, CO 80206
Tel: (303) 393-7282 or (888)3636287
Fax: (303) 393-7290
Technologiepark-Zwijnaarde 3B-9052 Gent, Belgium
Tel: 32 9 241 57 05 Fax: 32 9 245 03 04
www.enfocus.com
Enfocus "Ferrari" is a server application for print production. Normalize and preflight PostScript to a reliable format and also convert it to PDF and EPS if needed. Includes numerous automatic correction functions such as spot to process and font inclusion. Optimize your PostScript and PDF workflow. With Enfocus Ferrari you can preflight, correct, convert, and normalize your PostScript, PDF, and EPS files before going into prepress production.

Preflight Pro
Extensis Corp.
1800 S.W. First Ave., Suite 500, Portland, OR 97201
Tel: (503) 274-2020 Fax: (503) 274-0530
www.extensis.com
Preflight Pro automates the preflight process, finds errors in all leading page layout and illustration programs, and helps correct problems with the unique Pilot feature before the job is output. After preflighting, the job can be distilled into a clean, error-free PDF file, increasing the speed and reliability of digital workflows.

Preflight Designer
Extensis Corp.
1800 S.W. First Ave., Suite 500, Portland, OR 97201
Tel: (503) 274-2020 Fax: (503) 274-0530
www.extensis.com
Preflight Designer eliminates rework by allowing designers to prepare error-free files for printing. Inspects files and displays key information related to RGB images, missing

fonts, and more. Users can then collect all the elements needed to print, including embedded fonts and graphics. An electronic Job Ticket helps streamline communication with service bureaus. Additionally users have the option to distill a PDF directly from Preflight Designer, and collect it with a job for output.

FileOpen PDF
FileOpen Systems Inc.
101 W 85th St. #1-4, New York, NY 10024
Tel: (212) 877-3183 Fax: (212) 712-9543
www.fileopen.com
FileOpen PDF is a system for publishing secured PDF files on the Web or on CD-ROM. The system allows publishers to define access privileges for collections of PDF documents, to set rules for document expiration at an absolute or relative date, embed the copyright owner's contact information in the file, embed Digital Object Identifiers (DOIs) for copyright management and usage tracking, and automatically create an installer for the client software and PDF collection. The FileOpen client, at the user end, invisibly stores permissions data in the user's operating system and opens files for users without any password entry. The FileOpen PDF security system blocks unauthorized users from accessing FileLock'ed or expired files.

Enterprise Solution Module
HAHT Software
4200 Six Forks Road, Raleigh, NC 27609
Tel: (888) 438-4248 or (919) 786-5177
Fax: (919) 786-5250
www.haht.com
The HAHTsite Enterprise Solution Module (ESM) for Adobe Acrobat provides a rapid and powerful way to connect Adobe PDF documents to server-side data and applications over the Web. The ESM for Adobe Acrobat is a wizard that runs in the HAHTsite Integrated Development environment to allow developers to point and click to associate PDF form fields with databases and applications. PDF forms can now quickly and easily be integrated in any Web application. The ESM for Adobe Acrobat requires the HAHTsite IDE, and is available as a free download from the HAHT Website.

PDF Handshake
HELIOS Software GmbH
Steinriede 3, D-30827, Garbsen, Germany
Tel: 49 5131 709320 Fax: 49 5131 709325
www.helios.com
U.S. distributor EMC, www.ugraf.com
Helios PDF Handshake is an extension for EtherShare and/or EtherShare OPI servers. It allows you to print PDF documents with proper colors to any PostScript device and to use PDF as hi-res input format for the OPI workflow. PostScript Type 1 and 3 as well as TrueType fonts are supported. Comes with the standard PostScript fonts (apx. 340), Berthold font faces, and aprx. 30 MB highest quality ICC profiles. Users can print PDF documents with a Helios-supplied Acrobat plug-in or UNIX tool separated for final print or matched for proof print, to any PostScript device, incl. Level 1 RIPs, with optional merging of spot to process colors, and with registration marks. In case of OPI, PDF Handshake generates color-correct EPS lo-res images of PDF originals. These lo-res representations can be used like any other EPS. During output, the Helios server swaps EPS lo-res by PDF hi-res and sends it as color attached/separated PostScript to the printer.

PDF Handshake gives prepress and printing customers all the benefits of PDF as a universal exchange format for their existing applications and their currently installed output devices, without any need for costly and time-consuming upgrades.

Iceni Technology Ltd.
82 St Philips Road, Norwich, Norfolk UK
NR2 3BW
Tel: 44 1 603 474 831 Fax: 44 1 603 474 832
www.iceni.com
Software to enable the repurposing of the content of PDFs, both text and images. It uses an "intelligent content recognition" engine to automatically determine the different content component parts of a document. This information is then used to tag and extract the content from the PDF page. For example, it is able to identify and link together the heading, by line, caption, and body text of an article on a page of a newspaper or magazine. It can automatically associate captions with images to enable searching of images using the caption within an "asset management system." This process is automatically carried out for each separate article on the page. Thus, the different articles on a page are identified, tagged, and extracted as separate files from the same PDF page. The tags that are applied to the content components are user configurable for different end uses such as XML, HTML, RTF, or input for search engines.

AdStract
Iceni Technology Ltd.
82 St Philips Road, Norwich, Norfolk UK
NR2 3BW
Tel: 44 1 603 474 831 Fax: 44 1 603 474 832
www.iceni.com
AdStract—Extracts and tags the content of ads that have been supplied in PDF format, distilled into PDF from EPS files, and/or have been converted to PDF from camera-ready artwork using Capture. Software has been optimized for auto and job ads. For example, the software is able to extract and format lists of autos, with their prices, from dealer ads. The tags that are applied are user configurable for different uses such as HTML output as well as for Web ad sites, such as Auto Hunter and Job Hunter.

TEP
Iceni Technology Ltd.
82 St Philips Road, Norwich, Norfolk UK
NR2 3BW
Tel: 44 1 603 474 831 Fax: 44 1 603 474 832
www.iceni.com
TEP extracts text from PDFs and formats it into XML, HTML, RTF, or user-defined Tagged Text format. Supports automatic embedding of PDF image links in XML & HTML. Software is also used as a front end to provide search engines with high quality and very structured input. Recognizes and separately tags headings, paragraphs, footnotes, title, page number, author, and creation date. Gives more accurate and relevant captions in search results fields. Uses "hot" folders and/or standalone processes.

PEP
Iceni Technology Ltd.
82 St Philips Road, Norwich, Norfolk UK
NR2 3BW
Tel: 44 1 603 474 831 Fax: 44 1 603 474 832
www.iceni.com

PEP extracts images from PDF as Progressive JPEG, EPS, or TIFF. Able to preserve or convert color spaces and supports image compression schemes. Supplied with macros for automatically naming images and embedding information into image header files. Can be used in combination with TEP software to provide full PDF to XML or HTML output including images, with links. Available as a plug-in to Exchange that uses "hot" folders and/or standalone processes.

PressWise
Imation Publishing Software
1011 Western Avenue, Suite 900, Seattle WA 98104
Tel: (206) 689-6700 Fax: (206) 689-6701
http://ips.imation.com
Imation PressWise produces plate-ready signatures in minutes, for use on web- or sheet-fed presses. It includes the ability to RIP files to screen, which allows detailed, on-screen review of font, ink, and page specifications. PressWise comes with customizable sets of page, form, and sheet marks, including the option to use EPS art as a mark. PressWise 3.0 imposes PDF files, allowing you to mix PDF, EPS, and PostScript pages within the same signature. PDF support allows PressWise users to benefit from the application independence and small files sizes of PDF.

OPEN
Imation Publishing Software
1011 Western Avenue, Suite 900, Seattle WA 98104
Tel: (206) 689-6700 Fax: (206) 689-6701
http://ips.imation.com
With Imation OPEN software, you can automate time-consuming, repetitive tasks within a distributed server environment. OPEN can automate repetitive steps in a PDF workflow, such as creating PDFs on a server, converting PDF to PostScript, or distributing PDF files to multiple recipients. Users can send files into the Pipeline from anywhere on the network, letting OPEN control their progress each step of the way. Whatever your production needs, OPEN can scale up to handle the heaviest workload.

Media Manager
Imation Publishing Software
1011 Western Avenue, Suite 900, Seattle WA 98104
Tel: (206) 689-6700 Fax: (206) 689-6701
http://ips.imation.com
Cross Platform w. Microsoft SQL Server, Imation Media Manager spares you the tedium of managing valuable digital resources. As a client/server database system, Media Manager manages text, image, sound, video, and other digitized media files from a high-performance server, while users control operations from the comfort of their own workstation. With the Media Manager PDF I Piece plug-in, users can transparently catalog, preview, locate, and retrieve their PDF documents from the Media Manager database.

InfoLink
Infocon America
620 Newport Center Dr. Suite 1100, Newport Beach, CA 92660
Tel: (714) 721-6662 Fax: (714) 759-8391
www.infoconamerica.com
The InfoLink Publishing Enhancement Software converts documents to PDF, greatly enhances with many navigational capabilities, bookmarks, and links, edits, preflights, indexes

for full text search, and secures for sale and distribution to subscribers and customers.

Virtual File Cabinets
Infodata Systems/Ambia Corporation
12150 Monument Drive, Fairfax, VA 22033
Tel: (703) 934-5205 Fax: (703) 934-7154
www.infodata.com
Virtual File Cabinet (VFC) is a family of client/server, intranet-based products that allow users to collaborate on mixed file type documents across the enterprise. Utilizing a familiar Web browser interface, VFC allows workgroups to annotate and share Adobe Acrobat PDF documents in real time.

Infodata Systems/Ambia Corporation
12150 Monument Drive, Fairfax, VA 22033
Tel: (703) 934-5205 Fax: (703) 934-7154
www.infodata.com
Infodata's Acrobat division, Ambia, a developer of Acrobat products and services, has a full line of Acrobat tools for publishers (Compose), workgroups (Re:mark) and individual end users (Aerial). Ambia also develops custom solutions for organizations needing specialized Acrobat features, or integration of Acrobat software into a systems solution.

VBShelf
Ivy International
270 West Center St., Orem, UT 84057
Tel: (801) 227-3447 Fax: (801) 227-3478
www.virtualt.com
Java/Internet server version VBShelf enables publishers to create complete publishing solutions by allowing both control of documentation presentation and the contextual organization of every electronic document. Using VBShelf, an Acrobat plug-in, PDF files are programmed with information that makes them "Intelligent." They are arranged by date, collection, volume, issue, or article. Being Intelligent, these documents can reside anywhere: hard drive, CD-ROM, floppy disk, corporate intranets, or the Internet. End result, readers no longer need to remember cryptic file names, where files are located, or their relationship with other documents you've published or will publish in the future.

Kuehling Buerokommunikation GmbH
Schleefstr. 2e44287 Dortmund, Germany
Tel. and Fax: 49-213-45991-0
www.kuehling.de
Server Application for archiving and printing spool files from UNIX or IBM (converting their native formats) or Windows (using PDF). Features document separation, page handling, long document splitting, thumbnail insertion. Permits tunneling of index info to the archival system. Does text extraction for full text indexing. Can control import into archival system. Text field extraction capabilities like in classical COLD. Document type classification based on contents: used for deciding where the document goes.

Crackerjack
Lantana Research Corporation
39560 Stevenson Pl. #220, Fremont, CA 94539
Tel: (510) 744-0282 Fax: (510) 744-1307
www.lantanarips.com
Crackerjack version 2.0 and Crackerjack Pilot, both for the Macintosh & Windows (95 and NT) platforms. It provides the user with output control over positioning, scaling, separation, screening, and more. It is the link between the natural preflighting environment of Exchange and production printing equipment,

such as imagesetters, digital proofers, and digital presses. Release 2.0 provides an enhanced feature set over the previous version, including the ability to select any output device on your network directly from Crackerjack menus.

Crackerjack Pilot is an automation option to Crackerjack. PDF print production can be streamlined to a simple drag-and-drop operation. Pilot allows the user to set up hot folders. Each folder can be associated with a different output device and/or application-specific output parameters. Folders can be established by output device, application, customer, or combinations of these. Pilot plug-in scans the folders and ensures that each new document is processed using Crackerjack's technology. The suggested retail price for Crackerjack is $495 and $795 for Crackerjack Pilot when purchased separately. Bundled, the suggested retail price is $1150.

Muscat Limited
St. John's Innovation Centre, Cowley Road
Cambridge CB4 4WS UK
Tel: 44 1223 421222 Fax: 44 1223 421223
www.muscat.com
Web-server-based UNIX and NT. A scalable PDF indexing and search product that indexes large collections of PDF's either document by document, or page by page, and preserves positional information for term highlighting. Natural language searching with relevance ranking with Search by Category (Dates, Authors, Sections).

DigiScript, DigiServer
OneVision
Florian-Seidl Strasse 11, D-93053, Regensburg, Germany
Tel: 49-941-78004-0 Fax: 49-941-78004-49
438 Division Street, Sewickley, PA 15143
Tel: (412) 741-4811 Fax: (412) 741-4818
www.onevision.de
DigiScript opens, checks, and corrects digital data and enables you to pass it along as error-free PostScript or PDF files to your production environment. It offers the capability to amend image, text, and graphic elements without regard from which system environment the files originate. Accepts and edits EPS, PDF, separated and unseparated PostScript files. Zooms up to 80,000 percent, may also be set in dpi (WYSIWYG). Processing of image, text, and graphic elements. Changing colors for selected elements, selected pages, or entire documents. Extraction of all embedded fonts.

DigiServer software enables you to proof data files from customers in PDF, EPS, AI, TIFF, and PS formats for a fully automated and error-free production process, from order entry to the final print. A log file gives you detailed information about the incoming files. Faulty files can be rejected. Necessary corrections and enhancements for image, text, and graphic elements can be done using DigiScipt. Automated interpretation of PDF, EPS, AI, TIFF, and separated and separated PS files. Data formats independent of hardware architectures and applications. Rejects files containing PS errors before entering the production process and will not disturb your workflow. Automated order processing and controlling. Logs faulty data files, which can then be amended with DigiScript. Both DigiScript and DigiServer allow you to use OneVision Imposition to impose documents from any hardware architecture and/or application making it possible to process data that has entered the production in PS, EPS, PDF, AI, or

TIFF format. Also supports OPI. No import filters required. Folding schemes.

PenOp
PenOp Inc.
One Penn Plaza, Suite 2407, New York, NY 10119
Tel: (212) 244-3667 Fax: (212) 244-1646
www.penop.com
Provides secure electronic sign-off, approval, and authentication for documents and forms within Acrobat Exchange. PenOp technology enables the safe and legal execution of electronic documents through the innovative combination of cryptography and biometrics. Designed to be the legal equivalent of a handwritten signature on paper, PenOp captures the signing event using an inexpensive digitizer and links it to an Acrobat Exchange document or form, creating a Biometric Token—an evidentiary record of who signed what, when, and why. PenOp allows users to sign Acrobat Exchange documents and forms using the PenOp plug-in for Acrobat Exchange. PenOp's Software Development Kit, as well as a number of other plug-ins or PenOp-enabled document management and workflow solutions, are also available for customization of the particular environment.

Quite Software Ltd.
105 Ridley Road, Forest Gate, London E7 0LX UK
Tel: 44 181 257 1044 Fax: 44 181 522 1726
www.quite.com
Quite Imposing and Quite Imposing Plus provide a toolkit for performing imposition. Rather than adapting existing imposition technology to PDF, these plug-ins are exploiting the new possibilities and new ways of working that PDF makes possible.

Quite Imposing
Quite Software Ltd.
105 Ridley Road, Forest Gate, London E7 0LX UK
Tel: +44 181 257 1044 Fax:+44 181 522 1726
www.quite.com
Quite Imposing Plus' extra features include "Step and Repeat," manual imposition, page numbering, and electronic masking tape.

P/Comp
Radtke Consulting
4707 140th Avenue N., Suite 103, Clearwater, FL 33762
Tel: (813) 531-8205 Fax: (813) 531-9141
rradtke@gte.net
A PDF Comparison Plug-In. Using P/Comp will build bookmarks and links that describe the differences between two PDF files. P/Comp uses different colors of links to highlight differences in font types, size, position, and most importantly, new or missing words. Bookmarks are organized into New Words and Missing Words by page in the PDF.

Bookworm
Radtke Consulting
4707 140th Avenue N., Suite 103, Clearwater, FL 33762
Tel: (813) 531-8205 Fax: (813) 531-9141
rradtke@gte.net
Allows a user to select fonts, sizes, attributes, and/or strings to be used to create Bookmarks in a PDF document. The Bookworm searches through a document and when a match is found it creates a bookmark to the location of the Match in the document.

RC:Splitter
Radtke Consulting
4707 140th Avenue N., Suite 103, Clearwater, FL 33762
Tel: (813) 531-8205 Fax: (813) 531-9141
rradtke@gte.net
RC:Splitter—An Automated PDF Splitter and Combiner Plug-In. Based on selected criteria, this plug-in searches a PDF and when the criteria changes the plug-in creates a new PDF document with all the pages up to the changed page. The tool can optionally recombine the newly created PDFs into a reorganized complete document.

PDM
Radtke Consulting
4707 140th Avenue N., Suite 103, Clearwater, FL 33762
Tel: (813) 531-8205 Fax: (813) 531-9141
rradtke@gte.net
PDM—PDF Document Manager. Allows a collection of PDFs to be organized for delivery. The PDM keeps track of where PDFs are located: network drives, removable CDs, jukeboxes. Selection criteria can be searched to find PDFs. When the documents are selected the proper device and location is automatically selected or requested, and the document is opened. This can be used for controlling links across devices or for delivery on CD-ROM.

RTSDuplex
Round Table Solutions
PO Box 211, South Melbourne, 3205 Victoria, Australia
Tel: 61 3 9693 6401 Mobile: 0419 889 751 Fax: (61) 3 9893 3290
www.roundtable.com.au
Double-sided printing made easy, and moreover it halves the amount of paper you would normally use. RTSDuplex doubles your printing options in Acrobat Exchange. RTSDuplex will allow you to print odd, even, and double-sided copies from any printer, even the most archaic, whether in Acrobat Exchange or a Web browser. This plug-in runs only in Acrobat Exchange and Reader.

RTSJoust
Round Table Solutions
PO Box 211, South Melbourne, 3205 Victoria, Australia
Tel: 61 3 9693 6401 Mobile: 0419 889 751
Fax: (61) 3 9893 3290
www.roundtable.com.au
RTSJoust is a streamlining plug-in for Adobe Acrobat Exchange providing three powerful functions, including Send Mail, Save, and Edit/Transfer. RTSJoust makes editing, annotating, and sending a Web-based PDF document a simple, one-click process. This plug-in runs only in Acrobat Exchange and Reader.

LegacyXCHANGE
Solimar Systems Inc.
3940 Fourth Avenue, Suite 300, San Diego, CA 92103
Tel: (619) 294 4960 Fax: (619) 294 5973
www.solimarsystems.com
LegacyXCHANGE is a Windows NT-based print server solution that converts print data intended for Xerox LPS production printers to PDF, PostScript, and PCL. The print server connects directly to legacy host systems including IBM mainframes, AS/400s, RS/ 6000s, Unisys A-series, and UNIX hosts. The emulation is modular and allows automated conver-

sion in a production environment. LegacyXCHANGE translates Xerox resources to the desired output format on-the-fly, providing accurate, simple conversions that can be installed and maintained by the user. Converted data can be delivered to destinations by file, Internet, print queue, or direct connect.

Sys-Print
Sys-Print, Inc.
4151 Memorial Drive, Suite 111-D, Decatur, GA 30032
Tel: (404) 296-7812 or (888) 698-4767
Fax: (404) 296-0884
www.sysprint.com
High-speed transformation software to convert mainframe, legacy data to PDF and/or PostScript. Accepts a variety of data input types, including Xerox DJDE and Metacode, IBM AFP, HP PCL, TIFF and "sys-out" line data. Mainframe and PC operating versions are available, allowing organizations to easily retrieve and view documents for selective printing and archiving. Sys-Print converts mainframe "Sys-Out" data to either a PostScript file for printing, or a PDF file for viewing and storage. The system provides automatic indexing, forms merge, font changing, and graphics. The conversion is accomplished on-the-fly, without distillers, and is up to 40 times faster than alternative methods. Sys-Print software accepts a variety of data input types, including Sys-Out, Xerox DJDE, Xerox Metacode, IBM AFP, and HP PCL. Sys-Print software also offers automatic creation of an index for use as a navigational tool, also referred to as bookmarks. Three levels of indices may be extracted on-the-fly. Users may define the "zoom" variable and the geometric position of the viewable data on the screen.

Techno Design
Koraalrood 1002718 SC Zoetermeer, The Netherlands
www.techdesn@knoware.nl
This XTension for QuarkXPress allows you to create Acrobat Bookmarks, Hyperlinks, and Articles in QuarkXPress. Create Bookmarks and Hyperlinks manually as in Acrobat Exchange or you can create them automatically based on typography by defining so-called Auto Bookmark definitions and Auto Link definition. The PDF Design also allows you to combine a number of QuarkXPress documents into one PDF file via a PDF project manager.

Posta
Tumbleweed Software
2010 Broadway, Redwood City, CA 94063
Tel: (650) 369-6790 Fax: (650) 369-7197
www.tumbleweed.com
Posta is an Internet document delivery solution that allows business users to control and protect the delivery of their important, time-sensitive documents. Posta offers real-time tracking capabilities and several levels of security to the delivery of documents, including encryption, authentication, and password protection. Posta converts files to Adobe Acrobat PDF automatically while sending to let recipients easily view document regardless of what applications or OS they're using.

Ultimate Server
Ultimate Technographics
1 Westmount Square, Suite 1700, Montreal,

QU Canada H3Z 2P9
Tel: (514) 938-9050 or (800) 363-3590
Fax: (514) 938-5225
www.ultimate-tech.com
The Ultimate Server is a new concept in PDF workflow for prepress. The Ultimate Server uses the technologies of Impostrip, UltimateFlow, and Trapeze and combines them into a single powerful PDF workflow. The Ultimate Server is designed to have multiple processes on one machine, with load balancing in mind (Mac or NT). The Ultimate Server's main concept is to only move the data once by processing the data through an integrated workflow stream. The benefits of this workflow will have a revolutionary impact on time saving, productivity, and prepress resources.

Sonar Bookends
Virginia Systems, Inc.
5509 West Bay Court, Midlothian, VA 23112
Tel: (804) 739-3200 Fax: (804) 739-8376
www.virginiasystems.com
Automatic index generation software for PDF and other types of documents. Indexes can be created for single files or multiple files. The index can be single or multilevel. Sonar Bookends can detect and index proper nouns, produce an index of all words based on their frequency, or build an index based on a user-supplied word/phrase list.

Virginia Systems, Inc.
5509 West Bay Court, Midlothian, VA 23112
Tel: (804) 739-3200 Fax: (804) 739-8376
www.virginiasystems.com
High-speed text retrieval system that can search through the text in PDF and other format files at over 12,000 pages per second. Supports Boolean, proximity, wild card, synonym, phonetic, and quorum searches. Reports generated automatically.

xToolsOne
xman Software
350 Pacific Ave., 2nd Floor, San Francisco, CA 94111
Tel: (415) 986-1773 Fax: (415) 438-4905
http://www.xman.com
xToolsOne Plug-ins for Acrobat Exchange aim to enhance productivity and save valuable work time. Create a floating window that provides detailed information about each annotation in an Acrobat document. It can assign creation dates to all annotations and export lists of document annotations. Bend a page's corner for reference. Copy text to clipboard in footnote format. Mark a page as a home page for future reference. Quickly and easily create links and bookmarks. Put marks on a page with nonprinting ink. Focus print area to a user-defined rectangle.

We cannot guarantee the accuracy of this list.

12

OTHER ISSUES

A number of organizations and individuals are keeping track of minor problem areas with PDF workflows. Here is a compendium of those problems that we have seen on at least two lists:

1. There is a limit of 45 inches on viewing page sizes in Acrobat Reader/Exchange. However, pages greater than 45"x45" should still print correctly to a PostScript printer. This is important if you are printing to a wide-format printer.

2. Imagemasks (images with transparent backgrounds) can display incorrectly in Reader and Exchange. They "show through" on preseparated plates where they shouldn't. This can be avoided by unchecking the *smooth text and mono images* box, and is only a display problem.

3. Acrobat Reader/Exchange cannot preview pattern fills on screen. They will probably print OK.

4. Some monochrome images are displayed with a white background when *smooth text and monochrome images* is turned on. Change in Quark's *General Preferences*.

5. Distilling EPS files may give different page sizes when you turn *Use prologues/epilogue* on or off. Turning it off makes Distiller honor the bounding box info by turning it into page params. Turning it on uses the default page size. When exporting as EPS, some files have printed and displayed incorrectly with respect to the bounding box info. There is a new plug-in for Export PS, available on the Adobe Website, which may address some of the problems. New plug-in as of 3.01 update.

6. Screen shots placed in Acrobat may display badly, but the printout is usually OK. One thing to try is turning off the feature *smooth images*. This feature of smooth images can also create display problems with imagemasks (i.e. colored line art). If they display incorrectly, try turning this off.

7. Using compression can cause problems in the images, depending on the level of JPEG compression used. For Windows documents, switch to ZIP 8-bit compression, and switch off subsampling, to ensure that the PDF contains exactly the images that went into it and still have a healthy compression. Never use *subsample*, always *downsample*. For monochrome bit maps, use manual compression, CCITT Group 4.

8. When viewing certain graphic images or screens, the images or screens will be incomplete or inaccurately displayed. The display error can be eliminated by increasing the zoom factor. Under *Preferences* there is a new option called *Smooth text and monochrome images*. The default is to have this feature on (checked). By changing the default to off (clearing the check), the problem (inaccurately displayed screens) is eliminated without any loss of fidelity to the displayed PDF pages.

9. Some text rendered in a TrueType font may not appear when viewing a PDF file. Turn off *greek text below xxx pixels* in the Reader/Exchange options. Some TrueType fonts do not distill correctly and characters are replaced by rectangles. This usually indicates the original font had bad encoding. It could also be a viewing problem, due to exceeding the GDI TrueType complexity limit. Distiller's handling of poor TrueType fonts is pretty good.

10. When viewing a rotated page using paragraphs of TrueType fonts, Reader often will not rotate the text. This is a Windows TrueType rendering deficiency. It appears Windows cannot display text with arbitrary transformation matrices. The PDF file usually prints correctly to a PostScript printer.

12. Acrobat Distiller will never embed the standard Base 13 PostScript fonts, even when *embed all fonts* is chosen. This may be addressed in future versions. In a perfect world, this would be OK, since all PostScript RIPs ship with the Base 13 installed. However, if a customer has chosen to edit one of the Base 13 fonts without renaming it, a PDF workflow will result currently in the modified font being replaced at output time by the original font installed at the RIP. And it really is 14 since Zapf Dingbats is included.

13. On the Macintosh, the LaserWriter driver gives preference to fonts loaded in the System Folder. If the System Folder has TrueType Helvetica, or even an old version of PS Helvetica from pre-TrueType days, and you also loaded a PS version of Helvetica using a program like Suitcase, when creating the PS file, the TrueType version (or older PS version) from the system folder will be used. Likewise, if both PS and TrueType are loaded in the System folder, the OS will give precedence to the TrueType version.

14. Type 3 fonts are bitmap fonts, and may be used for things like Frames in Quark. Acrobat does not like Type 3 fonts, and probably will not work. Do not use the *smooth text and graphics* option in the QuarkXPress *print setup* box. This creates bitmap areas around the edges of fonts, and is designed for laser printer output, not imagesetter. Do not use Type 3 fonts (including Geneva, New York, etc.).

15. In Distiller making the choice of *subsetting below 99%* means subsetting whenever there are *less than* 99% of the full complement of glyphs. This means that even for fonts with large complements of glyphs, you will get a subset unless all but a few characters are used.

Proposal for handling bleeds in PDF by Aandi Inston

Bleeds are almost unknown in the world of desktop printing, but are an everyday essential for high-end users. Because the cutting and binding of paper is not infinitely accurate, page contents extend off one or more of the edges of a trimmed page. The excess is set to be larger than the tolerances in the page cutting.

At their simplest, bleeds are almost a "non-issue" since the image is made larger and printed on a larger sheet. This is trimmed after printing. Bleeds become a production issue when they are combined with the automatic addition of trim marks (rather than including them in the design); or with automatic cutting; or especially with imposition, where pages are combined onto a larger sheet, which may be folded and trimmed in a variety of ways.

Although some applications allow the user to adjust for bleeds when printing or imposing, there is a lack of uniformity. There seems no public, widely adopted standard for specifying bleeds in either PDF or PostScript files. In practical terms, there is no use defining any sort of standard if nobody uses it. However, there is a need to define processing of bleeds for imposition applications which work with PDF.

The simplest proposal requires no effort or changes. That is to reuse two existing concepts in the PDF specification—the media box (usually the original page size, and almost no applications allow this to be changed); and the crop box (which

Two examples: 1. Default subsetting (35 percent), "always embed," standard glyph complement (229 glyphs). If the file uses from one to 145 glyphs from the font, a subset will be embedded. If the file uses from 146 to 224 glyphs, the whole font (without a name change) will be embedded. 2. 99% subsetting, "always embed," Expert glyph complement (165 glyphs). If the file uses one to 163 glyphs, a subset will be embedded. If it uses 164 or 165 glyphs, the whole font will be embedded. Subsetting fonts and using the recommended *subset below 99%* will result in editing problems of the eventual PDF file, if a glyph is needed that is not contained in the subset.

This can be worked around if the font is available to the system at the time of editing, but could result in changes. If using a font resident in the system to provide editing of a subsetted font, "exporting as PostScript" results in the RIP sometimes reporting a missing font, and defaulting. The 99 percent figure does not mean that 99 percent of your font is included. It means that "a subset of the font, representing only the used characters, is included, unless more than 99 percent of the characters are used, in which case the entire font is included."

Exporting PS does not work if there is an embedded font. If you print to file with the LaserWriter driver it will download the TT font scaler and embed the TT font in the stream. No Courier substitution takes place. However, printing to a PostScript file from Exchange will usually result in the newly used system-accessed font being embedded. It is possible to re-embed the font in the PDF file. When preparing a PDF file for blind exchange, it may be advisable to subset when creating the document, and afterwards, use PitStop to embed only those fonts you know are likely to be edited.

16. TrueType fonts pose problems for Distiller and Exchange. A normal printer driver on a Mac platform will create Type 1 outlines of TrueType fonts when creating PostScript, in order to support the majority of output devices that do not have a TrueType rasterizer. Unfortunately, Distiller strips out these Type 1 outlines leaving only the TrueType in the file. If the

resultant PDF is then exported as PostScript or EPS out of Exchange, there is no Type 1 font information, and the job fails at the RIP if no TrueType rasterizer is present.

17. Distiller could emit incorrect definitions for spot colors, in situations where the color is never used at 100 percent in a job. The job will rip properly, but a downstream trapper or separator might have trouble with it. To fix this, place a block of 100 percent color off the page limit (as color bars, for instance).

18. The default setting when Acrobat is loaded is to turn CMYK images to RGB images. It is possible to create a new PPD for Distiller that changes the default option to retain CMYK.

1. Open the Acrobat Distiller PPD (in Printer Descriptions) in a text editor.

2. Alter the default color space value from RGB to CMYK. % —Device Capabilities ColorDevice: True. DefaultColorSpace: CMYK.

3. Locate the line of text above "Device Capabilities" which reads: PCFileName: ADISTILL.PPD Alter it to read: PCFileName: CMYKDIST.PPD.

4. Do a *Save As* to the edited PPD file in text only format, to the same location, using the name CMYKDIST.PPD, so that it is different from the original file.

19. To handle spot colors, use the prologue/epilogue option in Distiller when converting to PDF. Create EPS files with the PS-Export plug-in under Exchange (using 3.01) and import into QuarkXPress. These files (prologue.ps, epilogue.ps) are installed with Acrobat, but are not easily identifiable. Use *Find* to locate them, and move them into the same folder as the Distiller program. Also, you cannot Distill with Acrobat 2.1 compatibility, you must use the 3.0 format. Any application which requires the earlier version of PDF (PDF 1.1 spec) cannot support spot colors, which requires the 1.2 spec to work. (TrapWise, FreeHand, versions of Preps.) Some in-RIP separations do not support this, but CrackerJack from Exchange usually works.

20. OPI 2 comments are not preserved in Acrobat 3.01.

can be set using cropping tools in Exchange). Overloading of existing functions is dangerous. It would also be difficult to crop a large page and then define a bleed within the cropped area, which is a potential requirement. There is also the danger that users would provide carefully cropped pages for production, with unexpected and undesirable bleeds. This proposal does accommodate a simple rotation.

The proposal is to add a key to the page dictionaries of PDF files for which bleeds are to be used. (The PDF standard allows extra keys to be used; PDF viewers just ignore the ones they do not understand). This would contain information about how the bleeds on a page are to be managed.

It is proposed that the key /QITE_bleed_1 for this, initially (where the _1 indicates version 1 and allows for future developments). The keys can be added by a plug-in to Acrobat Exchange which provides an appropriate user interface (including the ability to define a bleed for all even pages). In the current release of Exchange, these keys survive the Document > Insert Pages and Document > Extract Pages facilities. When Document > Replace Pages is used, the keys from the original (replaced) page are used, which may be undesirable, but there are few options around this.

This is why there is a proposal for attaching page specifications to the page objects—it is about the only way we can keep the specifications as the documents are transformed.

21. In Acrobat Exchange, when you use *Save As a PDF document* with the *Optimize* check enabled, the PDF file is always saved in binary mode (i.e. using 8-bit ASCII characters) and using LZW compression for the page description. This occurs whether the original file was 7-bit ASCII only (which is more robust for transportation between plaftorms), or if the original file used ZIP compression (which is more compact than LZW). While this "optimization" may be appropriate for on-line Web viewing, it is almost always a bad idea for print production. Turn off the *Optimize* switch on the save panel when saving a PDF Document using *Save As*.

22. Do not use the ASCII option when creating PDF files. This is left over from an old version, and only Binary should be used.

23. Often, when a PDF file goes cross-platform or is transmitted over the Internet, it loses the creator field and Acrobat document icon on the Mac. On the Acrobat CD ROM is a small applet called 'PDF' (the file name includes the single quotes), which can be found in one of the Utilities folders. Dragging the PDF file on top of this applet will fix the problem. This applet is also known as "Acrobatizer." Going the other direction through e-mail from the Mac to the PC, do not use binhex to encode the file. Use AppleSingle or Base64 instead so the PC user is able to read the file.

This list was compiled from information distributed by Thad McIlroy at the Seybold New York event during the PDF Day session, and by an ad hoc group of PDFophiles from Europe, as well as material discussed on the PDF Web forum.

13

TO RECAP

Acrobat Distiller Job Options
From the Distiller menu, select *Job Options* and the *General* tab.
From the *Compatibility* list, select Acrobat 3.0.
If selected, clear the ASCII Format box.
Set *Default Resolution* and *Default Page Size* as required.

To select Compression options:
Select the *Compression* tab.
Select the *Compress Text and Line Art* check box.
Clear *Downsample to* or *Subsample to* check boxes for *Color Bitmap Images*, *Grayscale Bitmap Images* and *Monochrome Bitmap Images*.
For *Color Bitmap Images*, select the *Manual Compression* check box, and from the list select ZIP (8 bit).
For *Grayscale Bitmap Images*, select the *Manual Compression* check box, and from the list select ZIP (8 bit).
For *Monochrome Bitmap Images*, select the *Manual Compression* check box, and from the list select CCITT Group 4.

Fonts can be embedded in the PDF file. If they are not embedded in the PDF file, Exchange, or Reader may substitute Multiple Master fonts if the real outline font is not available.

To Select Font Embedding Options:
Select the Font Embedding tab.
Select the *EmbedAll Fonts* check box.
Select the *Subset Fonts Below* check box, and fill in the % box with the amount needed. We recommend 99%, to include maximum font information.
Add fonts to the *Always Embed* list and *Never Embed* list as they are needed.

To Select Advanced Options:
Select the Advanced tab.
Select the Distill with prologue.ps/ epilogue.ps check box.
Clear the *Convert CMYKImages to RGB* check box.
Select the *Preserve OPI Comments* check box.
Select the *Preserve Overprint* settings check box.
Select the *Preserve Halftone Screen Information* check box.
From the *Transfer Functions* list, select *Preserve.*
From the *Under Color Removal Black Generation* list, select *Preserve.*
Select *Unchanged* from the *Color Conversion* options.
Choose *OK.*

To Export PostScript from Acrobat Exchange:
From the File menu select *Export* then PostScript or EPS.
From the *Format* list select *PostScript Job.*
Select *ASCII* or *Binary* as required.
Select the page range to print.
From the *PostScript* list select *Level 1* or *Level 2* as required.
From the *Font Inclusion* list select *None* or *All*
Embedded Fonts as required.
Select *Include Halftone Screens* as required.
Select *Include RGB and Lab Images* as required.
Choose *Save.*

Saving the PostScript File:
Pick the location in which you want to save the PostScript file and enter a name.
Choose *Save.*

Font Substitution

Delete the file named superatm.db1 from the Fonts folder inside the Acrobat folder. This will prevent font substitution with Adobe sans and serif fonts if a font is not found. Other applications install this file as well, so as more apps become PDF-aware, you may want to do a search for this document after installing any Adobe apps, and delete it.

Embedding the Standard PostScript Fonts

Acrobat Distiller will never embed the standard Base 13 PostScript fonts, even when *Embed all Fonts* is chosen. This may be addressed in future versions. In a perfect world, this would be okay, since all PostScript RIPs ship with the Base 13 installed. However, if a customer has chosen to edit one of the Base 13 fonts without renaming it, a PDF workflow will result with the modified font being replaced at output by the original font installed at the RIP. Sorry to repeat ourselves, this is a recap.

Dealing with True Type

The Laserwriter driver gives preference to fonts in the System folder. If the System folder has TrueType Helvetica, or even an old version of PostScript Helvetica from pre-TrueType days, and you have also loaded a PS version of Helvetica using a program like Suitcase when creating the PS file, the TrueType version (or older PS version) from the system folder will be used. Likewise, if both PostScript and TrueType are loaded in the System folder, the OS will give precedence to the TT version.

Distiller will embed them as unPostScriptable gibberish names, so its easy to catch them in the font usage screen. Best bet is to trash the Apple-supplied fonts and replace them with the Base 13 from one of your Adobe application distributions.

Type 3 Fonts

Type 3 fonts are bitmap fonts, and may be used for things like Frames in Quark. Acrobat does not like Type 3 fonts, and probably will not work. Do not use the *Smooth text and graphics* option in the Quark print set-up box. This creates bitmap areas around the edges of fonts, and is designed for laser printer output, not imagesetters.

Subsetting Fonts

Making the choice in Distiller set-up of *Subsetting below 99%* means subsetting whenever there are less than 99 percent of the full complement of glyphs. This means that even for fonts with large complements of glyphs, you will get a subset unless all but a few characters are used. Two examples:

- Default subsetting (35%), *always embed*, standard glyph complement (229 glyphs). If the file uses from one to 145 glyphs from the font, a subset will be embedded. If the file uses from 146 to 224 glyphs, the whole font (without a name change) will be embedded.
- 99% subsetting, *always embed*, Expert glyph complement (165 glyphs). If the file uses one to 163 glyphs, a subset will be embedded. If it uses 164 or 165 glyphs, the whole font will be embedded.

Subsetting fonts and using the recommended Subset below 99% will result in editing problems of the eventual PDF file if a glyph is needed which is not contained in the subset. This can be worked around if the font is available to the system at the time of editing, but could result in changes. If using a font resident in the system to provide editing of a subsetted font, exporting as PostScript results in the RIP sometimes reporting a missing font, and defaulting.

Exporting PostScript does not work if there is an embedded font. If you print to file with the Laserwriter it will download the TrueType font scaler and embed the TrueType font in the stream. No Courier substitution takes place. Printing to a PostScript file from Exchange will usually result in the newly used system-accessed font being embedded. It is possible to re-embed the font in the PDF file by using Pitstop 1.5. To prepare a PDF file for blind exchange, subset when creating the document, and use PitStop to embed only those fonts likely to be edited.

Startup Options for Distiller

In the Acrobat folder, there is a startup folder, which preconfigures Distiller. It is possible to customize the startup so Distiller is preconfigured correctly. It is also possible to create preconfigured hot folders which Distiller watches.

Do not use the ASCII option when creating PDF files. This is left over from an old version, and only Binary should be used.

CMYK Images to RGB Images
The default setting when Acrobat is loaded is to turn CMYK images to RGB images. It is possible to create a new PPD for Distiller, which changes the default option to retain CMYK.

1. Open the Acrobat Distiller PPD (in Printer Descriptions) in a text editor.
2. Alter the Default color space value from RGB to CMYK

*% ==== Device Capabilities ===
*ColorDevice: True
*DefaultColorSpace: CMYK

3. Locate the line of text above Device Capabilities which reads

*PCFileName:ADISTILL.PPD
and alter it to read
*PCFileName: CMYKDIST.PPD

4. Do a *Save As* to the edited PPD file in text only format, to the same location, using the name CMYKDIST.PPD, so that is is different from the original file.

Distilling EPS Files
Distilling EPS files may give you different page sizes when you use prologues/epilogue, either on or off.

Turning it off makes Distiller honor the bounding box info, by turning it into page params. Turning it on, uses the default page size. Also, when exporting as EPS, some files have printed and displayed incorrectly with respect to the bounding box info.

There is a new plug-in for Export PS, available on the Adobe Website, which may address some of the problems. The new plug-in will be loaded standard with the Acrobat 3.01 update.

Turning Single-page EPS Files into a Multipage PDF
Read the file named "RunDirEx.txt" (WIN), or RunfileEx.ps (MAC) in the Acrobat:Xtras folder for how to distill an entire directory of PostScript or EPS files into a single PDF. This will cause the files to be processed oldest to newest by default. Rundirex.txt and all the other examples end up with an extra end on the stack if prologue/epilogue is used so the job errors out. Below is modified code that gets around this.

```
%!
/prun {/mysave save def dup = flush RunFile clear cleardict-
stack mysave
restore} def
mypsfile1.ps RunFile
mypsfile2.ps RunFile
%%RunFile is used instead of prun. This prevents dictstack-
underflow error
%%when distilling with epilogue.ps and prologue.ps
%EOF
```

Dealing with Duotones
Acrobat Distiller does not correctly handle duotones, and similar constructs such as colored monochrome TIFFs, etc. This is because duotones are usually produced using a separation effect, as well as a transfer function. The separation will not hold true in PDF, which is a composite workflow. Transfer functions can be maintained through a Distiller setting, although most prepress instructions are to turn this feature off. There is no good workaround for this except going back to the files and resaving them as EPS files in Photoshop, and changing any instruction which relies on creating a separated file. In theory, this should be fixed by PostScript 3 RIPs.

Using CrackerJack for Separations
Crackerjack relies on in-RIP separation, and therefore will not work on many Level 2 laser printers which do not provide this capability. Level 3 printers should fix this problem. Using Luminous Preprint Pro can get around this issue, since Preprint provides for on-host separation, as opposed to in-RIP. The new Laserwriter and PS Printer drivers available from Apple and Adobe respectively (8.5.1) can also call in-RIP separations.

Display Bugs
Screen shots placed in Acrobat display very badly, however, the printout is usually OK. One thing to try is turning off the feature smooth images. This feature of smooth images can also create display problems with imagemasks (i.e., colored line art) If they display incorrectly, try turning this feature off.

Cross-Platform PDF Files Losing Creator and Icon
Often, when a PDF file goes cross-platform or is transmitted over the Internet, it loses the creator field and Acrobat document icon on the Mac. On the Acrobat 3.0 CD-ROM, is a small applet called 'ŒPDF1' (the file name includes the single quotes), which can be found in one of the *Utilities* folders. Dragging the PDF file on top of this applet will fix the problem. This applet is also known as Acrobatize. Going the other direction through e-mail from the Mac to the PC, do not use binhex to encode the file. Use AppleSingle or Base64 instead, and the PC user should be able to read the file.

Compression Tip
Using compression can cause problems in the images, depending on the level of JPEG compression used.

For Windows documents, switch to ZIP 8-bit compression, and switch off subsampling, to ensure that the PDF contains exactly the images that went in to it—and still have a healthy compression. This may work for Mac documents but needs to be tested.

Never use *subsample*, always use *downsample*. For monochrome bit maps, use manual compression, CCITT Group 4 for the best results.

Spot Colors
Use the prologue/epilogue option in Distiller when converting to PDF. Create EPS files with PSExport plug-in under Acrobat Exchange (make sure you are using 3.01) and import that into QuarkXPress. These files (prologue.ps, epilogue.ps) are installed with Acrobat, but are not easily identifiable. Use *Find* to locate them, and move them into the same folder as the Distiller program.

You cannot Distill with Acrobat 2.1 compatibility, you must use the 3.0 format. Any application which requires the earlier version of PDF (PDF 1.1 specification) cannot support spot colors, which requires the 1.2 spec to work. (For example, Trapwise, Freehand, current versions of Preps) Some in-RIP separations do not support this, and you have to use CrackerJack.

Overprinting

Quark 3.3 does not hold the overprint instructions when printing as composite. One choice to get overprint from Quark 3.32 is to use the APX/LPX extension from Luminous, which creates DSC-compliant Quark. However, since this does not go through the printer driver, TrueType fonts are not embedded, and therefore do not work with PDF.

Imposition and PDF

You need to distill the output file from Preps, then use Crackerjack from Exchange to print to file. If you use Crackerjack before Preps you will receive a grayscale flat from Preps. If your RIP can do separations then you don't need CrackerJack. Sometimes when you *Distill* a flat all you see are the trim marks, color bars, etc. The rule of thumb used is:

If composite PostScript in then separate on the RIP.

If separated PostScript in, then you have to print separated from Preps, and Acrobat may not help you out.

14

ADOBE CAPTURE

Acrobat Capture software lets you easily convert one scanned page or thousands to Portable Document Format, while preserving all the original fonts, formatting, and images. Acrobat Capture is compatible with all the leading scanners. You can use the new Software Development Kit (SDK) to customize Acrobat Capture for your own paper-to-PDF conversion system. Document capture vendors can help you automate big paper-to-PDF conversion projects.

Convert Paper to PDF

Turn printed documents into instantly accessible resources instead of artifacts awaiting rediscovery. Adobe Acrobat Capture software makes it fast and easy to put paper documents online. Acrobat Capture lets you convert paper documents to electronic files in the Adobe PDF, which accurately reproduces the look and feel of the printed page, complete with fonts, graphics, formatting, and color, black-and-white or grayscale images.

PDF files are searchable, and you can add annotations, cross-document links, and bookmarks to help readers navigate quickly using Acrobat.

The Acrobat Capture, Import, and Scan plug-ins for Power Macintosh were not available when Acrobat 3.0 was released but are included in Acrobat 3.01. The Acrobat Import and Scan plug-ins can be used within Exchange to create PDF Image Only documents. The Capture plug-in converts PDF Image Only documents to PDF Normal document. The Macintosh Import plug-in supports PICTas well as TIF, GIF, PCX, and BMP formats on Windows.

Adobe Capture and the Acrobat 3.0 Capture Plug-in: The Same But Different

Both Adobe Acrobat Capture and the Acrobat 3.0 Capture Plug-in, which is included with Adobe Acrobat 3.x, are designed to create electronic documents from scanned originals.

Batch Processing
Capture can process multiple documents into PDF format at once when used with batch processing scanners; the Capture Lite Plug-in onlyonly handles one page at a time.

Editing
Both Capture and the Capture Plug-in use Optical (or Object) Character Recognition to convert bitmap text to text that can be corrected, indexed, searched, or copied to other files. When you use Capture to process a document to PDF format, it creates an ACD (Adobe Capture Description we think) file. You may correct or edit text in an ACD file before saving it to PDF or a word processing format. The Capture Plug-in, however, does not create ACD files. To edit text in a PDF file created using the Capture Plug-in, use the Acrobat Touch-up Plug-in, which is also included with Acrobat 3.x. You can change a single line of text at a time, including font size or typeface.

Color Scanning
Acrobat Capture 2.0 supports RGB, Indexed, and Grayscale TIFF color images. The Capture Plug-in supports up to 8-bit, 400 dpi, color images.

How Capture Works

1. Scan a printed page of any document—from contracts and spreadsheets to brochures, books, or magazine articles. Acrobat Capture supports many scanners. The image is captured right in Acrobat Exchange.
2. Acrobat Capture converts the scanned image to an electronic copy in PDF.

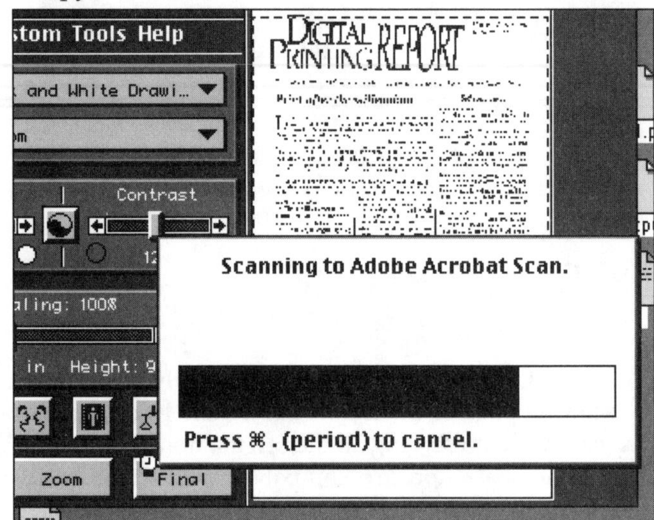

3. Once your document is in PDF, it is completely platform- and application-independent. Now, here is the magic: Capture converts the scanned image into OCR'd text which underlays the scanned image.

Automated Page Recognition

Acrobat Capture 2.0 offers improved page recognition, including support for black & white, grayscale, and color documents—which means improved searchability on highly formatted content such as tables and forms. Acrobat Capture 2.0 also provides automatic downsampling of photos and artwork. The Acrobat Capture 2.0 Reviewer has been improved to include more tools for customers to enhance and alter converted documents, giving them options such as changing text fonts and colors, or importing and placing images. Acrobat Capture 2.0 captures documents in eight languages (U.S. English, U.K. English, German, French, Swedish, Dutch, Spanish, and Italian).

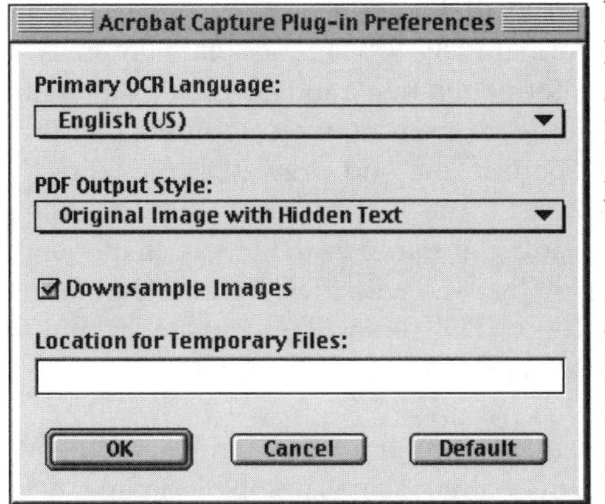

You specify the language for OCR and the level of PDF output in a *Preferences* dialog box.

Adobe Acrobat Capture 2.0 uses a hardware key to monitor throughput (i.e., the conversion of paper to electronic documents). When Capture processes a page, the Acrobat Capture server window opens and displays the number of pages that can be processed with the current hardware key. When you anticipate running out of pages, order another hardware key (page pack).

Most popular desktop and high-volume scanners are supported through ISIS and TWAIN drivers. Convert documents to PDF from common image formats, such as TIFF (including G3, G4, and LZW formats), PCX, BMP, PDF Image. Scan and convert pages up to 27"x27". Scan and convert up to 20,000 pages in batch-processing mode.

OCR, Font, and Page Recognition

Convert paper documents to PDF Normal: for compact, searchable files—the ideal Web format PDF Image: for a cross-platform image of the entire scanned page PDF Image+Text: for an image of the entire scanned page with OCR'd text hidden behind, creating a searchable bitmap—the ideal format for meeting legal requirements to preserve the original scanned image.

Other formats: HTML, ASCII, Rich Text Format (RTF), Microsoft Word version 6 for Windows, and WordPerfect versions 5 and 6 for Windows. Convert paper documents to black-and-white, grayscale, and color files. Schedule scanning and conversion at your convenience with delayed processing.

Capture 2.0 includes a Software Development Kit with information on how to integrate Capture with other products. The Application Programming Interface (API) gives you direct access to the Capture server, which converts TIFF, BMP, and PCX images to PDF and other formats. As an enterprise market application, you can use Capture in any number of workflows, such as:

Network Fax Server. *Connect Capture to your network fax server and convert incoming faxes to PDF. You can easily distribute PDF files so others can read them from a variety of computer systems. Distribution of faxes converted to PDF Normal format requires less network bandwidth than distribution of fax images.*

Network Scanner Use. *Capture with the software for a network scanner (e.g., HP Network Scanjet 5, or Kofax Netscan), and convert files from TIFF to PDF before attaching them to e-mails or posting them to a network drive or departmental Web server.*

Database. *Integrate Capture with a document workflow or management application to automatically convert TIFF files to PDF, then store the PDF files in a document system or database so you can retrieve them using a full-text search.*

The Capture plug-in uses the current PDFWriter settings for font embedding and subsetting when it creates PDF files. To avoid problems when correcting a captured document, be sure that font subsetting is not selected in PDFWriter before capturing the document.

Increase available memory to process complicated grayscale or color images: Necessary memory = Uncompressed Image Size X 3. During Capture processing versions of your document will also be stored as temporary files on your hard disk.

During installation the Microsoft C Runtime Library, Microsoft Controls Library, and Microsoft Portability Library are placed in the Extensions folder within the System folder and are necessary for the Capture, Scan, and Import plug-ins to load and function. Have your scanner's TWAIN driver installed prior to scanning. Some TWAIN drivers have a default setting to store a copy of the preview scan. You may have to increase the memory allocation for Exchange to accommodate the TWAIN driver's stored preview image. Scanning via ISIS drivers is not available on the Macintosh. The Capture plug-in launches the application "Adobe Acrobat 3.0: Capture: Capture Server." The Capture plug-in will not function if the overall path name to the application is longer than 128 characters. Do not nest Exchange in a folder that will cause it to exceed this limitation.

View, Navigate, and Print PDF Files

Portable Document Format PDF Web libraries place volumes of important business information just a mouse click away. With free Acrobat Reader software, users on any computing platform can navigate, scale, zoom in on, and print PDF files directly within their Web browsers. And PDF files can be indexed and searched with the leading intranet search tools. Experience high-quality printing on the Web with PDF! Because they aren't limited to 72 dpi resolution, PDF files will print at the maximum resolution of your black-and-white or color printer.

The Capture plug-in is installed from the Acrobat CD-ROM. Use the Capture plug-in to convert small numbers of paper documents to PDF. If you need to convert large collections of paper documents or electronic images to PDF, upgrade to the full Acrobat Capture product with automated processing features.

Choose *Capture Pages* in Acrobat Exchange. The plug-in uses optical character recognition (OCR) to convert bitmap text to text that can be corrected, indexed, searched, or copied to other files. The text it converts is in PDF image documents that were scanned directly, or imported, into Acrobat. The Capture plug-in can recognize any of eight languages, hide recognized text behind a document image, and downsample images to minimize file size. After you capture a document, you can use the touch-up tool in Exchange to review and correct text.

Capture produces three styles of PDF documents:

1. PDF Normal contains text that is scalable and can be indexed, searched, and copied. Page formatting and images are preserved. Create this kind of file with Acrobat Distiller, PDFWriter, or the Capture Pages command in Exchange. Normal files are significantly smaller than PDF Image Only files.
2. PDF Image Only contains only a bitmap picture of the original document. PDF Image Only files are produced by the Scan and the Import commands in Exchange.
3. PDF Original Image with Hidden Text combines features of PDF Image Only and PDF Normal documents. They contain a bitmap picture of the page, but with OCR recognized text hidden behind the picture. This provides the advantages of searchable text while ensuring that a document is identical in appearance to the original. Great for for legal or archival

purposes. PDF Original Image with Hidden Text files are created only with the *Capture Pages* command in Exchange.

The last format is the most desireable since it preserves the visual integrity of the page while providing an underlying searchability.

When you capture a PDF Image Only file, it usually reduces file size significantly. In most cases, PDF files captured with the PDF Normal setting are smaller than those captured with the PDF Original Image with Hidden Text setting.

Capturing Documents

Documents that you capture are image files that are scanned or imported into Exchange—PDF Image Only files:

1. File > Scan. Choose a scanner and document type; click *Scan.*
2. After the page has been scanned, choose *Document > Capture Pages.*
3. Determine which pages you want to capture by selecting *All Pages, Current Page,* or *Specified Range* and entering page numbers in the text box.

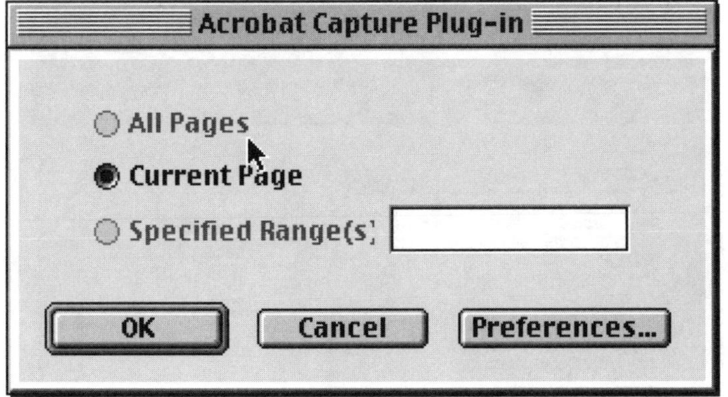

4. To change the Capture preferences, click *Preferences.* The document will be captured with the new settings.
5. Click *OK.* The Capture progress window shows the page, character, and word recognition process. In order for the process to be successful, the resolution of the captured PDF Image Only file must fall within the following ranges:

If you only need to process a few pages at a time, you can use the Capture plug-in included with Acrobat Exchange 3.0. If you need to process large volumes of pages, Acrobat Capture 2.0 provides throughput for 20,000 documents. When more throughput is required, optional packages are designed to fit specific needs.

• *Acrobat 3.0 (Retail Price: $295.00) Acrobat 3.0 includes the Capture plug-in, which lets you convert documents to PDF without using a hardware key. It converts one TIFF file at a time (TIFFs may have multiple pages) using a two-step process, but has an unlimited capacity. The Capture plug-in is available for Windows 3.1 and Windows 95.*

• *Acrobat Capture 2.0 (Retail Price: $895.00) Acrobat Capture includes Capture Reviewer, which lets you edit your captured image before saving it as PDF, and a 20,000-page capacity hardware key. This option offers a high volume of batch conversion on the desktop at an affordable price.*

• *Acrobat Capture 2.0 Volume Edition (Retail Price: $14,995.00) The Volume Edition can process up to one million pages, and includes Capture and Reviewer.*

If you require capacity for more than one million pages, contact your Adobe Sales Representative or Adobe Customer Services at (800) 833-6687 for additional pricing options.

Acrobat Capture 2.0 is available at the suggested retail price of $895 and includes the ability to convert up to 20,000 pages. Additional page packs are available for 20,000 pages and for converting 200,000 pages. Customers will be able to purchase Acrobat Capture 2.0 from Adobe Authorized Resellers or directly from Adobe by calling (800) 272-3623. Registered licensees of Adobe Acrobat Capture 1.0 or 1.01 will be able to upgrade to Acrobat Capture 2.0 at the suggested retail price of $169.

- Monochrome images, 200–600 dpi
- Grayscale or color images, 200–400 dpi

Text should be dark against a light background. Text on a dark or shaded background, or on a page with complex color gradients may not be recognized.

Watching Capture work is quite amazing. After the scan is done you select *Capture Pages*. The box below comes up and indicates each step in the process of OCR'ing the page. Each area of the page is highlighted as it is being read (OCR'd).

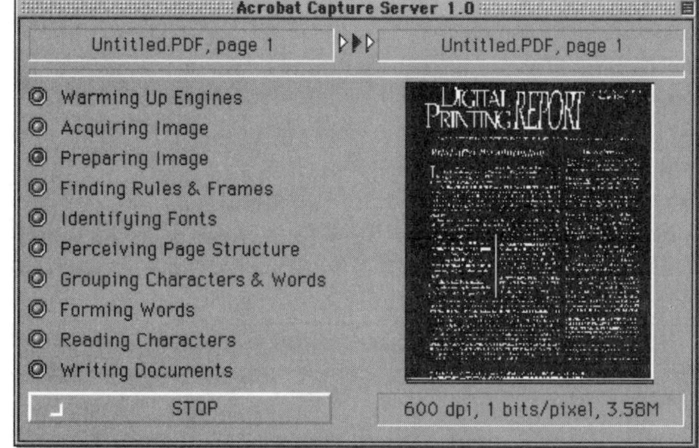

Correcting Captured Documents
When Capture suspects it has not recognized a word correctly, it displays the bitmap image of the original word in the document and hides its best guess for the word behind the bitmap. This ensures accurate reproduction of the original, even without correction. You can review and correct suspect words in Exchange with the text touch-up tool. This is useful when you want your document to be fully searchable.

Remember, you are creating two files in one: the scanned bitmap of the page and the underlaying text for searchability. File sizes could get a bit high. Here are some sample file sizes for comparison purposes with *Downsampling* off and on. The examples are at 300 dpi but OCR and image quality are best at 600 dpi.

Downsampling Off 300 dpi	**TIFF File**	**PDF Image**	**PDF Normal**	**PDF Original Image + Text**
Black and White	1043K *190K*	202K	161K	213K
4-bit Grayscale	8335K *606K*	421K	222K	328K
8-bit Grayscale	8333K *796K*	1183K	756K	884K
24-bit RGB Color	2499K *3085K*	2531K	1832K	2044K

Downsampling On 300 dpi	**TIFF File**	**PDF Image**	**PDF Normal**	**PDF Original Image + Text**
Black and White	1043K *190K*	202K	61K	94K
4-bit Grayscale	8335K *606K*	421K	222K	325K
8-bit Grayscale	8333K *796K*	1183K	113K	309K
24-bit RGB Color	2499K *3085K*	2531K	500K	616K

The italic number is LZW Compression. Group 4 Compression is even greater.

Build a Business

Here is a great example of Acrobat Capture in action:

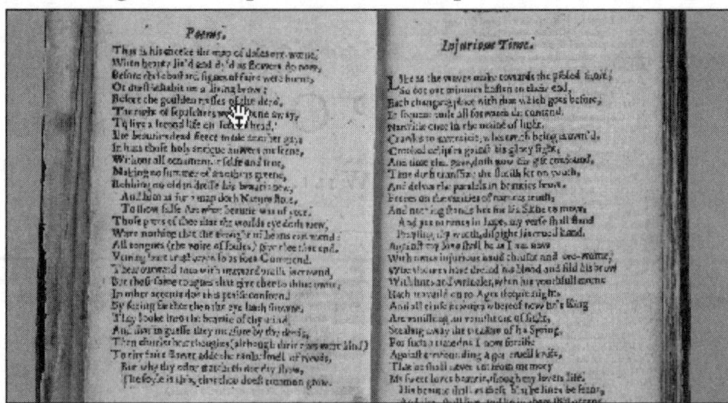

The illustration is the Shakespearean First Folio in all its glory. Scanned, OCR'd, and PDF'd by Octavo (www.octavo.com). You can buy the book on CD-ROM in PDF form.

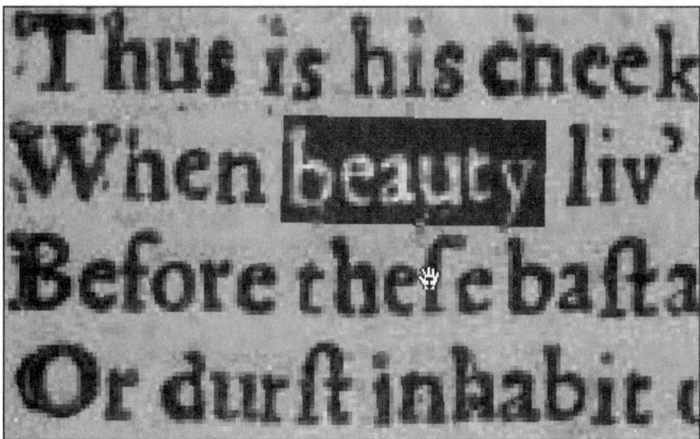

Even at 800% zoom you can read the text which is the exact replica of the First Folio. But when we searched for a word the underlying OCR'd text matched up with the image and both were highlighted. Think of the new market this technology opens for archival materials in paper form. Now they can be electronic.

15

APPENDIX

Some areas of the Adobe Acrobat PDF require a little more detail and we have placed that detail in this Appendix. Some of it repeats material already covered.

The Threshold

We now recommend 99 percent as the "subset below" threshold. Why didn't we recommend 100 percent? Because if you make the "threshhold" to where a font is subset, it will not subset—it will embed the entire character set with the same name. To create PDF files that are very reliable, then subsetting at 99 percent is your best bet.

Let us say I use Hobo and embed it (without subsetting). I have an old version of Hobo and you have a newer (possibly different) version of Hobo loaded. You open my PDF document on your system and Exchange or Reader "tells" your system it needs Hobo and the system says fine here it is—it loads your Hobo, and ignores the Hobo in my PDF—and if it is different, well, it will display and print differently. If I force all embeded fonts to subset by setting it to 99 percent—meaning "as long as you do not use more than 99 percent of the character set, make a subset and rename the font." This forces your system to download the fonts embeded inside my PDF file, since you will not have this custom-named font in your system, making it display and print the way I intended.

Because the 1986 version of Adobe's Palatino that came with your original imagesetter is not the same as the 1997 version that I bought from my Type on Call disk last month. Honest!

If Distiller runs into a needed font while distilling a PostScript file and the font is
• neither a currently active Type 1 font
• nor a font embedded in the PostScript code
• nor in any other way accessible for Distiller
then Distiller tries to look it up in the superatm.db (short form of SuperATM Database, though we'll never understand why the Acrobat team chose to name the same file 'distsadb.dos' for the Wintel version) to retrieve the metric information needed to convert the PostScript pages into PDF (the font outline is actually not needed, because Distiller does not do any rasterizing).

The advantage is:
• If you are ok with Adobe's font substition approach, you'll get a file with properly measured fonts (characters siting where they should sit). If on the taget machine Reader or Exchange have the respective original font available, they will use that original font, and you'll see perfect character shapes, etc. If the target output machine does not have the respective original font loaded, Adobe's font substitution machinery will jump in and simulate the font fairly well—well enough for tech docs, internet use, etc.

The disadvantage is:
• If you are creating PDF files for prepress production, font substitution definitely is not your preferred option. In this case it is better to force Distiller to not use substitution information, but at least issue a message "Font not found—using Courier" (in the log window, log file, and message file) and also arrive at a file that has Courier instead whatever font was missing. If you remove superatm.db, Distiller will not alert you, but also will not be able to retrieve font metrics for otherwise missing fonts at all.

Font Descriptor
The PDF Language manages fonts through the use of a "font

descriptor," a small object including enough information to allow a PDF-based application to find or simulate a font needed in the document. PDF also allows an actual font (either a complete or subset font) to be included in the document. Details are found in Chapter 7 of the PDF Reference Manual.

PDF defines a base set of 14 fonts for which no font descriptor is required in a PDF document. These fonts are treated as universal, because they are "guaranteed" to be available with the Acrobat Reader and other Adobe-produced PDF-based applications. The base 14 fonts are *never* included in a PDF document.

Although the PDF Reference Manual discusses font substitution, and identifies font descriptors as the means to accomplish font substitution, substitution is really a feature of applications attempting to generate, display, or print PDF, not of the language itself. This is because substitution is a "behavior," rather than a language feature. In other words, different applications may implement different behaviors when handling a PDF font descriptor for which they cannot find the original font.

In Acrobat Distiller, font substitution may be managed through use of a font database. This font datatbase is essentially the PDF font descriptors for several thousand commercially available fonts. Distiller uses the font database to construct font descriptors and manage metrics for fonts referenced but not available when creating a PDF document from a PostScript file. ("Available" means included in the PostScript file in such a way as to be defined by Distiller, or available through ATM, or in the usual places on the system.)

If, while converting a PostScript file, Distiller encounters a reference to a font which is not available, Distiller will attempt to look the font up in the font datatbase in order to correctly place characters on the page. If Distiller finds the font in the database, it will insert the font's descriptor into the document. The resulting PDF file will be identical to what Distiller produces when the font is present, but not embedded.
If Distiller does not have the font database available when it is converting, and a font is not available, Distiller will produce an

error message, and will use Courier instead of the font. This will usually result in incorrect page appearance when the resulting PDF document is viewed or printed, even if the system used to view or print the file has the originally missing font available. This is why some users do not recommend removing superatm.db. One can discover the missing font and correct it, but once the file has been Distilled with a missing db, there is no fix except for re-Distilling.)

Acrobat Reader and Acrobat Exchange use the font descriptors in a PDF file, both for viewing and printing, in much the same way as Distiller uses the font databse. This only happens when a font is not available at the time of viewing/printing ("available" here meaning the font, full or subset, is included as a resource in the PDF document or is found on the system where Reader/Exchange is running).

If a font is available, Reader/Exchange will use the font for viewing and printing. If a font is not available, Reader/Exchange will use the PDF font descriptor in conjunction with Adobe Type Manager to simulate the appearance of the font onscreen. When printing, Reader/Exchange will use a printer-resident font in preference to a simulated font, but will use an included subset or full font over a printer-resident font.

Reader provides the facility, through the *Fonts...* sub-selection of the *Document Info* menu, to get a list of all fonts, including substituted fonts, in a document. If a missing font is subsequently loaded onto the system where Reader is running and Reader (and the system itself, in the case of the Macintosh) is restarted, the Reader will no longer substitute, but will use the real font for viewing and printing.

Turning type into outlines at the desktop is an alternative... and a kludge. You can live with it for short bits of display type in Illustrator EPS files, but it is not the cure, especially where designers set running copy in TT in a DTP application like Quark or PageMaker. A font policy for Type 1 is:

- Always use the client's version of every font to avoid subtle changes including reflow and font variations, and

• Wherever possible download fonts to printer disks and omit fonts from print-to-disk and Quark APX exports for PressWise. You cannot download a TrueType font to the printer's disk. Same problem arises for Multiple Master fonts. It is usually not an option for us as a service bureau either to convert a TrueType font into PS type 1 format (font gets altered, hinting dies or changes), nor to force the DTP application to substitute a comparable T1 font (text will reflow, client may not agree, often no equivalent Type 1 available.) Nor is it practical to compel clients to stop using TrueType.

The PDF file does embed the 7- and 8-bit custom encoding differences even for the standard fonts, which is why it prints correctly on a PostScript printer. However, the 8-bit re-encodings cannot be read on screen and therefore do not print on inkjets.

TrueType Fonts

A Type 42 PostScript font is a TrueType font that's just had a little "wrapping" put around it. It's still a TrueType font; a PostScript interpreter has to include a TrueType rasterizer (which all PostScript Level 2 interpreters do, although this capability was added to Level 2 after the Red Book was published) in order to do anything useful with the font. TrueType fonts are often converted to a PostScript readable format by adding code which makes a PostScript interpreter able to handle them. Whether or not there is any alteration of the TrueType code itself still appears to be a question in the quadratic vs. cubic PostScript interpretation is unknown.

The Microsoft PostScript driver has three basic choices:

1. Send TrueType fonts according to the font substitution table. This does not specify how the fonts will be sent, just which ones will be sent a "TrueType" and which ones substituted with the PostScript fonts on the printer, such as Times, Helvetica, etc.
2. Always use buit-in printer fonts instead of TrueType fonts. This may not be a useful option, unless you stick to the Base 14 fonts. The driver does not interrogate the PPD to find out which fonts the printer has, it just uses the Base 14.

3. Always use TrueType fonts. This doesn't tell you how the fonts will be sent, it just means that if you are using Times-Roman, and the driver should download the Times-Roman TrueType font instead of using the PostScript version.

There is a *Send fonts as* button as well, and this tells you what will actually happen to the fonts when they get downloaded. If you choose *Bitmaps* the the fonts are rasterised on the PC, using the Windows TT rasteriser, and sent as Type 3 bitmap fonts. If you select *Outlines*, then the TrueType font outlines are converted into Type 1 font outlines, and the font is downloaded as a Type 1 font. This is done by the PostScrip driver. You lose the hinting information both ways. This is only a problem if running at low resolution. The Adobe driver has the same basic options, but the *Send fonts as* is different. If your PPD's PostScript version is at the right point then you also get the ability to send fonts as Type 42.

Type 42 fonts are essentially the same as TrueType fonts. The actual character data is the same, although the layout of the font is different. Any Level 2 RIP with a TrueType rasteriser will handle Type 42 fonts. This should apply to any commercial Level 2 RIP in the last few years. Type 42 fonts are hinted, so the output will look good at any resolution. The Adobe driver also re-encodes the text, and downloads the fonts in various interesting ways. This is complex and actually looks like an attempt to prevent people from ripping off the embedded font. Again the resulting PDF file can be viewed and printed, but the text in it cannot be indexed or searched for.

For a PDF file to be a portable document you must convert TrueType to PostScript fonts using the print drivers. Not embedding fonts as Type 1 may cause print failures, unless the printer can handle the "Type 42" wrappers. Since PDF documents are allowed to embed TrueType fonts, it is perfectly permissible to embed the original TrueType font in the document, and this is what both PDFWriter and the Macintosh equivalent do. PDF readers must either contain a TrueType rasteriser, or run on an OS with a rasteriser, and pass the work to the Operating System.

When it comes to printing, either the RIP must be able to render the TrueType font as-is, or convert it to Type 42, and then render it. PostScript RIPs, of course, cannot read PDF files directly. If you load the PDF file into Exchange you will need to print it through the PostScript driver to send it to a RIP, which will replace the TrueType fonts with some form of outline.

A PDF cannot embed TrueType, and create a portable document at the same time. You must embed, and convert, the fonts in order to create a file usable by any prepress house on any of their devices. PostScript RIPs are not PDF RIPs (unless they are Adobe Level 3 RIPs, not Language Level 3, but PostScript 3 systems).

PDF and Compression

- Using LZW or ZIP will never cause a loss in quality.
- Using Low JPEG should practically always be ok, and for high quality sheet-fed and web-fed printing—the loss is hardly ever noticeable.
- Using Medium JPEG should practically be okay for newspaper printing (again, the loss is seldom noticeable).

PDF and Downsampling

A big file size saver is the downsampling option in Distiller for images—set it to the value you'd usually use for scans etc. (for grayscale and color images: newspaper: 150 to 200 dpi, sheetfed, etc. around 300 dpi).

Experiments with complete (editorial and ads) pages from newspaper production have shown the following average decrease in file sizes:

PostScript file	100%
Plain PDF	77%
Downsampling to 200 dpi	47%
ZIP compression	27%
Low JPEG instead of ZIP compression	17%
Medium JPEG instead of ZIP compression	7%

Distiller compression settings confuse reduction of bit depth and compression algorithm. ZIP4 uses lossless compression, but only after reducing bit depth of images. ZIP8 uses lossless compression and does not reduce image bit depth. JPEG compression is lossy, and may affect image quality.

1: The built-in Photoshop 4.0 *Save As...JPEG* option:

Quality

Low		*Medium*			*High*		*Maximum*		
1	2	3	4	5	6	7	8	9	10

Small file — *Large File*

File Size

The EPS *Save As* option:

- ASCII
- Binary
- JPEG (low quality)
- JPEG (medium quality)
- JPEG (high quality)
- JPEG (maximum quality)

The JPEG levels under EPS Format appear to exactly mirror the *Save As...JPEG* levels.

Photoshop's "Maximum" quality (minimum compression) setting of JPEG is not lossy (i.e. there is no discernible loss of image quality—all 8-bit per-channel pixel color values are unchanged from the original).

Do the numbers 1 through 10 represent an absolute set of compression algorithms, or is it just a relative scale of values some programmer threw in there to make the user feel good?

2: An older "Photoshop JPEG" plug-in, if put into Photoshop's Plug-ins>Import/Export folder, also shows up in the *Save As...* menu as JPEG, right above 4.0's built-in JPEG option:

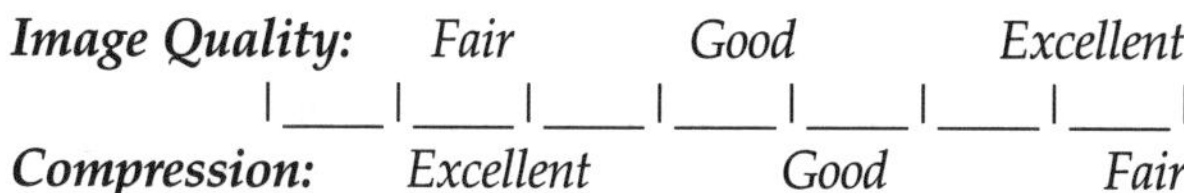

3: In Acrobat Distiller, under Job Options>Compression:

JPEG High
JPEG Medium-High
JPEG Medium
JPEG Medium-Low
JPEG Low
LZW (4-bit)
LZW (8-bit)

In Distiller, "High" means high compression, which means low image quality—not the same as Photoshop's "High" quality setting.

Users archive and retrieve large EPS/CMYK images with Photoshop's *Save As...JPEG* option—and there is absolute fidelity maintained at the "Maximum Quality" setting. It is true that Low, Medium, and High levels are lossy—i.e., artifacts and irregularities appear at color boundaries and within detailed areas. There seems to be a difference between Acrobat Distiller's JPEG compression engine and the Photoshop JPEG engine. They should all implement the same standards of the "Joint Photographic Experts Group."

ZIP and LZW Compression

ZIP is a file format which includes a number of compression options, a directory structure for creating a multifile archive, and some information to guide decompressors and control file attributes when a file is decompressed. The Flate compression scheme is the only thing the ZIP format and compressed PDF (or PostScript 3) data share. ZIP also permits (for compatibility puposes) the use of LZW, although many programs do not support this option in reading and writing ZIP files.

What exactly does 8-bit mean and how does this relate to 24-bit images? A 24-bit image is 3 x 8 bit channels, each of which is compressed without loss. CMYK is 32-bit or 4 x 8-bit. Four-bit

ZIP is lossy. It loses the four least significant bits in each channel, then compresses. ZIP means LZW compression. LZW is not related to JPEG, and is certainly not lossy. The position is confused by the fact that Distiller has two ZIP compression options—4-bit and 8-bit. This is the part that suggests some loss of image data since it implies subsampling. Both of these job options set LZW Encode as the image compression filter, but set Color ImageDepth to four or eight respectively. The Adobe document on Distiller parameters says that this parameter only takes effect when image subsampling is on (i.e. the *Downsample to:* box is checked, and DownsampleGray Images/DownsampleColor Images is true).

To get the best compression with no possibility of loss (i.e., for high-end press work):
- uncheck *Downsample to:* and *Automatic Compression*
- check *Manual Compression*
- choose *ZIP (4 bit)* or *ZIP (8 bit)*—both will have the same effect

Strictly speaking, ZIP and LZW are different animals. The important thing for a user is that ZIP is typically 10 percent better than LZW and is still lossless. The reluctance to trust it is most odd; the same people will happily use PKZIP or STUFFIT which do ZIP compression. ZIP is public domain, while LZW is, according to Unisys, owned by Unisys and you have to pay them for each program that uses it. At least the developer does.

When you select ZIP compression, the corresponding key (GrayImageFilter or ColorImageFilter) really is set to LZW Encode. When you distill a test file with a gray image in it, you get an image XObject encoded using FlateEncode. There's another key lurking in the distillerparams called UseFlateCompression. When "true" (the default), FlateEncode is silenty substituted for LZWEncode in all cases. Since Flate is almost always technically better than LZW, and the public domain nature of Flate makes it much nicer. Both LZWEncode and FlateEncode could just about be called "ZIP" since LZW or closely related cascaded Lempel-Ziv (the L and Z of LZW) methods are used in PKZIP files, and Flate is used in the GNU gzip format.

Trapping
Adobe's PostScript LanguageLevel 3 RIP software offers extensibility to perform other prepress-related functions in the RIP. One of those functions is trapping. There are two types of elements that get processed in the RIP. One is raster, resolution-dependent, such as scanned data files like a picture. The other is vector, resolution-independent such as type, borders, or drawings—anything that is bezier curve based. Each element is treated as a separate object in the PostScript language.

What happens in a RIP? First, the file is interpreted. This means that each object is processed separately and a new list of information is created by the RIP. This Interpreted List is used to create a Render, or raster file. The final stage is then screening. Look at the Interpretive stage. In Adobe's PostScript 3, trapping is applied in the Interpretive stage. This means that trapping is applied to the objects themselves. Since anything digital is binary, trap is either on or off. If it's on, then it's either choke or spread. If it's spread, then it's either one color or another.

QuarkXPress and Trapping
Quark states that traps will not get lost in composite print files in 4.0. This is not true. What QuarkXPress 4.0 does is to make a certain PostScript function (together with the desired amount of trapping) part of the (composite) PostScript code it creates.

QuarkXPress does not use the "setoverprint" operator to define its trapping. Quark uses a proprietary PostScript operator called "settrap" which is not specified in the PostScript Language Reference Manual (LanguageLevel 2) or the PostScript 3010 Supplement (LanguageLevel 3). Therefore, when interpreting a Quark composite PostScript stream in a Adobe PostScript 3 Interpreter the "settrap" commands are lost, not the "setoverprint" commands. The same things happens when converting Quark composite PostScript to PDF using Acrobat Distiller.

Quark implemented the settrap feature in a very clean way: it never breaks anything if digested by a consumer that does not "know" settrap, but can be useful for those consumers that know how to deal with it. It is only contained in composite Post-

Script/EPS (in separated PostScript/DCS output from QuarkXPress the trapping is done through regular imaging operators). This approach (to set up pseudo language operators) can be found in many PostScript producing applications (including Adobe's). At the time when Quark "invented" the settrap operator there was no PostScript 3, and PostScript Level 2 did not offer anything in terms of trapping.

When you go from QuarkXPress via a preseparated PostScript file and Distill to PDF, the traps are kept. Traps are done through regular imaging operators, and will not get lost when run through Distiller.

Acrobat PostScript and Illustrator PostScript

There is a difference between Adobe Illustrator PDF and Distiller PDF; Illustrator PDF looks like Illustrator PostScript (mostly) and can be easily manipulated. Distiller PDF looks like binary. Distiller is a powerful program to "distill" PostScript—convert a PostScript file to the essence of itself with any extraneous byte avoided. That's why it is compressed and binary and looks like a weird sequence of bytes if you open it in a text editor. We remember the disadvantages of PostScript files—the file size.

Turn compression off in Distiller, and select ASCII instead of binary—the files become much more "readable" for hackers, but also less efficient. Do not do this for production. Illustrator is an application for a specific purpose: to assemble a single ensemble of elements into a graphic file.

Distiller has to digest every flavor of PostScript, but there is a more straightforward road from Illustrator PostScript to PDF: no distilling needed with a more direct conversion of PostScript to PDF equivalents. PDF code was never designed for manual creation/editing. Illustrator PDF is usable in most environments, but Distiller PDF built from suspect PostScript is usually unreadable in Illustrator. PDF is the cross-platform, single-format language that PostScript was thought to be. Adobe itself has two different versions of it. It is efficient PDF code in both cases and the differences may be much much smaller than we think.

Optimization
The optimize option gets rid of any unused commands that were discarded when the PDF is heavily edited by Exchange. It's very important to use this because it will greatly reduce the size of files if they have been heavily edited. A regular *Save as* without optimize will collect all of the deleted items. Optimizing will occasionally reduce file sizes, especially of multi-page documents with common backgrounds. You should presume that transmission of a message via SMTP (e-mail) across any network will be treated as a 7-bit ASCII message and not an 8-bit binary file at some point. If that happens and your file is not encoded properly, it will have a problem. Your file must be encoded.

If you're mailing the file, this should happen automatically. There are problems with some products encoding (notably Base64 encoding of e-mail attachments from Netscape's mail client). It has been known to encode some characters that reset or hang communications equipment. You should also use a third-party compression utility to reduce transmission size, and add a CRC integrity check to the file that will fail immediately on attempting to unzip or unstuff it if it was corrupted in transmission. If you're a PC user with those peksy HQX and .sit files, get StuffIt Expander, the free decode/decopress utility from Aladin; they will handle all the major encoding and compression standards: PC, Mac, and UNIX.

The PDF Forum
There is a Web Forum for PDF people. It is quite active and lively and you can usually get the information you want. Here is their message to new members:

If you want to join this mailing list, you can send mail to <majordomo@infomania.com> with the following command in the body of your email message:
  subscribe pdf-prepress-l
If you ever want to remove yourself from this mailing list, you can send mail to <majordomo@infomania.com> with the following command in the body of your email message:
  unsubscribe pdf-prepress-l

or from another account, besides paul@vivacolor-inc.com:
unsubscribe pdf-prepress-l paul@vivacolor-inc.com

If you ever need to get in contact with the owner of the list, (if you have trouble unsubscribing, or have questions about the list itself) send e-mail to
<owner-pdf-prepress-l@infomania.com>.
This is the general rule for most mailing lists when you need to contact a human. Here's the general information for the list you've subscribed to, in case you don't already have it:

This list is intended for discussion of the Adobe PDF file format as it relates to prepress production. To submit e-mail to the list itself, and therefore the many people that subscribe to the list, send e-mail to:
<pdf-prepress-l@infomania.com>

Please note that there is a digested version of this list available. The name of that list is:
pdf-prepress-d
and can be subscribed to in much the same manner that this list was by sending e-mail to
<majordomo@infomania.com>
and placing "subscribe pdf-prepress-d" in the body.

To maintain the list's quality, you will be automatically mailed a message at frequent intervals with the words "Subscription Verification" in the subject of that e-mail. If that mail bounces for any reason, or if you reply to that message, you will be automatically unsubscribed. Please use proper etiquette when posting to the list. The whole purpose of the list is to promote free flow of ideas and information. If you don't agree with a post, feel free to tell everyone why you don't agree, but personal attacks on a poster will be frowned upon by all, and will not be in anyone's best interest.

Index

A

B

C

D

Index

E

F

G

H

I

J

K

L

M

N

O

P

Q

R

S

T

U

V

W

X

Y,Z